A
DICTIONARY
OF
AFRICANISMS

CONTRIBUTIONS OF
SUB-SAHARAN AFRICA
TO THE ENGLISH LANGUAGE

GERARD M. DALGISH

Greenwood Press
Westport, Connecticut • London, England

Library of Congress Cataloging in Publication Data

Dalgish, Gerard M.
    A dictionary of Africanisms.

    1. English language—Provincialisms—Africa, Sub-
Saharan—Dictionaries. 2. English language—Foreign
elements—African—Dictionaries. 3. Africa, Sub-Saharan—
Languages—Glossaries, vocabularies, etc. 4. African
languages—Glossaries, vocabularies, etc. I. Title.
PE3401.D3 1982   442'.496   82-9366
ISBN 0-313-23585-6 (lib. bdg.)

Library of Congress Catalog Card Number: 82-9366
ISBN: 0-313-23585-6

First published in 1982

Greenwood Press
A division of Congressional Information Service, Inc.
88 Post Road West, Westport, Connecticut 06881

Printed in the United States of America

10 9 8 7 6 5 4 3 2 1

A
DICTIONARY
OF
AFRICANISMS

To my wife, Lynda, and my children,
Anne and Barbara

CONTENTS

ACKNOWLEDGMENTS

It was C. L. Barnhart who first gave me the idea of writing a book about Africanisms, seeing the project as a logical extension of my teaching, research, and linguistic experience in Africa combined with my newer work in the field of lexicography, editing, and publishing. But if I had not had the great good fortune to work with Sol Steinmetz, Senior Editor at C. L. Barnhart, Inc., this book simply would never have been written. His patience, insight, and experience impacted on every aspect of this book, from content to format. He has been a sharp but understanding critic, quick to point out mistakes but also patient enough to finish reading a sentence before attacking. In the three years of working in my spare time on this book, I often wondered if it would ever be published, but Sol never doubted that it would be. I'm glad he was right.

Lee Abramson was also a great help to me, often devoting her lunch hours to assisting me in typing, mailing, and the like. Her practical assistance, too, was invaluable.

I wish to thank also several professionals in the fields of African linguistics and lexicography. Professors L. Zgusta, R. Schuh, M. Lionel Bender, B. Kachru, and J. E. Gates, and Mr. Robert Barnhart all read parts of this work or were otherwise encouraging. I am particularly indebted to Professor Bender for his help in Amharic.

I am grateful to members of various missions to the United Nations in the New York area who were gracious enough to assist me. Mr. Kwapong (Ghana), Mr. Samb (Senegal), Habiba Bensouda (Gambia), and Jane Muchuku (Kenya) were all most generous in giving their time. B. Teweldeberhan, one of my students, helped me with some Amharic and Tigrinya data.

My wife and I met Charles Whitmore and Chris Nicolai while we were in Tanzania together, and our lives have been the richer for it. They have been good friends, godparents to one of our daughters, and careful critics. I have needed their encouragement as well.

For some reason it is customary to mention last the one who has been most important to the author. Although this book is dedicated to my wife,

Lynda, she deserves mention here again. She typed the entire manuscript and the camera-ready copy, and somehow in the process managed to cope with first one, then two little girls. She gave me a great deal of encouragement and understanding; I could never have finished this without her. I owe her much more than I can say.

PREFACE

This dictionary is a lexical index of terms from African languages that have entered the general vocabulary of the English-speaking world. It also includes Africanisms that are not yet so widespread as to be recorded in standard dictionaries of English, but are nevertheless well known or reasonably common among English speakers in Africa, or fairly familiar to Africanists, and thus may someday come to be part of the general vocabulary. But more than this, the dictionary is an attempt to present a representative view of the African continent through its contributions to the English language. Such contributions in the form of lexical entries come from all aspects of life: social, religious, economic, cultural and political organizations, concepts, and titles; zoological, botanical, agricultural, and geographical terms; clothing, food, and crafts; Afro-American terms relating to the emerging interest in black cultural identity, and others.

The approximately 3,000 entries were collected from a reading of a wide range of sources: novels, newspapers, magazines, and texts, including African, Afro-American, American, British, and Canadian publications. The definitions are often accompanied by illustrative quotations from these sources showing how these terms are used and indicating to some degree the extent to which these terms have entered the common, general English vocabulary. The extensive and authoritative files of C. L. Barnhart, Inc., are the major source of these quotations and were indispensable in preparing this book. Some forty dictionaries of African languages were consulted; experts in areas of Africa outside the author's expertise were helpful; the author's personal files obtained from firsthand linguistic research in Africa were also drawn upon.

The system of pronunciation used in this book is based on the symbols of a broad transcription of the International Phonetic Association (IPA) alphabet.

It is my hope that this book will be a useful addition to the reference libraries of all those who wish to be kept informed on African and Afro-American affairs, on the historical, social, and cultural aspects of the

African continent, and on Africa's continuing and increasingly relevant influence on the English language and on the Western world in general. I hope that Africanists, linguists, and word aficionados alike will find it useful, informative, and interesting reading.

EXPLANATORY NOTES

CONTENTS OF THE DICTIONARY

This dictionary is intended to be a record of terms from the African languages that have become a part of the English language. In addition the dictionary lists many new words from African languages—new in the sense that they are not recorded in standard English dictionaries, though the words themselves, of course, may have been in existence in their respective African languages for some time. Many such words have been of great importance to Africans but only recently have begun to filter into English, their use being restricted perhaps to the English-speaking expatriate living or working in an African country. The editor has attempted to record the most well-known items of this type in the belief that such items are most likely to become fully "mainstreamed" into the English language. Items relating to recent important political, social, or economic events, organizations, and concepts rank high among such items.

The emphasis of this book is on the contribution of African languages of the sub-Saharan region to the English language. Lexical items that have originated from each of the four major language families of Africa are included: Niger-Congo (many West African languages, as well as the widespread Bantu languages); Nilo-Saharan (Nilotic languages of Central and East Africa); Afro-Asiatic (Ethiopic and Chadic languages); and Khoisan (Hottentot and others).

In addition, Africanisms that originated in one of these African languages but have entered English via some other language (such as French, Afrikaans, or Arabic) are also included. Conversely, lexical items that originated in a non-African language (such as Hindi, Persian, or Arabic) and then passed through an African language into English are also included. Words coming directly and only from a non-African language into English are not included in this dictionary.

PRINCIPLES OF SELECTION

The entries of this dictionary are based on a reading program that encompassed eight major encyclopedias, a dozen English dictionaries, scores of history, sociology, geography, ethnology, and linguistic texts, in addition to travel books, novels, journals, newspapers, magazines, and other media concerning Africa and African affairs and produced by Africans, Afro-Americans, and non-Africans alike. Items were checked for their lexicality (most proper names are excluded), frequency (number of occurrences in print), and distribution (number of different sources); finally the entire list was checked against the quotation files of C. L. Barnhart, Inc. If an item occurred only once in this program, it had to be excluded; however, seemingly obscure items have appeared in a number of mainstream publications, and while their frequency and distribution do not yet qualify them as entries in standard dictionaries, they are quite appropriate for a book of this sort. As suggested above, many may find their way into the common English vocabulary.

MAIN ENTRIES

Main entries appear in enlarged type in alphabetical order, whether the entry is written as one word or two, hyphenated, or compounded.

Variant spellings occur often among even the established African terms. Following accepted lexicographical practice, the spelling found to be most frequent is listed first, followed by the less common spellings. In some cases very frequent variant spellings will each appear as main entries; the more frequent spelling will usually contain the definition, pronunciation, etymology, and so forth. However, there is another consideration in the decision concerning the primary variant spelling, and this has to do with the modernization or standardization of orthography of the African source language. When it can be determined that a particular variant spelling more closely follows the orthographical (romanized) system of the source language, then that variant will usually be chosen as the primary main entry. This also allows for a degree of sophistication, because the user of the dictionary can then determine which spelling is more authentic in terms of its resemblance to the source language. Thus, although *foo-foo*, a West African food, is the most frequent variant in my files, the primary entry is *fufu* because this spelling is coming to be recognized as the one more closely resembling the spelling given in many of the (West) African languages in which it is found. In fact there is a general tendency to substitute *i* for *ee* (cf. *impi*, *impee*); *u* for *ou* and *oo* (*bubu*, *boubou*, or *booboo*), and other changes, as writers attempt to follow the accepted orthography of the source language.

A common feature of many African languages is the use of different prefixes to indicate (among other things) the singular and plural forms of a noun. Thus, Swahili *mzungu*, a European, has as its plural *wazungu*, and both are entries in this book. For convenience one of these forms is given pronunciation, a full definition, etymology, and so forth, with a note referring to the other form; the other form is given a pronunciation followed by the definition: "singular (or plural) of _____." Most entries will have corresponding singular or plural forms listed as entries.

PRONÚNCIATIONS

All new or unfamiliar terms are given a pronunciation enclosed within slashes (/. . ./) immediately following the head word. The pronunciation is usually an Anglicized one representing that of native English speakers; where Anglicization is not established the African pronunciation is given. The pronunciations are rendered in a broad transcription based on the symbols of the International Phonetic Association. For full details see the Pronunciation Key, page xvii.

DEFINITIONS

The definitions have been kept simple, using nontechnical language whenever possible. Discrete meanings of an item are given separate definitions, labeled 1, 2, and so forth, but closely related meanings are incorporated in one definition.

basenji, . . . an African breed of dog . . .; a dog of this breed.

ekhimi, . . . a tropical African tree . . .; the wood derived from this tree.

QUOTATIONS

Whenever possible entries are given illustrative quotations to show the term's use in a natural context, to furnish details about the term that cannot be supplied by the definition, and to demonstrate the range of use that an item enjoys, thereby giving an indication of the degree to which the item has become integrated into the English vocabulary. The author(s), the title of the book, magazine, or other publication, date of publication (month/day/year), and page number are included.

ETYMOLOGIES

Etymologies giving the source and history of a word follow the last quotation and are enclosed within brackets. The symbol ◄ means "derived from" or "taken from;" the symbol ~ means "related to;" the symbol + means "and." The name of the language is given first, followed by the italicized word (or part of the word) relevant to the etymology, followed by its gloss.

CROSS REFERENCES

Cross references appear immediately after the etymology and refer the reader to other items of related interest in the dictionary.

APPENDIX

An appendix in which items are grouped by subject area is included, so the reader may determine equivalent or similar terms for related items across Africa.

PRONUNCIATION KEY

A. VOWELS AND DIPHTHONGS

i	*i* in *bit*	u	*oo* in *book*
i	*ee* in *meet*	u	*oo* in *boot*
a	*a* in *car*, *father*	o	*o* in *dog*
	o in *hot*		*aw* in *raw*
ai	*i* in *mice*	oi	*oi* in *oil*
au	*o* in *pout*	ou	*o* in *go*
æ	*a* in *hat*	ə	*a* in *about*, *u* in *cup*
e	*e* in *bet*	ei	*a* in *plate*

B. CONSONANTS

(1) Ordinary Letter Values

b in *banjo*	n in *no*
d in *did*	p in *put*
f in *fat*	r in *run*
g in *go*	s in *sit*
h in *hat*	t in *top*
k in *kit*	v in *van*
l in *low*	w in *win*
m in *map*	y in *yes*
z in *zoo*	

(2) Special Symbols

ʃ	*sh* in *shaman*	ð	*th* in *this*
tʃ	*ch* in *chin*	ʒ	*s* in *pleasure*
ŋ	*ng* in *wing*	dʒ	*j* in *joy*
ə	*th* in *thick*	x	in German *ach*
/	dental or alveolar click (as in "tsk-tsk" sound of disapproval)		
!	palatal click (imitative of a cork popping)		
//	lateral click (as if urging on a horse)		

C. ACCENT

′ primary stress, as in *banjo* /ˈbænd͡ʒou/

, secondary stress, as in *chimpanzee* /ˌt͡ʃimpæn'ziː/

A
DICTIONARY
OF
AFRICANISMS

A

'aano geel /'ano ,gi:l/, n̲ camel's milk (in Somalia).
Fresh camel's milk ('aano geel), ... is a taste sensation and need not be pasteurized. P. Allen & A. Segal, Traveler's Africa, 1973, p 215
[< Somali 'aano milk + geel camel]

abafazi /,abə'fazi:/, n̲ pl women (in southern Africa).
[< Nguni aba- plural noun pfx + -fazi ~ Luyia (omu)xasi woman]

abakwetha /,abə'kweitə/, n̲ pl recently circumcised Xhosa or Fingo males ready to pass into manhood.
[< Xhosa, Fingo aba- plural noun pfx + -kwetha (root for) a circumcised youth]

abatembuzi /,abatem'bu:zi:/ n̲ pl Ugandan chiefs ruling in the fourteenth century.
The Abatembuzi are said to have had a great influence in northern Uganda, and to have continued to be powerful until the coming of the Luo after 1450. B. Davidson, History of East & Central Africa, 1969, p 41
[< Luganda aba- plural noun pfx + -tembuzi ~ Bantu -tem- cut, decide] See NTEMI

abathakathi or abatagati /,abəta'kati: or -ta'ga-/, n̲ pl

evil wizards among the Zulu.
The enemies are the abathakathi, evil human beings, wizards who cause untold misery - taking human life, sending illness, creating drought, making the cattle sicken and die. National Geographic, 12/71, p 760
[< Zulu aba- plural noun pfx + -thagati ~ -thagat- work magic, bewitch] See TAGATI

abelungu /,abei'lungu:/, n̲ pl whites (in southern Africa).
[< Nguni abe- plural noun pfx + -lungu ~ Swahili (WA)ZUNGU]

abibiman /ə'bi:bi,mæn/, n̲ the archtypical black African (a literary term).
The problems of today are caused by the gross neglect of "Abibimans'" [sic] roots. The poet laments thus: Pluck down the essence/ of the stump of your back. In the face of the sun/ I see only darkness/. Herein contained is the scathing attack on those alienated blackmen who claim they are civilized. Weekly Review (Nairobi), 6/8/79, p 32
[< Akan abibi-man African man < abibi African; coined as a literary term by the Nigerian-born author Gabriel Okara; man converging with but not related to English man]

3

abiku /a'bi:ku:/, n an evil spirit
of the Yoruba who inhabits the
body of a child. The child soon
dies and the spirit reenters the
mother's womb, to be born and die
again.
> I am Abiku, calling for the
> first/ And the repeated time
> .../ Whet the heated fragment,
> brand me/ Deeply on the breast.
> You must know him/ When Abiku
> calls again./ W. Soyinka in C.
> Brooks, African Rhythms, 1974,
> p 175
[< Yoruba]

abiru /a'bi:ru:/, n pl (formerly)
hereditary experts of ritual and
taboo in Rwanda. Sg: MWIRU.
[< Kinyarwanda ab- plural noun
pfx + -iru (root for) these ex-
perts]

aboloo /a'boulu:/, n a West African dish of steamed and fermented
cornmeal patties.
> Kenkey, with its slightly bitter
> beer taste, has so much more
> character; aboloo is so bland
> and light that it has meaning
> all its own. S. Boone, West Af-
> rican Travels, 1974, p 235
[< a West African language, ?
Akan aburo maize, Hausa aburu a
cereal grain; cf. dialectal Jamaican English aburu cornmeal
mush]

aboma /ɔ'boumɔ/, n any of various
large constrictor snakes of South
America.
[< Portuguese, French, and American Spanish ; alteration of Kikongo mboma python]

abou-san /ɔ'bu:,sa(n)/, n =
ABUSA.
[< French < ABUSA]

abuna /ɔ'bu:nɔ/, n the title of
the head of the Ethiopian Orthodox
Church.
> During a visit to Ethiopia last
> year, Rev. Meshesha was elevated
> to the rank of Bishop and is now
> known as Abuna Athanasius.

Sunday Guardian, 4/15/73, p 11
[< Amharic abun(ɔ) < Arabic
abuna our father]

abura /ɔ'burɔ/, n a West African
tree (Mitragyna ciliata); its
soft, fine, close-grained reddish-brown wood.
[< Yoruba abura]

abusa /ɔ'bu:sa/, n a sharecrop-
ping system in the Ivory Coast
and Ghana in which the land
rights are divided into three
parts and shared by the landown-
er and tenant.
> "...But because they are the
> same Akyem people as my master,
> they get the abusa deal from
> him, by which a third of the
> gross amount of money that is
> obtained from their cocoa is
> given to them, whereas I am on-
> ly paid ... three shillings a
> day." C. Doudu in C. Brooks,
> African Rhythms, 1974, p 130
[?< Akan (cf. sensan to mark the
extent of); ? < Ewe]

abusua /,abɔ'su:ɔ/, n an exoga-
mous matriclan among the Ashanti.
> The key to the social structure
> of the Fante is the ... abusua.
> All members of the clan are be-
> lieved to be related through
> descent from a common ances-
> tress, though this relationship
> is often more mythical than
> real...All members of the abu-
> sua consider themselves related.
> J. Christensen in E. Skinner,
> Peoples and Cultures of Africa,
> 1973, p 513
[< Akan abusũá]

Abyssinia /,ǝebǝ'sini:ǝ/, n the
earlier name for Ethiopia, the
country in northeastern Africa.
[< an Afro-Asiatic language <
Habashat name of a group of early
inhabitants of Ethiopia < Arabic
habaši Ethiopian]

Acholi /a'tʃouli:/, n Also, Acoo-
li. a people of Uganda and western
Kenya; their Nilo-Saharan (Chari-

Nile, Eastern Sudanic) language, akin to LUO.

ackee /'æki:/, n = AKEE.

ackey /'æki:/, n a former British silver coin used in West Africa.
[< AKEE, the seed of which was used as a unit of weight]

adalu /æ'dalu:/, n a West African dish of smoked fish, corn and beans mixed with vegetables and pepper.
[< a West African language]

addax /'ædæks/, n a light-colored, ox-like antelope of North Africa.
[< Latin < an African language]

addra /'adrə/, n a large African white gazelle (Gazella dama) with reddish hair on the neck.
22 species of rare mammal have been hunted down...for zoos and museums, including the Addra gazelle, the sassaby, and...the white oryx. Time, 4/21/61, p 100
[< a West African language ∼ Akan adowa antelope]

adinkra /a'diŋkrə/, n a type of patterned, colorful fine dyed cloth or linen worn in Ghana. Pieces of carved calabash are often used as hand stamps for the dyed patterns.
Adinkra is a patterned fabric made by stamping designs on the surface of cloth. It is an Asanti craft...used to make magnificent wraparound costumes which are worn like Roman togas. E. Dendel, African Fabric Crafts, 1974, p 35
[< Akan adinkara (originally the name of an Ashanti king) ∼ dinkra goodbye (because the cloth was worn during mourning)]

adire /a'di:rei/, n resist-dyed calico from Nigeria, usually 2-1/2 yards long and occurring in pairs, colored white and indigo.
Yoruba adire is still popular

and sold all over West Africa. The Times, 12/1/77, p XI
[< Yoruba, literally, to take, tie and dye] See ETA.

--adire eleko, cloths patterned with starch paste, made in the adire fashion.
--adire eleso, tied and stitched cloths, made by hand in the adire fashion.

Adontenhene /ə,dontən'heinei/, n a sub-chief (formerly a military leader) among the Akan in Ghana.
Nana Ekwam VII, chief of the town and Adontenhene of the Gomoa Adjumako Traditional Area, said damage to the property was estimated at ₵5,000. Ghanaian Times, 4/16/73, p 5
[< Akan adɔnten main body of an army + -hene king, chief]

Afar /'afar/, n the Danakil, a people of Ethiopia and Djibouti; their Afroasiatic (Eastern Cushitic) language akin to GALLA and SOMALI; hence, Territory of Afars and Issas, former name of DJIBOUTI. See AFRICA.

afara /ə'farə/, n a species of tree from Nigeria; its light-colored, teak-like wood; LIMBA.
Afara, an unusual wood, naturally light and with a grain similar to that of teak, is used for a group by the White Furniture Company. New York Times, 2/20/55, p 38
[< Yoruba afara]

afarsata /ə'farsətə/, n an investigation or trial by ordeal to identify a wrongdoer (in Ethiopia).
A few weeks later I had a chance to see just how the afarsata works. In this kind of trial, everybody in town where the trouble occurred is shut up within a fence of thorny bushes. No one may go out, even to milk a cow....The villagers, all of whom are suspect, wail and moan. They then select eight to ten

agents called "birds" who take an oath... There is then a weary waiting period, sometimes lasting a month, during which the agents quietly circulate in the crowds... Finally a "bird" tells the judge the name of the thief. National Geographic, 9/35, p 317
[< Amharic afərsəta]

Afar triangle /'afar/, n a triangular region of northeastern Ethiopia, thought to be evidence of continental drift from Arabia (near the Red Sea and the Gulf of Aden).
The insert shows details of the Afar Triangle - the lava covered junction between the Red Sea, the Gulf of Aden and the East African Rift System. Science, 8/69, p 41

afe negus /a'fei 'neigəs/, n a chief justice in Ethiopia.
[< Amharic afə ngus literally, mouth of the emperor]

afo /'afou/, n a festival in West Africa.
They have a big market in Abame on every other Afo day and, as you know, the whole clan gathers there. C. Achebe, Things Fall Apart, 1958, p 126
[< Ibo, ~ Akan ɛfa, afa festival]

Afo-a-kom /,afou a 'koum/, n a large, bead-covered, iroko wood carving of the Kom in Cameroon, representing the people's political, spiritual, and religious heritage.
Although considered sacred, the Afo-A-Kom is not an object of worship by the Kom. Rather, the 62-1/2-inch-high wood carving is invested with symbolisms. Assigned to the care of the Fon, it becomes a symbol of royal authority and the promise of continued succession within the dynasty. Put on public display, it becomes a symbol of the history, culture, and traditions

of the Kom people. ...[and] a symbol of the endurance of African tribalism. National Geographic, 7/74, p 143
[< Kom afo- thing + a- of (connective) + Kom the Kom]

Africa, n the continent south of the Mediterranean, bounded by the Atlantic and Indian Oceans.
[< Latin Afrī ancient people of Africa, singular Afer, though perhaps a back formation, ? < AFAR]

Afroasiatic /,æfroueiʃi'ætik/, adj of or relating to a language family of Africa comprising the Semitic, Chadic, Cushitic, Berber, and ancient Egyptian languages, once labelled HAMITO-SEMITIC.
[coined by J. Greenberg in Studies in African Linguistic Classification, 1955, p 54: "I rather hesitantly suggest the name Afroasiatic for this family as the only one found both in Africa and Asia."]

agahuza /,agɔ'hu:zə/, n =DAGAA (in central Africa).
I watched an old Hutu magician burn about three pounds of agahuza - little herring-like fish that came all the way from Lake Tanganyika where the Congolese call them ndagala. The theory behind this smelly operation was that the potent fumes of the burning fish would penetrate into the banana trees, which would then have as many babies as the herring. J. Hallet, Congo Kitabu, 1964, p 116
[< Kinyarwanda aga- diminutive pfx + huza (root for) these fish]

agala dzemkpele /ə'galə dzem-'kpeilə/, n a Ghanaian dish of soft-shell crabs boiled with ginger, served with a tomato and vegetable sauce and a mixture of fish stock, cornmeal and vegetables.
[? < Ewe]

agba /'agbə/, n a large African
tree (Gossweilerodendron balsami-
ferum); its heavy wood used for
furniture.
   There are symbols in this present room, if one uses his imagination. The 300 year-old agba log from French Equatorial
   Africa is a symbol of man's dependence upon God for his material well-being. Time, 12/1/52,
   p 4
[< a West African language]

agbada /ag'badə/, n a two-piece
full-length patterned cotton robe
of the Yoruba, open at the sides.
   They were talking to Bassey...
   who was now almost unrecogniz-
   ably dashing in a sky-blue silk
   agbada, or long cape, worn over
   sky-blue trousers and soft
   leather slippers. On his head he
   wore a red awo, or skullcap.
   New Yorker, 11/10/62, p 225
   Boldly colored agbadas of kenta
   cloth, the bubus worn by African women, and gossamer saris
   were gay relief from the traditional black tie. New York
   Times, 10/21/67, p 36
[< Yoruba] See LAPPA.

Agni /'agni: or anyi:/, n Also,
Anyi. a people of the Ivory Coast
and Ghana; their Niger-Congo (Kwa)
language related to AKAN.

agushi or agushi soup /ə'gu:-
ʃi:/, n a Ghanaian sauce made from
ground melon seeds to accompany
cassava, yam, and other main
dishes.
   Try groundnut (peanut) stew...
   or fried spiced plantain (kelewele), jollof rice, agushi
   "soup" (a melon seed sauce). P.
   Allen & A. Segal, Traveler's
   Africa, 1973, p 493
[< a West African language]
Called EGUSI in Nigeria.

Ahobaa /ə'houba/, n a festival in
Ghana, a special time of goodwill
for families.
   The next day was Ahobaa. It was
a day of rejoicing for everyone. In the morning, old family quarrels were being patched
up. In Maami Ama's family all
became peaceful. ...I sympa-
thized with the kids, I could
not give them a holiday, although Ahobaa was such an important festival for them. A.
Aidoo in C. Brooks, African
Rhythms, 1974, p 218
Harper's International Travel
Planner 1979. Ghana. June:
AHOBAA KAKRABA FESTIVAL, Abura,
Central Region. Harper's,
3/79, p T29
[? < Akan]

ahyewa or agyewa /a'gyeiwə/, n
a type of music among the Akan
of Ghana.
   If in Akan society someone
   scraped off mud on a bottle
   with the lid of a cigarette
   tin, he would produce noise as
   a by-product. If he performed
   this act of scraping in the
   performance of ahyewa music,
   the sound, though similar,
   would have a different meaning.
   J. Nketia in E. Skinner, Peoples & Cultures of Africa,
   1973, p 583
[< Akan agye(so)wa a certain
tone or melody in music]

akadja /a'kadʒə/, n a type of
edible fish in Benin.
[< Akan akadeaa kind of small
fish]

Akan /ə'kan/, n a people of Ghana
and the Ivory Coast, including
the FANTE, TWI and others; their
Niger-Congo (Kwa) language including FANTE and TWI.

akara /ə'karə/, n a West African
dish of bean cake(s) made from
mashed black-eyed peas mixed
with water and onions, fried in
palm or peanut oil.
   The fad of the future, a real
   protein gain over French fries
   and the myriad tidbits of the
   fast-food world, may well come

to be West African akara:little
balls of a spicy mixture of
mashed beans with onion,crisply
deep-fried. Scientific American,
11/72, p 28
[< Yoruba, Ibo, Efik; cf. Jamaican English ackra this dish]

--akara awon /ə'wan/, akara with
okra.
--akara ijesha /i'dʒeʃə/, akara
using less water;drier akara.

akassa /ə'kasə/, n a dish of
boiled flour or fried corncakes,
served with spicy sauces in Benin
and Togo.
[< a West African language]

akee /'æki:/, n a tree (Blighia sa-
pida)of western Africa whose
fleshy aril attached to the seed
is edible;its fruit; ACKEE.
[< Kru akee ⌢ Akan ànkyẽ wild cashew tree]

akida /ə'ki:də/, n a black or Arab
subordinate official or agent working for a colonial power (in East
Africa), especially during the
German occupation of Tanganyika.
The akida has a bad name in Tanzanian history. He is usually
portrayed as the son of a slave
trader, an Arab or half-caste
with a whip, terrorising and exploiting the people he ruled.
Many akidas were like this,es-
pecially before Maji Maji. But
in the later years of German
rule the akida was usually an African, an educated young man lit-
erate in Swahili. J. Iliffe in I.
Kimambo and A. Temu, History of
Tanzania, 1969, p 153
[< Swahili < Arabic]

akil /ə'ki:l/, n a government appoi-
nted headman of a village or town
in Djibouti and Somalia,
[? < Somali]

aklama /a'klam /, n a type of stat-
uette made by the Ewe.
[< Ewe]

akori /ə'kori:/, n a porous coral,

or an ornament made from it (in
West Africa).
[? < Akan akot(on)i kind of cowry]

akpeteshie /,akpə'teiʃi:/, n a
potent alcoholic drink of Ghana,
distilled from palm juice.
Bishop Amissah's thesis at St.
Peter's College in Rome was a-
bout a comparison between Catholic canon law and native customs on marriage; he is currently investigating the native
custom of pouring libations on
important occasions (English
gin, schnapps or potent akpeteshie). Time,]2/23/57,p 44
The greater share of sugar allocated to the region was being diverted to Egya villages
where they were being used to
distill akpeteshie. Ghanaian
Times, 2/26/72, p 16
[? < Akan ahwié-sã palm wine or
rum poured as a libation]

akuaba /,aku'abə/, n pl small,
carved dolls carried by young A-
shanti girls. The head is lens-
shaped and elongated,sloping backward; the body is cylindrical.
They are said to embody the A-
shanti ideal of beauty...;a
less realistic representation
of a human head can hardly be
imagined, yet one sees in Ashanti, as among no other people, a
higher proportion of children
(notably in the royal families)
whose high, wide foreheads do
at once remind one of the akua'-
ba.W. Fagg & M. Plass, African
Sculpture, 1964, p 13
[(Ashanti) Akan]

akuammine /,aku'ami:n/, n a crystalline alkaloid substance derived from the seeds of a West
African tree (Picralima nitida).
Formula: $C_{22}H_{28}N_2O_4$
[< Akan akúamã the tree + English -ine]

Akwasidae /a,kwasi'daii:/, n a
festival held on Sunday every forty days in Ghana.

The Annual Festival Celebration
for this year will begin on Saturday, 2nd Feb. 1980 and will
last for two weeks. Highlights
of the occasion will be Pouring
of Libation on AKWASIDAE Sunday
3rd Feb. 1980 at Asoneyeso at
5:30 a.m. Followed by firing of
musketry and drumming through
the principal streets. Ghanaian
Times, 1/23/80, p 3
[? < Akan Kwasidae Sunday; cf.
Akwasi name for a female born on
Sunday]

Akwete /a'kweitei/, n a type of
embroidered cloth from Nigeria.
The Akwete cloth with its beauty and colourfulness still
needs to be made known in a manner that its sister counterpart,
the Kente cloth of Ghana, is
known and appreciated round the
world. J. Sofola, African Culture and the African Personality, 1973, p 165
[< Akwete town in Nigeria where
this cloth is made]

aladire /alə'di:rei/, n a person
who makes ADIRE patterned cloths.
It is an absolutely engrossing
sight to watch an expert aladire make hundreds of freehand,
small circles with a feather...
There is one adire artist in
Ibadan whose hands are so beautiful in motion that it is worth
the trip just to watch her. E.
Dendel, African Fabric Crafts,
1974, p 123
[?< Yoruba al- person pfx +
ADIRE]

alafin /'ælǝfin/, n a chief or
leader of the Yoruba in the former kingdom of Oyo in Nigeria.
[< Yoruba]

alari /ǝ'lari:/, n a type of red
cloth made in Nigeria. See the
quotation under ETA.
[?< Yoruba]

alecha or alecha wat /a'leitʃǝ/,
n a moderately spiced WAT (stew)

of Ethiopia, with cumin and herbs.
A gentler alternative stew,
which never contains berbere
is the alecha. Alechas in
their various forms are fa-
vored by many European and
American visitors in Ethiopia
precisely because they are not
so incendiary as wats, and
they are delicious in their
own right. The most popular
base for an alecha is chicken.
L. van der Post et. al., African Cooking, 1970, p 38
[alecha < Amharic alece any
sauce without hot peppers (also,
slang for impotent man)]

amad(h)lozi /,amǝ'dlouzi:/, n pl
ancestral spirits of the Zulu
and other Nguni peoples who are
believed to look after their
descendants.
[< Nguni ama- plural noun pfx
+ dhlozi (root for) ancestral
spirit]

amadinda /,amǝ'dindǝ/, n a xylo-
phone-like instrument of East
and Central Africa.
[< a Bantu language < ama- plural noun pfx + -dinda~MARIMBA]

amandla /a,mand'la/, n a rallying cry or slogan in South Africa, used especially by black
nationalists, meaning "power."
As the coffin was brought before the altar in the open sta-
dium, the crowd rose to chant
the black anthem "Nkosi Sike-
lele Afrika" (God Bless Africa).
Then their clenched fists rose
into the air with a massive
shout of amandla. The Times,
9/26/77, p 6
[< Zulu]

amasi /ǝ'masi/, n sour milk (in
South Africa).
This porridge [uputhu] is the
favourite of the Zulu, Swazi
and Xhosa people who traditionally serve it with sour milk
(amasi) or wild green vegetable stew (imfino). Flying

Springbok, 10/79, p 83
[< Nguni <u>ama-</u> (mass) noun pfx +
-<u>si</u> (root for) milk]

amatungulu /ˌaməˈtuŋgulə/, <u>n</u> a
shrub or spiny plant (<u>Carissa</u>
<u>grandiflora</u>) of South Africa, used
especially for hedges and its
fruit, which is also called NUM-
NUM.
[< Nguni <u>ama-</u> (plural) noun pfx
+ -<u>tungulu</u> (Zulu -<u>thungulu</u>)]

amba /ˈambə/, <u>n</u> a large, flat-
topped mesa in Ethiopia.
"This is rough country. Tonight
I have an unobstructed view in
every direction of a succession
of ... <u>ambas</u>. There are many of
these gray outliers of rim rock;
sheer cliffs join steep-sided
valleys deeply indented with
minor drainage. Side ravines are
close together; terrain more
difficult to traverse than can-
yon country of the United States,
differences of elevation being
greater. General tone is brown
and gray; no timber. <u>National</u>
<u>Geographic</u>, 9/35, p 298
[< Amharic]

ambasha /amˈbaʃə/, <u>n</u> a kind of
Ethiopian bread, usually of wheat.
For a day's work, each miner receives 1-1/2 Ethiopian dollars
(roughly 60 U.S. cents), one
<u>ambasha</u>, or large loaf of Ethi-
opian bread, and one goatskin of
water. <u>National Geographic</u>,
2/70, p 194
[< Amharic <u>ambasa</u>]

Ambo /ˈæmbou/, <u>n</u> a people of
northern Namibia also called OVAM-
BO; their Bantu language.

americani or amerikani /əˌmerəˈka-
ni:/, <u>n</u> = MERIKANI.

Amhara /amˈharə/, <u>n</u> a people of
northern Ethiopia speaking AMHARIC;
a former kingdom, now a province
of northern Ethiopia.

Amharic /æmˈharik/, <u>n</u> Also <u>Am-</u>
<u>harinya</u>. the Afroasiatic (Semit-
ic) language of the Amhara, the
official language of Ethiopia,
akin to TIGRINYA.

amiwo /aˈmi:wou/, <u>n</u> a dish of
boiled poultry browned in oil
and served over corn meal mixed
with tomatoes, onions and spices
in Benin.
[< a West African language]

Anansi-tori /əˈnænsi:ˌtori:/,
<u>n</u> = NANCY-STORY (in Surinam).

Angola /æŋˈgoulə/, <u>n</u> a country
in West Africa bordering on
Zaire, Zambia, Botswana and Namibia.
[< Portuguese, ? alteration of
<u>Ngola</u> title of a Mbundu king;
the Portuguese are said to have
mistaken his title for the name
of the territory]

angolar /ˌæŋgouˈlar/, <u>n</u> a former unit of currency of Angola.
Monetary unit: angolar, at par
with the escudo. (Escudo val-
used at 3.5 cents U.S.). <u>Brit-
annica Encyclopedia</u>, 1959, p
557
[< Portuguese, literally, of
Angola]

angoni /æŋˈgouni:/, <u>n</u> an East
African strain of zebu cattle.
[< <u>Angoni</u>land plateau region of
Malawi < <u>Angoni</u> the Ngoni people
of the area]

angwantibo /æŋˈgwantibou/, <u>n</u> a
small lemur of West Africa with a
long snout.
The "forest" will feature a
wide range of animals...the African galago...potto (only
three in America)and the stubby-
tailed angwantibo, also from
Africa. <u>New York Times</u>,7/31/65,
p 23
[< Efik]

ankole or ankoli /æŋˈkouli:/,<u>n</u>

a breed of long-horned cattle from East Africa.

Some African breeds, such as the Ankole, differ from European and zebu cattle in possessing enormous, bulbous horns. Scientific American, 6/58, p 54

[< Ankole the plateau region in Kenya and Uganda < (a)Banyankole the Bantu people of this region]

Ankyeamehene /an,tʃeəmə'heinei/, n a sub chief of the Akan (in Ghana).

[< Akan ankyeafo person of repute ⁓kyeame speaker, reporter + -hene king, chief]

Anyanya or **Anya Nya** /a'nyanyə/, n a former guerrilla organization of the non-Arab southern Sudan that fought for autonomy from the Arab-dominated north.

The [Uganda Liberation Front] Committee ... should bring relief to the countryside, which has been used to illiterate thugs recruited from Anyanyas in the Sudan and Nubians in Kibera. New York Times, 4/8/79, Sec. 4, p not known

3,000 former guerrillas adopted the uniform of the police and were integrated into the forces of order in the three southernmost provinces of the country. The Anya Nya guerrilla fighters had spent 17 years in the maquis: now they were moving to the other side of the fence. Manchester Guardian, 2/10/73, p 18

[< a central African language, said to mean poison of a snake]

Anyoto /a'nyoutou/, n a notorious secret society in Zaire whose members masqueraded as leopards and performed ritual murder.

The Anyoto, or Leopard men, practitioners of ritual murder ...still operated some distance south of Pawa, draping themselves in leopard skins and leaving feigned leopard tracks near their victims. New Yorker, 4/18/59, p 130

[< KiMabudu, a language of the Mabudu in Zaire]

aoudad /'audæd/, n a type of wild sheep of North Africa.

[< French < Berber audad]

aoul /'auəl/, n the Abyssinian gazelle.

[< an Ethiopian language]

ardo /'ardou/, n a chief or leader of the Fulani, especially a leader of a self-regulating community.

[< Fulani]

Arusha /ə'ru:ʃə/, n Also **Arusa**. a people of northern Tanzania; their Nilo-Saharan (Chari-Nile), Eastern Sudanic) language akin to MAASAI.

Arusha declaration, n an important proclamation issued by President Julius K. Nyerere of Tanzania in 1967, outlining the goals of Tanzanian socialism (UJAMAA) such as self-reliance, the elimination of exploitation, and democratic elections.

The Arusha declaration has, none the less, initiated a wave of nationalization, under very varying conditions, throughout black Africa. The Times, 10/29/70, p 10

Coming to the Arusha Declaration I want to state that many of our leaders just pay lip service to the "socialism" ideology. They cannot openly oppose socialism. This is because they need their daily bread. Sunday News (Dar es Salaam), 9/19/76, p 6

[Arusha the name of the city in northern Tanzania where the declaration was issued 2/5/67 < ARUSHA]

asafo /a'safou/, n a men's association in Ghana, formerly a military company but nowadays a political organization.

[< Akan asafo company, society]

Asafohene /a,safou'heinei/, n a
head of the ASAFO; a chief of an
Ewe clan (in Ghana and Togo).
[< Akan ASAFO + -hene king,
chief]

Asantehene /ə,santə'heinei/, n
the paramount chief of the Ashanti of Ghana.
Some of these subject monarchs
were powerful, such as the
Asantehene in Ashanti, the Kabaka of Buganda, the Sultan of
Zanzibar, the Emirs of Northern
Nigeria. The Times, 7/27/63, p9
The Golden Stool, repository of
the souls of all the people...
became the recipient of blood
sacrifice, held yearly before
the Asantehene in his palace at
Kumasi. Scientific American,
6/68, p 138
[< Akan (Ashanti) asante the
Ashanti people + -hene king,
chief]

Ashanti /ə'ʃanti:/, n Also Asante
a people of Ghana famous for
their weaving and gold works, formerly united in a kingdom in central Ghana; their language, a
dialect of AKAN.
[< Akan (Ashanti) Asante]

Ashia /a'ʃi:ə/, n a "corn-row"
hair style (short braids or pigtails flat against the scalp in
rows) popular among Africans and
Afro-Americans.
The Ashia, from Kenya, the Nzinga from Nigeria, and the Umoja
from Egypt...adhere to corn-
rowing basics - stick-up or
tied-down short braids, or Me-
dusa-like strands sliding down
the head. Time, 12/24/73, p 84
[< a place name in Kenya]

asikloe /asi'kloue/, n a festival
or celebration of the Ashanti.
The asikloe is a festive day of
reunion, in Ghana, explained
Sandra Michael...."It's a day
for meeting old friends and
greeting new ones," she said.
New York Times, 5/21/61, p B2

[< Akan]

askari /ə'skari:/, n a policeman,
soldier, guard or watchman in
East Africa.
The askari...from our field
station helped me with my load
while lighting the way with
his flashlight. National Geographic, 4/78, p 546
The small boat manned by two
askaris - rangers in khaki
shirts and shorts, rakish safari hats, and long puttees -
pushed through reeds and scud-
ding nympheas to the open water. P. Matthiessen, Tree
Where Man Was Born, 1972, p29
[< Swahili < Arabic askari]

aso-oke /,asou'oukei/, n a
brightly-colored, toga-like cotton garment from Nigeria, traditionally worn by men and women.
Down Whitehall, along the pave-
ments of clubland in St. Ja
James's, and under the drip-
ping plane trees in Kensing-
ton, the taxis have been dis-
gorging loads of cheery men
and women wearing aso-oke, the
graceful toga garment which
is handwoven in brilliant rain-
bow colours. Manchester Guardian, 10/6/60, p 6
[? < Yoruba]

assegai /'asə,gai/, n a short,
slender spear, introduced by Shaka in southern Africa.
This is where they made his in-
fernal invention, the stabbing
assegai. Before his time,the
tribes used long throwing
spears. Each man carried several, and the warriors would toss
them at one another until they
were all used up. Then one army would chase the other one
home without too much harm done.
Shaka changed all that.He short-
ened the spears, put stout hafts
on them, and taught his warriors a revolutionary battle tac-
tic-- to close with the enemy
and sink the blade into the

chest. <u>National Geographic</u>,12/71, p 748
[< southern Bantu languages <Arabic <u>al</u>- noun pfx + Berber <u>zaghaya</u> lance, spear]

assin /a'sin/, <u>n</u> a metal ornament on a grave for food offerings to the dead (in Benin).
[< a West African language]

asunrara /ə'sunrarə/, <u>n</u> a praise-singer of the Yoruba.
The functions of music are apparent in songs sung in praise of chiefs. The <u>asunrara</u> sings in praise of the Oba. J. Şofọla, <u>African Culture and the African Personality</u>, 1973, p 7
[<Yoruba] See IMBONGI

ata sauce /'atə/, <u>n</u> a very hot,spicy pepper sauce of Nigeria and Ghana, made from green and chili peppers and vegetables fried in palm or peanut oil.
One recipe I have for <u>ata sauce</u> points up cultural differences between countries: it suggests ata sauce be served with boiled starch for <u>breakfast</u>! H. Hachten, <u>Kitchen Safari</u>,1970, p 87
[< Akan, literally, hot]

athimaki /,aθi'maki:/, <u>n pl</u> important guerrilla leaders among the Kikuyu and related peoples who resisted colonial rule in Kenya.
These leaders were not priests or prophets, as were the <u>orkoiik</u> of the Nandi and the <u>laibons</u> of the Masai, nor were they chiefs like the <u>ruoths</u> of the Luo, but fighting men who had proved their courage and fitness to command in time of danger. Among the Kikuyu, they were called <u>athimaki</u>. These never became chiefs or kings, but were able to unite different villages in self-defense. The Kamba also developed a kind of <u>athimaki</u>. B. Davidson, <u>History of East and Central Africa</u>, 1969, p 174

[< Kikuyu <u>a</u>- plural noun pfx + -<u>thimaki</u> ~ Swahili <u>(m)simamizi</u> overseer, director]

athuri /a'θu:ri/, <u>n pl</u> Kikuyu elders.
The last time Gati had seen Gaichuhie was in August 1954, when he had been chosen by Kimathi as one of the four so-called <u>athuri</u>. I. Henderson, <u>Man Hunt in Kenya</u>, 1958, p 77
[< Kikuyu <u>a</u>- plural noun pfx + -<u>thuri</u> (root for) these elders]

atieke /a,tie'kei/, <u>n</u> a dish of pancakes or porridge made of cassava flour (in Ivory Coast).
[< a West African language]

awo /'awou/, <u>n</u> a skullcap worn by men in Nigeria. See the first quotation under AGBADA.
[< Yoruba]

Axum or Aksum /ak'su:m/, <u>n</u> an ancient kingdom of Ethiopia, or ca. 1st to 8 century A.D., or its capital city, an important center of Ethiopian Christendom.
[< an Afro-Asiatic (Ethiopic) language, ? ultimately < Arabic (because south Arabians may have first founded it)]

ayous /ei'yu:s/, <u>n</u> = OBECHE.
[< French < a West African language ~Yoruba <u>awusa</u> a similar tree]

Azania /ə'zeini:ə/, <u>n</u> the name adopted by black nationalists for South Africa.
When the UN gave its mandate for armed struggle in Namibia, The News was dismayed by what it saw as an endorsement of bloodshed. Well, black blood is shed every day in Namibia, Zimbabwe (Rhodesia) and Azania (South Africa) by men, women and children. <u>Daily News</u> (<u>N.Y.</u>), 12/29/76, p 41
The struggles of the peoples of Guinea-Bissau, Mozambique,

Angola, Zimbabwe and Azania
have inspired progressive people everywhere and have struck
...fear in the hearts of the
ruling classes of the imperial-
ist nation [sic] everywhere.
Daily News (Dar es Salaam),
1/30/77, p 4
[< the name of an Iron Age civilization of southern Africa from
ca. 500 to 1500 A.D.; see the
quotation under Azanian for the
suggested relation between Azania
and Zanj an Arabic term for certain black Africans]

--Azanian, n: Derived from the
Caucasoids, it appears were the
"Azanians" found along the coast
of "Zanj" - tall bearded men,
"red" in color, a piratical tribe
of fishers who traded tortoise
shell, soft ivory, and aromatic
gums for iron blades and beads
and cloth. Perhaps by this time
the Azanians had mixed with those
early Indonesians who brought the
outrigger canoe and the marimba

to the Indian Ocean coast and were
to colonize Madagascar. P. Matthiessen, Tree Where Man Was Born,
1972, p 33

azikhwela /ˌaziˈkweilə/, n a rallying cry or slogan of a South
African boycott of public trans-
portation over apartheid policies.
The pamphlets named the stay-
at-home campaign "azikwela," a
Zulu term meaning "we will not
get on." This was a reference
to the cars, buses and trains
that carry most black workers
from the townships to adjacent
white areas. New York Times,
8/23/76, p 3
[< Zulu, literally, we will not
board, climb (on) < a- subject pfx
+ -zi- negative pfx + -khwela
jump on, ride   KHWELA]

azmari /azˈmari:/, n a travelling
musician or bard of Ethiopia.
[< Amharic < zəmmər he chants
or sings] See GRIOT.

B

B, abbreviation of BIRR.
The Ethiopian birr, divided into 100 cents, is the unit of currency... It consists of notes of EB1,5,10,50... The former dollar notes were replaced by the new birr in Oct. 1976. Statesman's Year-Book, 1980, p 436

baba /'babə/, n the title or a term of address for an elder male; father.
In Nairobi, crowds of young Africans filled the streets to cheer Mr. Kenyatta, 73 years old, as "Baba Wa Taifa" - "the Father of the Nation." New York Times, 5/28/63, p 2
'Women could not do work like that, mam. It is too difficult for them.' 'Women are no good at all, are they, baba?' J. Cary, American Visitor, 1963, p 9
[< any of various African languages, Swahili, Yoruba, etc.~ Mandingo baaba my father]

babalawo /,babə'lawou/, n a diviner or specialist in forecasting techniques of the Ifa cult, especially the technique of manipulating and interpreting throws of palm kernels.
By means of a corpus of prophetic verses coded by 2^8 binary chance results, the professional diviner, or babalawo uses 16 smooth black palm nuts. He

grasps them between his hands and tries to take them all in his right hand. Scientific American, 6/71, p 134
[< Yoruba, literally, "father has secrets"]

backra /'baekrə/, n = BUCKRA.

badza /'badzə/, n a short-handled, ax-like farming or digging implement (in Zimbabwe).
The lepers of Mutemwa ... battle along with wooden legs; others can only crawl. But every morning sees them out in their small patches of land, somehow managing to grasp their badzas between the stumps of fingers, cultivating, tending vegetables, beans and mealies. Rhodesia Herald, 2/23/73, p 29
[? < Shona < a Bantu language~ Luyia -baatsi ax] See JEMBE.

bafaro /bə'farou/, n a type of stonebass (Polyprion) of southern Africa.
[< Afrikaans < an African language]

bafumu /,ba'fu:mu/, n pl of UMU-FUMU (magician).
Not only did the bafumu prevent the banana trees from being struck by stray bolts of lightning, but they dealt confidently with all of the evil omens lurking in the fields, bushes and groves. J. Hallet,

Congo Kitabu, 1964, p 116
[< a Bantu language of Zaire <
ba- plural noun pfx + -fumu (root
for) magician]

Baganda /ba'gandə/, n (pl) (a)
people of Uganda, speaking the
Bantu language of LUGANDA.
[< Luganda ba- plural noun pfx +
ganda (root for) these people]

bahar zaf or bahr zaf /bə'har
zaf or bar/, n a eucalyptus tree
found near water in Ethiopia.
[< Amharic bahir ocean + zaf
tree]

bahtawi /ba'tawi:/, n anchorite,
usually attached to an Ethiopian
orthodox monastery.
[< Amharic]

bakombozi /,bakom'bouzi:/, n pl
Tanzanian soldiers who, together
with Ugandan refugees, drove Idi
Amin from power in 1979.
  This was not the Uganda I re-
  membered. We didn't see any
  smiles in the capital, Kampala.
  Amin was gone, yes, but the Tan-
  zanian bokambozi - liberators -
  remained, an army in our midst.
  National Geographic, 7/80, p 77
[< Swahili, literally, rescuers
< ba- plural noun pfx + -kombozi
ransom, redeem; Mkombozi title of
Jesus Christ]

baku /'baku:/, n an African tree
(Mimusops heckelii); its hard,
heavy wood.
[<a West African language ∿ Akan
abákó type of shea tree ? ∿ bakua
banana or plantain stalk]

bakungu /,ba'kungu:/, n pl important chiefs acting as advisors of
the Buganda and Bunyoro kingdoms.
[< Luganda, Lunyoro ba- plural
noun pfx + -kungu ? ∿ Swahili
mkunga confidential advisor]

balabbat or balabat /balə'bat/,
n a local chief or village official in Ethiopia; formerly, a

squire or landlord of a share-
cropping farm.
  They will not cut my throat
  during my sleep, I decide, but
  neither will they be of much
  help if I am attacked. As in-
  surance, Mahmud goes to see a
  Danakil balabat, or local chief,
  who announces that I am under
  his protection. National Geographic, 2/70, p 195
  But there was no question of
  ruining the propertied classes,
  who would then be a burden to
  the community. The case of
  each balabat was accordingly
  debated in public. A collective
  decision was taken to impose a
  kind of "revolutionary tax" on
  each individual, calculated according to his past record, his
  wealth, and any injustices he
  may have committed. Manchester
  Guardian, 8/8/76, p 12
[< Amharic balə abbat ∿ Hebrew
ba'al habbayith lord of the house]

balafon or balaphon /'bælə,fan/,
n a type of xylophone with hollowed gourd resonators.
  The shows they have given consist of their own entertain-
  ments as enjoyed when they are
  back home - wild festival or
  ritual dancing and chanting to
  tom-toms and balafons. New
  Yorker, 4/23/60, p 145
[< French balafon < Bambara balafo play xylophone, cf. bala xylo-
phone] Also, balafo.

Balante /bə'lant/, n a people of
central Guinea-Bissau; their Niger-Congo (West Atlantic) language
akin to Wolof.
[< Balante Bulanda]

balleh /'bale(x)/, n a temporary
pond over impermeable soil (in
Somalia).
[< Somali]

balopwe /ba'loupwei/, n pl members
of a dominant lineage or ruling
group, some of whom are believed

to be the founders of the Luba
people of West Africa.
  All candidates to the throne or
  to lesser posts of authority in
  the political system...called
  themselves balopwe. By a confla-
  tion of their own beliefs about
  legitimacy with the beliefs of
  those they ruled, balopwe gathered power to themselves in this
  and in neighboring Luba-type
  states. B. Davidson, Angola's
  People, 1972, p 61
[< Chiluba ba- plural noun pfx
+ -lopwe (root for) these rulers]

balq or belq /bælk/, n the
short rainy season in Ethiopia
during April and May.
[< Amharic balq]

Bambara /bam'barɔ or 'bambərə/, n
Also Bamana. a people of Mali, the
Ivory Coast, and the upper Niger
River; their Niger-Congo (Mande)
language, called Bambara-ka, used
as a lingua franca in Mali.

bambarra nut /'bambərə/, n a
leguminous creeping herb with
edible fruits that ripen underground.
[< BAMBARA]

bamboula /bam'bu:lə/, n a type of
tambourine or drum used in New
Orleans jazz and in the West Indies; the vigorous dance to which
it is the accompaniment.
[< French Creole < a West African
language, ?~ Chiluba bambula beat,
hit, strike a surface]

bami /'bami:/, n pl of MWAMI.
[< Kirundi ba- plural noun pfx +
-ami (root for) king]

Bamileke /bami'leikei/, n a people
of the grasslands of Cameroon;
their Bantu language.

bana-bana /'banɔ'banə/, n pl urban street hustlers (in West Africa).
  The government has declared war

on the squadrons of beggars,
lepers and contraband hustlers
(bana-bana) who have heretofore
dogged tourists' steps throughout the city [Dakar]. P. Allen
& A. Segal, Traveler's Africa,
1973, p 639
[?< Wolof bahna-bahna, literally, it is good-good (cries
made by these vendors)]

banana, n the well-known fruit.
[< Spanish or Portuguese < a
West African language ~ Mandingo
or Wolof banána, baránda plantain]

banco /'baŋkou/, n a type of adobe
made of water and a claylike lat-
erite soil, used in dwellings in
West and Central Africa.
  She had tried to reconstitute,
  in this French villa spun of
  sub-Saharan materials, the
  rectilinear waterproof comfort
  of a Wisconsin living-room. But
  the tile floor, the banco walls,
  the rattan furniture betrayed
  the illusion, which termites
  and the breakage occasioned by
  our terrible dryness had further undermined. J. Updike,
  The Coup, 1978, p 133
[?< an African language, ?<
Italian, accumulation of detritis
from the bottom of the sea or a
river]

Banda /'bandə/, n a people of the
Central African Republic; their
Niger-Congo (Adamawa-Eastern) lan-
guage.

banda /'bændə/, n a thatched hut
or dwelling, often circular or
rounded, in many parts of Africa.
  The social aspect of life in
  the area is of course important
  too. "Amboseli is very special,"
  Lee says. "There are lots of re-
  searchers scattered around in
  camps and bandas and there's
  Ol Tuki (the Park headquarters)
  and three safari lodges nearby.
  Everyone in the local community
  is friendly. New Scientist,
  5/17/79, p 530

Another new facility, an airy thatched shed, or banda, where visitors may enjoy a picnic lunch, stands at the cliffside. Its walls are decorated with large color photographs...of the Leakeys' finds. *National Geographic*, 11/66, p 705
[< Swahili and other Bantu languages]

bandji or **Bangui** /'bandʒi or 'bangwi/, n a type of palm wine popular in the Ivory Coast.
[?< Bangui capital city of the Central African Republic]

bangi /'baŋgi/, n marijuana (in Zaire and the Congo).
The Congo was represented by a handful of military police headed by [a] bustling Security Inspector who frequently retreated behind a hedge to stuff his pipe with bangi. *Time*, 12/5/60, p 26
[< numerous West African languages < BHANG]

bango /'baŋgo/, n a type of East African reed or grass used in BANDA construction or in woven mats.
[< an East African language]

banjo, n the popular musical instrument.
[< a West African language ∿ Kimbundu mbanza ∿ Chiluba mbanzi stringed musical instrument]

banto faros /'bantou 'farous/, n a swampy lowland floodplain along the Gambia river in Gambia.
Above Kuntaur the grassy swamp belt known as the banto faros is used for rice growing. Two-thirds of the country's rice is now produced internally and Chinese advisers are encouraging more cultivation. R & E. Steel, *Africa*, 1974, p 56
[< Mandingo, literally, area where one farms]

Bantoid /'bæntoid/, adj of or relating to a group of languages within the Niger-Congo (Benue-Congo) family, of which the Bantu languages are a sub-group.
[< Bantu + -oid resembling, because some of the languages within this group have certain features highly reminiscent of Bantu languages]

Bantu /'bæntu/, adj of or relating to a large group of closely affiliated languages (and the peoples speaking them) of western, central, eastern, and southern Africa whose most striking characteristic is a system of noun classes in which noun stems are preceded by sets of prefixes, usually one for the singular and one for the plural. Adjectives, connective particles, verbs and other elements related to a noun are also preceded by these same prefixes (or ones phonologically related to them), and together form an agreement or concord system that is the hallmark of these languages. The term Bantu was coined by W. Bleek, and was a conscious effort on his part to stress the close interrelationship of these languages. The word literally means people, and is composed of the common Bantu plural noun prefix ba- (often used with noun stems denoting animate, human beings) plus the stem or root -ntu which may loosely be translated as "being, entity." Thus, ba-ntu means literally "plural/human/animate-being/entity."
--n As a noun, the term Bantu, despite its etymological plural meaning, is often used as an offensive term for a black person, especially in southern Africa.

Bantustan /'bæntu:stæn/, n a region in South Africa set aside by the government for blacks, now referred to as a homeland.
Until the mid-1970's, South Africa planned a so-called "bantustan" system for South-West Africa - like the scheme being

implemented in South Africa itself - which would have divided
the land along racial lines. Pre-
toria abandoned the bantustan
plan under threat of international sanctions. New York
Times (Sec. 4), 4/30/78, p 1
[< BANTU + Hindi -stan place,
country]

--bantustanization, n: The years
of colonialism have in any case
made reference back unreal. Only
the peculiar dogmas of apartheid
- and the exigencies of bantustan-
ization require that it be attempted. The Times, 11/24/73, p 15

Banyankore /,banyaŋ'korei/, n a
people of Uganda; their Bantu
language.

bao /bau/, n an African board game,
especially one which involves
moving pebbles through two rows of
parallel holes carved out of a
single piece of wood.
    Forms of bao are still played
    by primitive people all over
    Africa, for the game comes down
    out of the Stone Age. Each
    stone represents an animal, and
    each hole a stock corral or bo-
    ma; the point of the game, like
    the point of pastoral life, is
    to acquire more stock than one's
    opponent. P. Matthiessen, Tree
    Where Man Was Born, 1972, p 82
    There is a Bantu game - bao.
    It's a clever game - the best
    tribal game, I think. (Quoting
    Julius Nyerere in) New Yorker,
    10/16/71, p 56
[< Swahili, literally, large board
ubao wood]

baobab /'bau,bæb or 'beiəbæb/,
n a very common African tree (Adan-
sonia digitata) with a wide trunk
and gourdlike fruit.
    Baobab tree's rootlike branches
    make it appear to be growing
    upside down. National Geograph-
    ic, 9/63, p 336
[?< an African language ~ Swahili -bao wood]

Baoule /ba'u:l/, n Also, Baule.
a people of the Ivory Coast;
their Niger-Congo (Kwa) language,
a dialect of Akan.

baraza /bə'razə/, n a public meeting; a meeting-place, reception
area, veranda, etc. (in eastern,
southern and central Africa).
    Last week at a huge Baraza
    given in his honor, [Hastings]
    Banda watched members of the
    Angoni tribe perform their Li-
    guto war dance, for two hours
    accepted gifts from all over
    Nyasaland. Time, 7/21/58, p 24
    Greatly disturbed, Louis [Lea-
    key] called a baraza, or meet-
    ing, with the Masai elders and
    offered to build two cattle-
    watering dams in the gorge -
    provided the herds were kept
    away from the fossil beds. The
    elders agreed. National Geo-
    graphic, 11/66, p 701
    Things began to happen one af-
    ternoon as I was sitting on
    the back baraza, chatting with
    one of Michael's patients just
    discharged from the hospital.
    L. Kenney, Mboka, 1972, p 99
[< Swahili < Arabic]

Bariba /bə'ri:bə/, n a people of
northern Benin; their Niger-Congo
(Gur) language, used as a lingua
franca in northern Benin.

barisse /bə'risə/, n dish of
rice (in Somalia)
[< Somali]

Barotse /ba'routsei or ba'routsi:/,
n 1 LOZI 2 a breed of long-horned
cattle found in Africa.
[< Kololo (Bantu language of a
people who conquered the Lozi),
an adaptation of Aluyi the self-
designation of the Lozi < a-
plural noun pfx + -luyi group,
people ~ Luyia oluyia people,
army]

barshii /bar'ʃi:/, n a carved
wooden pillow or headrest, used
by nomads in Somalia.

[< Somali]

basaza /ba'sazə/, n pl local administrators or officials in the
kingdom of Uganda, ranking below
the KATIKIRO and KIMBUGWE.
    The entire kingdom was divided
    into ten districts, over each
    of which ruled a great official
    Basaza, or earl. Within his
    district the principal duties
    of the Basaza were to adminis-
    ter justice, maintain order,
    and supervise public works. He
    also had to provide a contin-
    gent of troops in time of war.
    R. Linton, Tree of Culture,
    1955, p 451
[< Luganda ba- plural noun pfx
+ SAZA]

basenji /bə'sendʒi:/, n 1 a breed
of small, brown, wiry-haired dog
from Africa, well-known because
they seldom bark; a dog of this
breed.
    - That's why we keep a basenji
    - no back talk. New Yorker,
    12/10/60, p 248
    If it's only the landlord's
    rules that stop you from owning
    a dog, here's one breed you
    might get away with: the basen-
    ji. It doesn't bark (honest)
    and has no doggy smell. Mac-
    lean's, 1/16/80, p 1
2 = BASHENZI.
    "Was any outsider there?" "There
    was nobody but the villagers.
    Busu Kwanga had its own cele-
    bration. Only the local basenji,"
    he said contemptuously. He
    would not call me a peasant, so
    he didn't know yet I had been
    there, too. L. Kenney, Mboka,
    1972, p 41
[< a Bantu language ∼ Lingala
basenji, literally, inhabitants
of the backward places < ba- plural noun pfx + -senji ∼ SHENZI]

bashenzi /ba'ʃenzi:/, n pl a derogatory term for black Africans
considered to be "uncivilized,"
"uneducated," or "heathen" (in
eastern, central, and southern
Africa).
    I slipped the precious forty-
    cent spectacles over my nose
    and peered intently. It was
    just like looking through win-
    dowpanes, for the frames con-
    tained ordinary glass. "Do
    things really look different
    to you when you put them on?"
    I asked him [a Congolese], a
    trifle mystified. "No, monsieur.
    I look different. Those bashen-
    zi - those ignorant natives -
    this way they have more re-
    spect for me." The only people
    who liked me, it seemed, were
    the bashenzi. J. Hallet, Congo
    Kitabu, 1964, p 21
[< a Bantu language < ba- plural
noun pfx + SHENZI ∼ Lingala ba-
senji]

basi nyebe /'basi 'nyeibei/, n
a Gambian dish of beef or chick-
en, beans, and steamed flour
balls.
    Local specialties include a
    Joloff rice dish called bena
    chin (a cousin of paella, with
    chicken and no seafood), domo-
    dah (meat in groundnut sauce
    eaten with rice), plasas (the
    headiest of the dishes: chunks
    of meat and smoked fish sim-
    mered in palm oil, eaten with
    pounded manioc or fufu), and
    basi nyebe. S. Blumenthal,
    Bright Continent, 1974, p 70
[< Wolof]

Basotho /ba'soutou/, n a people
of Lesotho, Botswana, and northern South Africa speaking the
Bantu language SOTHO.
[< seSutu ba- plural noun pfx
+ Sotho]

Bassa /'basə/, n a people of Liberia and Cameroon; their Niger-
Congo (Kwa) language.

basta /'bastə/, n spaghetti (in
Somalia).
[< Somali < Italian pasta]

Basuto /ba'su:tou/, n = BASOTHO; hence, Basutoland, former name of LESOTHO.

bataka /,ba'takə/, n pl traditional clan heads or sectional chiefs in the kingdom of Uganda.
Several hundred years ago the Bataka probably occupied the positions of greatest power within Buganda. This meant that the political system was far more decentralized and perhaps more equalitarian than it was in the 1870s when the first Europeans visited. By then the Kabaka had established his pre-eminent position. N. Kasfir in V. Olorunsola (ed.), Politics of Cultural Sub-Nationalism in Africa, 1972, p 89
[< Luganda ba- plural noun pfx + taka (root for) these chiefs]

batakari /,batə'kari:/, n a loose, striped smock worn by Ghanaian men, often in combination with Western-style trousers. Also, bate cari.
The best shopping is for the popular Ghana men's smock, batakari made of handspun, hand-woven country cloth. The selection is huge, the prices cheap, and the market amiable. S. Boone, West African Travels, 1974, p 271
[? < Ewe; ? < Hausa]

batuque /bə'tu:kə/, n a vigorous Brazilian courtship round dance of African origin.
[< Portuguese, ? < a West African language ⌣ Chiluba batukue, literally, they (people) who have become excited, wrought up < ba- plural noun pfx + -tukue ⌣ Swahili tuku(tiza) cause to quiver, shake (as during coitus)]

bayaye /bə'yayei/, n pl street hustlers, dealers in the black market, or young delinquents in Uganda.
The Bayaye came into their own with the growth of magendo (the black market) under the Amin regime when Bayaye were used as smugglers and middlemen. Today Mr. Sempangi...is trying to improve the lot of the younger hooligans by providing them with a refuge. The Times, 6/9/80, p 6
[? < Luganda ba- plural noun pfx + -yaye ⌣ (n)jaye marijuana]

bayethe or bayete /ba'yeitei/, n an exclamation of praise among the Zulu and Nguni; a traditional Zulu greeting to a great chief, meaning "Bring (or give) them (our enemies) to us."
"Thou who art great as the mountains! Cleaver of the heads of enemies! Thou whose wounds emit gunsmoke! Thou of the elephant! Thou who art black! Bayete! - All hail!" National Geographic, 12/71, p 738
Bayethe! We join the nation in rejoicing on the occasion of His Majesty's Birthday on Monday... We pray that those close to His Majesty are always worthy of the high honour and deeply conscious of their responsibility which extends, through the person of the King, to all his people. Bayethe! Times of Swaziland, 7/20/73, p 2
[< Zulu and siSwati ba- plural object pfx + -yete imperative form of bring, give]

bazimo /bə'zi:mou/, n = KISAMBILA. Uphof notes that African Maytenus (alias Gymnosporia) senegalensis has several colloquial names, among them bazimo, "confetti tree," kisambila, mmoza, and umiviesa. It is reportedly used as an aphrodisiac, for treating blennorrhagia, and for wounds. Science, 1/16/76, p 138
[< a Bantu language]

bazimu /ˌbaˈziːmu/, n pl spirits
or ghosts of ancestors among the
Tutsi and Hutu of central Africa.
A full crew of bazimu...had to
be feared, honored and at all
costs propitiated so that human life might survive. To deal
with those supernatural beings
the people resorted to the services of the bafumu - glib,
ingenious, money-grubbing
magicians. J. Hallet, Congo
Kitabu, 1964, p 115
[< a Bantu language in Zaire
< ba- plural noun pfx + -zimu
∿Swahili m-zimu ghost]

Bechuana /beˈtʃwanə/, n pl = TSWA-
NA; hence, Bechuanaland, former
name of BOTSWANA.
[< seTswana be- plural noun pfx
+ chuana Tswana]

beer /biːr/, n a Somali dish of
cooked liver.
[< Somali]

bega /ˈbeigə/, n the dry, hot seas-
on or summer in Ethiopia, from
September to June.
[< Amharic bəga]

beira or baira /ˈbeir/, n a
small,purplish-black antelope
(Dorcatragus) of Somalia.
[?< the Somali name ?<Amharic
bero polecat]

beisa /ˈbeisə/, n an antelope (Oryx) of northeastern and eastern
Africa.
The Beisa Oryx (Oryx beisa)...
varies in coat colouring from
grey to reddish brown. The face
is white and rather strikingly
marked with brownish black,hav-
ing a streak running from the
top of the head through the eye
and down the side of the jaw.
The Times, 5/20/55, p 6
[said to be< Amharic beˈzā]

Bemba /ˈbembə/, n a people of Zambia; their Bantu language widely
spoken there.

benachin or bena chin /ˈbenə-
tʃin/, n a dish of chicken and
JOLLOF rice stewed in tomatoes
and vegetables (in the Gambia).
Local specialities include a
Jollof rice dish called benachin (a cousin of paella, with
chicken and no seafood), domodah (meat in groundnut sauce
eaten with rice), plasas...
and basi nyebe. S. Blumenthal,
Bright Continent, 1974, p 70
[< Wolof, literally, one pot]

Benin /bəˈniːn or ˈbeiniːn/, n
a kingdom of West Africa in the
forest region of Nigeria, from
1400 to 1600, famous for its
brass, bronze and ivory sculptures; hence, a country in West
Africa bordering on Niger, Nigeria, Togo and Upper Volta, formerly known as DAHOMEY.
[< Edo]

benne or benni /ˈbeniː/, n sesame (in West Africa). In compounds: benne cake a kind of sesame cake; ben(n)iseed sesame.
One can always tell Tiv farming land by the great size of
the yam heaps. The old cash
crops of beniseed and soybean
have been almost entirely replaced by cultivation of food
crops for sale. The Times
12/1/77, p IX
[< a West African language ∿
Wolof, Mandingo, Bambara bene]

Benue-Congo /ˈbenə,wei/, n a group
of Niger-Congo languages including
Efik, Bantoid and the Bantu languages.
[< the name of the two rivers
bounding the area where many of
the (non-Bantu) languages of this
group are spoken]

berberine or berberin /ˈbərbər-
iːn/, n a yellow alkaloid derived from the barberry plant,
used as an antimalarial. Formula:
$C_{20}H_{19}NO_5$

The teen-age researcher has extracted cantharidin from powdered blister beetles, caffein from tea leaves, berberine and hydrastine from golden seal. Science News Letter, 2/26/55, p 134
[< Latin berberis barberry (< Arabic berber < Berber, the people of North Africa) + English -ine chemical suffix]

berebere or berber(r)e /bər,(e)-bə'rei/, n crushed, red pepper used in Ethiopian dishes.
She insisted on preparing her own berbere seasoning for her wat, and making berbere is no simple matter. Red peppers must be dried in the sun and pounded in a mortar; ginger and garlic are ground separately, along with a whole procession of spices both familiar and arcane. L. van der Post et al., African Cooking, 1970, p 35
[< Amharic bərbərre]

berele /bə'relə/, n a flask-like drinking vessel of Ethiopia.
Far more impressive vessels, notably some small silver decanter-shaped bottles with narrow necks are among the most beautiful traditional objects to be seen in wealthy households. But for all their beauty, these so-called bereles did not make the liquid they contained more welcome or more tasteful. L. van der Post et al., African Cooking, 1970, p 30
[< Amharic birille ? < Italian]

berimbau /bə'rimbau/, n a one-stringed musical instrument of Brazil.
Salvador...is the quintessence of African Brazil, a mellow, languorous city of rich, luminous colors that smells of dende oil, coconut milk and malagueta pepper and resounds to the throaty, metal-stringed strum of the African berimbau. Time, 4/21/67, p 43
[< Brazilian Portuguese, ? < a West African language ~ MARIMBA]

besa /'beisə/, n a bronze coin, or a copper coin, formerly used in Ethiopia, worth 1/100 of a rupee or talari respectively.
[< Amharic, said to be< Italian]

bhang /baŋg/, n marijuana.
Two men...denied a charge of being in illegal possession of 12 kilogrammes of "bhang" last Sunday. Standard (Nairobi), 11/23/79, p 2
[< Swahili and other East and West African languages < an Indian language]

bhanji /'bandʒi:/, n marijuana (in East Africa).
[< East African languages < BHANG]

Biafra /bi'afrə/, n an eastern region of Nigeria that attempted to secede in a war from 1967 to 1970.
[< Bight of Biafra eastern part of the Gulf of Guinea; or < Biafra small district in neighboring Cameroon, ? < Africa]

bibi /'bi:bi:/, n woman; a term of address for a woman (in eastern, central, and southern Africa).
How many Kikuyu bibis have you seen wearing goatskins in the last two years? ...Not a one of them but hasn't got a shuka made out of merikani or zanzibari. And shoes of a sort. And head kerchiefs. And houses with tin tops. R. Ruark, Uhuru, 1962, p 189
[< Swahili, or Zulu (i-)bibi< Hindi < Persian bibi lady]

biche /bi:ʃ/, n a bribe (in west Africa).
[< MATABICHE, ? < French]

biddy, n a female domestic fowl;
a young chicken, baby chick.
[? < a West African language ∿
Chiluba bidibidi small, yellow
bird]

birane /bi'ranei/, n pl early
Hausa walled cities; in modern
times, state capitals.
[< Hausa] See BIRNI.

birni /'bi:rni:/, n sg of BIRANE.
Hausa distinguish the state
capital (birni) from the capital of a village area or local
community (gari). M. Smith in
E. Skinner, Peoples & Cultures
of Africa, 1973, p 557

birr /bi:r/, n a unit of currency
in Ethiopia.
Monetary unit birr, with
(Sept. 19, 1977) a par value
of 2.07 birr to U.S. $1 (free
rate of 3.61 birr = Ł 1 sterling). Britannica Book of the
Year, 1978, p 378
[< Amharic]

bisabol /'bi:sə,bol/, n a myrrh-
like resin from the African
trees Commiphora kataf and C.
erythraea.
[< a West African language ∿
Wolof bisap (uala) a certain
tree]

bisabolene /,bisə'boli:n/, n an
oily terpene. Formula: $C_{15}H_{24}$
In matutinal sessions, the
students chant, "The terpens
are geraniol, limonene, borne-
ol, pinene, camphene, farnesol,
bisabolene, cedrene." New Yorker, 3/20/71, p 38
[< BISABOL + -ene chemical sfx]

Bobo /boubou/, n a people of Upper Volta, Ivory Coast and Mali;
their Niger-Congo (Gur) language.

bohor /bouhor/, n a small, rufous or fawn-colored reedbuck
(Redunca (reduca) bohor) of
eastern Africa. Also, bohur.

[< Amharic behor, bohor]

bojalwa /bou'dʒalwə/, n a popular
beer made from sorghum in Botswana.
[< seTswana ∿ Luyia (am)a-lwa
beer]

bokor /'boukor/, n a chief or
head of a clan in Somalia.
[< Somali]

bolis or bolilands /'bali:(z)-/,
n pl bottomlands or low-lying
grasslands that are seasonally
flooded (in the north of Sierra
Leone).
[? < Krio]

bolo-bolo /'boulou'boulou/, n a
West African tree of the bass-
wood family (Tiliaceae); the
jute-like fibre obtained from it.
[< a West African language ∿
Bini bolo to peel (bark off a
tree)]

boma /'boumə/, n 1 a corral, enclosure, fortification, or bar-
rier of thorn or other brush
material.
The pens of these bomas are
lined with grass so the oryx
...will be herded out in the
day and brought back to the
boma at night. (Transcribed
from the television program)
Mutual of Omaha's Wild Kingdom, WABC-TV, 10/21/79, 5:45EST
Two tuningforks of Cydonia
Chaenomeles Japonica...planted
against a wall amalgamated before long into a boma thicket
that stopped the mower dead in
its tracks. Punch, 7/4/62, p 26
2 a police or administrative out-
post.
The Governor...was recommending
that the Tanganyika Government
should offer the district commissioner's boma (administrative headquarters) at Bagamoyo
to the British school of ar-
chaeology. The Times, 8/22/55,
p 5

[< Swahili < Persian]

bonga /'baŋgə/, <u>n</u> a species of shad found in Sierra Leone.
  In bronze there are the one cent [coins] with a reverse of the fruit and leaves of the oil palm and the half cent with two bonga fish. <u>The Times</u>, 8/4/64, p 6
  [?< Mende or Vai]

bongo[1] /'boŋgou/, <u>n</u> a heavy-set chestnut-brown antelope with white stripes and open horns.
  [< a Bantu language ∿Lingala <u>mongu</u>, Bobangi <u>(m)banga(ni)</u> antelope]

Bongo[2], <u>n</u> a title or a term of address for a RASTAFARIAN.
  [< Jamaican English, ? variant of <u>bungo</u> a country bumpkin, offensive term for a black African, < Hausa <u>bungu</u> nincompoop; ?< <u>Bongo</u>, <u>Abongo</u>, <u>Obongo</u> names of peoples of West, Central Africa]

bongo[3], <u>n</u> the well-known drums of Africa and the Caribbean.
  [< a West African language ∿ Lokele <u>boungu</u> or <u>bongungu</u>]

bongo[4], <u>n</u> = BUNGO.

bongotol /,boŋgə'tol/, <u>n</u> pl small ingots made of dried powder mixed with clay and palm oil, used as money or offerings to the dead in Central Africa.
  Until fifty years ago, they [cowries] were the only currency used in Kasai except for the ingots of <u>bongotol</u>. (Shells and <u>bongotol</u> have now been replaced, for the most part, by <u>francs congolais</u>.) J. Hallet, <u>Congo Kitabu</u>, 1964, p 54
  [< a Central African language]

bonobo /'bounoubou/, <u>n</u> a small chimpanzee (<u>Paniscus</u>) found near the Congo river; pygmy chimp.
  Dr. Sue Savage, a very pretty psychobiologist...had been with three specimens of the very rare and interesting pygmy chimpanzee - the bonobo, or <u>Pan paniscus</u> - at the Yerkes Center. Her talk was about iconic communication - hand gestures that look like the actions they represent - among these animals. <u>New Yorker</u>, 4/24/78, p 80
  [< a West African language]

bonsella /ban'selə/, <u>n</u> a gift, present, gratuity (in southern Africa).
  He stood on one grayish, crusty leg. "Bonsella," he demanded. "Yes, even last day you don't forget bonsella." She gave him not one but two overflowing hands of popcorn. <u>Harper's</u>, 5/59, p 60
  [< Zulu <u>(i)bhanselo</u> a gift ∿ <u>-bansel-</u> give a (gift) to ∿ Swahili <u>-pa</u> give]

bontequagga /,bante'kwagə/, <u>n</u> Burchell's zebra.
  [< Afrikaans < <u>bont</u> spotted + QUAGGA]

boogie-woogie, <u>n</u> the popular blues music with repeated bass patterns.
  [said to be < a West African language ∿ Hausa <u>buga</u>, Mandingo <u>bugə</u> to beat drums]

Bophuthatswana /bə,putə'tswanə/, <u>n</u> a homeland (region in South Africa set aside by the government for blacks) for the Tswana, located in six scattered sections of the northern Cape. Although granted independence by South Africa in 1977, it is not recognized as a nation by the United Nations.
  A second African homeland, for Tswana-speaking Africans, joined the Transkei as an independent state on December 6. The new state is known as Bophuthatswana and is headed by Chief Lucas Mangope.

Collier's Encyclopedia Yearbook, 1977, p 490
[< seTswana, literally, that
which binds the Tswana]

Boran /'boræn/, n a breed of
cattle from East Africa.
The airport road into Dar es
Salaam is usually clogged with
herds of hump-backed Boran
cattle, handsome women in
gaudy tradecloth, and barbers
in nightgowns. Time, 6/11/65,
p 28
[< the Boran, the Nilotic pas-
toralists who herd these cattle
in the Lake Rudolf area of Kenya]

borele /bo'relei/, n the black
rhinoceros.
[< seTswana bodile]

bori /'bori:/, n pl spirits among
the Hausa who possess human beings and cause illness; the cult
involving such spirits; the
dances performed in the cult.
The pre-Fulani cult of spirit-
possession (bori) still flour-
ishes and has many devotees,
especially among women, the
prostitutes being its principal champions. It is of interest that bori is not uni-
versally regarded as being in
conflict with Islam. M. Smith
in P. Skinner, Peoples & Cultures of Africa, 1973, p 555
[< Hausa]

bority /'borəti:/, n a pole made
of mangrove, often used to support concrete roofs or ceilings
(in East Africa).
[< Swahili boriti, ? < Portuguese barrote beam]

botikela /,bati'kelə/, n an in-
terim chief in Zaire.
The village, I learned, was
without a chief. Since the
old one had died, the elders
said, the village had been
like a widow - there was no
one to apportion the land, to

settle the inevitable squabbles,
to provide guidance. Now they
had a candidate....Finally
Chief Basambi's spokesman
crossed the courtyard, placed
a crown on the new botikela's
head, and smeared a white line
down his forehead. A joyful
cry filled the courtyard. The
village was no longer a widow.
National Geographic, 3/73, p
401-6
[? < Kikongo]

Botswana /bou'tswanə/, n a
country in southern Africa bordering on Namibia, Angola, Zambia, Zimbabwe and South Africa;
formerly Bechuanaland.
[< seTswana bo- abstract noun
pfx + Tswana]

boubou /'bu:bu:/, n = BUBU.
The flocks of secretaries
working within the corridors
and anterooms of the Palais
de l'Administration des Noirs
were enjoined from wearing
tight skirts and blouses; the
corridors and anterooms were
obediently thronged with
loose boubous and kangas. Yet
underneath these traditional
wrappings, Colonel Ellellou
suspected, the women were
wearing elastic Western under-
wear, spicy brands called
Lollypop and Spanky. J. Updike,
The Coup, 1978, p 96

brubru /'bru:bru/, n a shrike of
the dry uplands in Africa.
We hear the liquid notes of
the tropical bru bru, a bird
seldom seen. (Cyril Connolly)
The Times, 11/24/68, p 50
[< an East African language]

buaze /'bwazei/, n a woody vine
(Polygalaceae) yielding a flax-
like fiber.
[< Chinyanja bwazi]

buba /'bu:bə/, n a blouse or
jacket-like shirt from West

Africa.

Thelma Steady...of Sierra Leone, ...was wearing a brightly
printed buba (blouse) over a
matching lappa (long skirt)
and a shocking pink turban.
New York Times, 6/21/67, p 46
[< a West African language]

bubinga /bu'biŋgə/, n African
rosewood; or, a tree yielding
this wood, such as Didelotia
africana, Copaifera, and others.

Besides old friends like cher-
ry, teak, rosewood, walnut,
chestnut, and mahogany, there
are samples of brown ebony,
bubinga, primavera, zebra wood,
padouk, limba, and a lot of
other splendid exotics - most
of them from Africa. New Yorker,
9/28/63, p 150
[< a Bantu language < bu- singular noun pfx + -binga (root
for) this tree]

bubu /'bu:bu:/, n a loose-fitting,
shapeless, full-length robe worn
in West Africa.

Whether the bubu, or cotton
robe, worn by the Fulahs de-
creases their resistance to
tuberculosis, I do not know.
National Geographic, 6/35, p
720

A babel of people in long
white Moslem robes and colored
bubus (tribal gowns) mingled
with those in formal tie and
tails wearing rows of medals.
Time, 1/17/69, p 28
[< a West African language]
Also spelled BOUBOU.

buchu /'bu:xu/, n a plant (Baros-
ma) of southern Africa with
leaves used for medicinal purposes.

The Buchu Family. A large Family, characteristic of the
"Cape" flora, most species being shrubs with aromatic leaves.
Some Buchus are used in official and patent medicines. R.
Compton, Our South African

Flora, 1940, p 31
[< Zulu bucu < Hottentot buku]

buckra /'bukrə/, n a white man.
Also, BACKRA.
[said to be < Efik mbakara one
who surrounds or governs]

Buganda /bu'gandə/, n a former
kingdom of the BAGANDA of Uganda.
[< Luganda bu- abstract noun
pfx + ganda (root for) the Baganda people]

buibui /,bu(w)i'bu(w)i:/, n a
full-length black robe traditionally worn by Muslim women.

Many women wear the buibui, a
loose black robe put over the
khanga, to conceal the contours
of the body. It may be hot,
but it's proper. National Geographic, 4/75, p 498

Perhaps she had been about to
go out, for she was muffled
head to toe in a dull black
buibui with the addition of a
face veil that covered even
her brow. A scattering of holes
smaller than the holes in a
cabbage-grater permitted her
to see, in speckled fashion.
J. Updike, The Coup, 1978, p 132
[< Swahili]

bukari /bu'kari:/, n a form of
UGALI (in central Africa).

A moment later, she brought us
a wooden bowl full of bukari
and a smaller bowl of sauce
that she ladled out of the
black pot. Following the Bantu
style of eating, I pinched off
a piece of the manioc dough
with my thumb and forefinger,
kneaded it into a ball, punched
a deep trough in the ball with
my thumb, forming a dough spoon
and used it to dip up the sav-
ory sauce. J. Hallet, Congo Kitabu, 1964, p 69
[< Chiluba bu- mass noun pfx +
-kari ~ Swahili UGALI]

bumbo /'bumbou/, n a West African

tree (<u>Daniellia thurifer</u>); a
soft, water-resistant wood, or
the fragrant resin, from this
tree.
[< a West African (? Sierra
Leonian) language, ?~Mende
<u>bogbo</u> a certain tree]

buna /'bu:nə/, <u>n</u> coffee (in Ethiopia).
>With some hidden logic, Ethi-
>opia is the one country where
>the word for coffee does not
>remotely resemble its inter-
>national root: here it is
>called <u>buna</u>. S. Blumenthal,
><u>Bright Continent</u>, 1974, p 365
[< Amharic <u>bunna</u>] See MBUNI.

bundu /'bundu:/, <u>n</u> open country;
the bush; wildlands (in eastern
and southern Africa).
>A family which has lived ob-
>scurely in the Rhodesian bun-
>du for generations can have a
>child who could, if the edu-
>cation were available, repro-
>duce the imagination and math-
>ematical genius of the archi-
>tect of the city of Zimbabwe.
><u>The Times</u>, 11/16/76, p 17
[< a Bantu language, said to
be < Swahili ~Shona <u>bundo</u>
grasslands]

bunduki /bun'du:ki:/, <u>n</u> a gun
(in eastern Africa).
>I better just get myself down
>there to the campfire and find
>a cosy place to rest my <u>bun-</u>
><u>duki</u> and be ready to open the
>betting if anybody else seems
>restless. I would say that a
>good safe range for elephant
>is thirty feet. R. Ruark,
><u>Uhuru</u>, 1962, p 56
[< Swahili < Arabic or Persian]

bunga /'bungga/, <u>n</u> the black African council or seat of government in the Transkei.
>For Prime Minister John Vor-
>ster, the fluttering of the
>blue, white and orange flag
>above the bunga, or seat of
>the government, will repre-

sent the fulfillment of a
political ideal. <u>New York</u>
<u>Times</u>, 9/8/76, p 8
[< Xhosa (<u>i-</u>)<u>bunga</u> ~ -<u>bung(ana)</u>
meet in council] See BUNGE.

bunge /'bungei/, <u>n</u> the national
assembly of the Tanzanian government.
[< Swahili]

bungo /'bənggou/, <u>n</u> a type of dug-
out canoe used in the southwest
United States.
>The most urgent steps were
>being taken to press every
>bungo and canoe to the imme-
>diate relief of the people
>along the coast. <u>Daily Pica-</u>
><u>yune (New Orleans)</u>, ca. 1848,
>p not known
[< American Spanish <u>bongo</u> < a
West African language ~Hausa
<u>bungubungu</u> canoe made from palm-
wood; cf. Jamaican English <u>bun-</u>
<u>gay, bungy</u> this boat]

Burundi /bu'rundi:/, <u>n</u> a country
of east and central Africa bordering on Zaire, Rwanda and
Tanzania; formerly, URUNDI.
[< Kirundi <u>bu-</u> abstract noun
prx + RUNDI]

busaa /bu:'sa/, <u>n</u> = BUZAA.
>Most of these teachers get an
>advantage of going to make tea
>in their houses with the re-
>maining milk and some turn
>back to nearby villages to
>drink busaa. At evening when
>the upper classes come back
>to their respective classes
>...teachers are very drunk.
><u>Daily Nation (Nairobi)</u>, 1/18/
>80, p 7

busuti /bə'su:ti:/, <u>n</u> Also,
<u>basuti</u>. a traditional cotton
full-length women's gown of
Uganda, with ruffled or puffed
sleeves and a double layer of
cloth around the middle.
>Another MP described how a
>woman at the party was made
>to wear a <u>busuti</u>, a rope was

tied around her neck and she
was pulled about to show how
'an African treats a woman.'
New Statesman, 6/27/75, p 817
This quaint, picturesque garment, basuti, with its voluminous ankle-length skirt and
leg-of-mutton sleeves, must
have gladdened the hearts of
the early Christian missionaries in Uganda. Punch, 3/29/67,
p 472
[< Luganda, ? < bu- singular
noun pfx + -suti ~ English suit]

butut /bə'tu:t/, n a unit of currency in the Gambia, equal to
1/100th of a DALASI.
The dalasi, which was divided
into 100 bututs, replaced the
Gambian pound. Collier's Encyclopedia Year Book, 1972,
p 254
[< Wolof]

buzaa /bu'za/, n Also, busaa. an
intoxicating liquor made of
honey (in eastern Africa).
I support the President of
Kenya, Mr. Daniel arap Moi's
directive that all buzaa clubs
in the country be closed down.
Alcohol brings life to the
sellers and death to drinkers.
A country like Kenya which
needs people with clear heads
to carry out national development projects cannot afford
to have drunk citizens. Weekly
Review (Nairobi), 2/16/79, p 3
[< Swahili buza < Arabic] Also,
BUSAA.

bwalo /'bwalou/, n a meeting hall
(in Malawi).
Workers constructed a small
city - Capricorntown - complete with refurbished hotel,
thatched huts, marked-off
lanes, a huge grass-thatched
bwalo and symmetrical rows of
small tents. Time, 7/2/56, p 22
[? < Chichewa]

bwana /'bwanə/, n a term of address to a man; "master"; "sir"'
boss; headman.
As we crossed the yellow plain,
togalike crimson robes appeared. Burnished steel flashed
in the sun. "Masai morani -
warriors," said Njovu. "Wild
boys, not civilized. Keep going, bwana." National Geographic, 9/60, p 340
In Montreal, the English-speak-
ers were the bwanas. They
stole the fur trade from the
French settlers. The Times,
11/20/78, p 16
One helpful farmer lined up
his Kukes and told them to
speak to me freely. The farmer
is a good bwana, they said,
but that isn't the point. The
land was always ours; now we
are hired laborers who can
never earn enough to buy a
farm. Time, 11/10/52, p 40
[< Swahili]

bwana mkubwa /...əm'ku:bwə/, n
(literally) a big boss; an extremely important boss.
General Amin said, "For a
black African like me to kick
the British out of the country,
he must be very strong and
tough....I will now be very
friendly to them because they
are no longer bwana mkubwas
[big bosses]." The Times,
1/8/73, p 1
[mkubwa < Swahili m- singular
noun pfx + -kubwa big]

bwana ya l'etat /...,ya lei'ta/,
n a government official (in
central Africa).
My career as a Bwana ya l'Etat
was about to begin, and I was
anxious to wear my new uniform.
Shyly but happily, like a virgin going to her inevitable
fate, I donned the khaki safari jacket, the kapitula
(tropical shorts), the long
khaki knee socks and the
sturdy walking shoes. Then,
the crowning touch: I put on

The Helmet. J. Hallet, <u>Congo Kitabu</u>, 1964, p 15
[literally, boss of the state < Swahili <u>bwana</u> + <u>ya</u> connective, "of" + French <u>l'etat</u> the state, government]

Bwiti /'bwi:ti:/, <u>n</u> an important cult of the Fang and related peoples of Cameroon and Gabon, noted for their ritual use of IBOGAINE.

In Yaounde, in the Cameroon, the Catholics allow drumming and dancing in their masses. This was felt necessary to side-step the Bwiti movement that has spread to 60,000 people of the Fang tribe in the Cameroon and Gabon. <u>New York Times</u>, 12/25/67, p 16
[< Fang < a Gabonese language]

C

C or ₡, abbreviation of CEDI.
Mr E.K. Antwi (in kente cloth),
best farmer of the Ashanti region, being congratulated by
Major-General D.K. Addo, former Commissioner for Agriculture, after he had been presented with a cheque for
₡1,000. Ghanaian Times, 3/20/
73, p 4

caama[1] /'kamǝ/, n a fox from
southern Africa; CHAMA FOX.
[< an African language]

caama[2], n a reddish hartebeest
from Southern Africa, also known
as the Cape hartebeest (Alcepha-
lus caama). Also, KAAMA.
[< seTswana < Nama //xamap]

cafuso /kǝ'f(y)u:sou/, n a Latin
American, especially in Brazil,
of mixed Indian and black (African) ancestry; ZAMBO.
[< Portuguese < a West African
language ∼ Hausa kafuri heathen]

cala /'kalǝ/, n a Creole dish of
fried rice cake.
[< a West African language ∼
Vai kolo (uncooked) rice ∼ Bambara kala cereal stalk]

Calabar bean /'kælǝ,bar/, n a
poisonous seed of a West African plant that yields ESERINE.
[< Calabar region and a river

in Nigeria, ? < KALABARI]

calinda or calenda /kǝ'lindǝ or
kǝ'lendǝ/, n a ceremonial stick
dance of the West Indies often
with mock battles and verbal
jousting, sometimes performed
while balancing a bottle or
glass of water on the head.
[< American Spanish < an African language, ? < Gũ (a West
African language) kalim a
slave (hence, a slave dance;
cf. Jamaican English calimbe,
calembe a stick dance]

calinut /'kæli:nǝt/, n the seed
of an African woody vine (Physo-
stigma).
[cali < a West African language
∼ Mende kale seed + English nut]

calumba /kǝ'lu:mbǝ/, n Also,
calombo, columba. the root of
an African plant that contains
COLUMBIN.
[< a West African language, ?
∼ Hausa kalumbo small tree]

calumbin /kǝ'lumbin/, n = COLUMBIN.
[< CALUMBA + -in chemical sfx]

camwood /'kæm,wud/, n barwood,
a hard, red wood from a tree
(Pterocarpus); or a similarly
colored and textured wood from
a tree (Baphia nitida).
These were small carved boxes

which are used to contain ra-
zors of native manufacture and
also the powdered red camwood,
takula, which is an important
African cosmetic. Atlantic,
4/59, p 60
[< Temne kám or another West
African language kam(bi) + English
wood]

candomblé /,kæ ndəm'blei/, n a
Brazilian fetish cult that com-
bines elements of African, American Indian, and Roman Catholic
beliefs; a dance, ceremony, amulet, incantation, etc. of this
cult.
     The African cult of candomble,
     a form of black magic, is
     still widely practised and its
     effects can be seen in the
     colourful dress of the street
     vendors or tasted in the spicy
     local food...African traditions
     still survive. The Times, 5/3/76,
     p XIII
[< Portuguese < an African language, ? ~Fon kanumɔ, Gũ kãlĩmɔ
a slave]

cashaw /kə'ʃo/, n a type of mes-
quite.
[~Yoruba kasha a running plant
~Bobangi nkasa a tree ~Akan
kasɛ a thorn]

cat, n the well-known domesticated
mammal.
[< Middle English < a Germanic
word borrowed < Late Latin cattus,
catta, thought to be < Nubian
kadis, Berber kaddîska]

Cattle Damara, n = HERERO.
[< a misapplication of the Nama
name Gomacha Dama, literally,
cattle-breeding black people, applied by the Nama to the Herero]
See DAMARA.

CCM, abbreviation of CHAMA CHA
MAPINDUZI.

cedi /'seidi:/, n a unit of currency in Ghana, equal to 100

PESEWAs.
     A revolutionary committee spokes-
     man has accused Lebanese and
     Indian businessmen of having
     offered ten million cedis (i.e.
     3 million U.S. dollars) for
     the assassination of Rawlings.
     ...The charges have been vehe-
     mently denied. Weekly Review
     (Nairobi), 6/15/79, p 18
[< Akan (Fante) sedi small
shell, cowrie]

chacma or chakma /'tʃakmə/, n
the Cape baboon, a large brown-
black baboon (Papio Comatus),
noted for its crop destruction.
     Although he was well past the
     age when his peers were said
     to grow cantankerous, and al-
     though he was a chacma - the
     largest of the baboon families
     - Mon Cul was considered a fit
     companion for the circus tots.
     "My friend has shared private
     amusements with children on
     five continents," Ziller as-
     sured the parents. T. Robbins,
     Another Roadside Attraction,
     1971, p 41
[< Khoi-Khoin]

Chagga /'tʃagə/, n Also, Chaga.
an agricultural people of northern Tanzania; their Bantu language.

chai /tʃai/, n 1 tea. 2 a slang
term for bribery (in eastern
Africa).
     The [unsold & missing] textile
     goods are sold to the "lucky"
     customers who can afford the
     "taxation of chai" and to re-
     cover this "chai" the "lucky"
     customers have to sell the
     goods in the blackmarket...
     If nothing is done to stop
     this "chai" I can guarantee
     that even in future we are go-
     ing to face the same old prob-
     lem of "unsold items piled up
     in godowns." Daily News (Tan-
     zania), 12/?/76, p 8
[< Swahili < Persian, Arabic

or Hindi]

Chama cha Mapinduzi /'tʃama tʃa ,mapin'du:zi:/, n the sole political party in Tanzania.
 The Tanganyika African National Union and the Afro-Shirazi Party in Zanzibar merged into one revolutionary party, Chama cha Mapinduzi, in Jan. 1977. Statesman's Year-Book, 1979, p 1169
 [< Swahili, literally, party of revolution or revolutionary party]

chama fox /'tʃamə/, n = CAAMA[1].

chambo /'tʃambou/, n a fish similar to perch (in Malawi).
 The hotel has a menu that includes succulent baked chambo, a fish unique to Malawi and one of 220 varieties in the lake. New York Times, 6/13/71, p 8
 [< Chichewa ~ Swahili chambo bait for fish]

chamma /'ʃamə/, n a white, toga-like garment worn in Ethiopia.
 Far down below us are sidewalks designed for and used by pedestrians; there's no mid-street milling of a white chamma-clad multitude. Moreover, we haven't seen a mule - or a camel. We miss them. National Geographic, 6/35, p 783
 [< Amharic šəmma]

changamire /,tʃangə'mi:rei/, n a king of the Rozwi, people who inhabited the Zimbabwe area.
 Great Zimbabwe became the capital of Urozwi. Here the changamires lived in a royal dwelling whose walls, rising to a height of more than thirty feet, are still the wonder of all who visit their tall grey ruins today. B. Davidson, History of East & Central Africa, 1969, p 254
 [< Shona]

cheka or chika /'tʃekə/, n a village chief or official in Ethiopia.
 [< Amharic chik'a (šum) literally, (mud) chief]

chere /'tʃere/, n a dish of millet-flour dumplings (in the Gambia).
 Local specialties include a Joloff rice dish called benachin...and basi nyebe (a ragout of beef or chicken, beans, and steamed millet-flour balls, or chere). S. Blumenthal, Bright Continent, 1974, p 70
 [? < Wolof]

Chewa /'tʃeiwə/, n Also, Cewa. a people of Malawi; their language, CHICHEWA.

chi /tʃi:/, n a personal god (among the Ibo) who determines one's fortune.
 If ever a man deserved his success, that man was Okonkwo. At an early age he had achieved fame as the greatest wrestler in all the land. That was not luck. At the most one could say that his chi or personal god was good. But the Ibo people have a proverb that when a man says yes his chi says yes also. Okonkwo said yes very strongly; so his chi agreed. C. Achebe, Things Fall Apart, 1958, p 25
 [< Ibo chi deity, cf. Chuku]

chibaro /tʃi'barou/, n a system of forced labor, especially in the mines of Zimbabwe and in southern Africa.
 Who or what was chibaro? "Chibaro-labour formed the most exploited group of an exploited class." "The words isibalo, cibalo, shibaru, and chibaro were widely used by Africans" throughout the southern African region. Manchester Guardian, 5/23/76, p 21 quoted from

Chibaro: African Mine Labour
in Southern Rhodesia by Charles
van Onselen
[< a southern Bantu language]

chibo /'tʃi:bou/, n a large, straw
torch formerly used by Emperor
Haile Selassie of Ethiopia to
light the DEMERA.
[< Amharic cibbo]

Chiboi /tʃi'boi/, n = CHILAPALAPA.
[< a Zambian Bantu language, ?<
Bemba < chi- singular noun (language) pfx + boi < English boy,
derogatory term for an African
man]

chibuku /tʃi'bu:ku/, n a potent
maize beer made in central, southern, and eastern Africa; the
trade name of this drink.
    I was so thirsty and I was
    really in great need for gulping
    several dozen of one day of
    chibuku, but I was able to
    utilize only one dozen (litres)
    after which I felt stomach dis-
    comforts characterised by some
    squeeling sound. So please chi-
    buku brewers make sure you
    sieve the beer. New Yorker,
    10/9/78, p 126
[< numerous Bantu languages]

Chichewa /tʃi'tʃeiwə/, n Also,
Cicewa. a Bantu language of the
Chewa of Malawi, used as a na-
tional language; CHEWA.
[< Chichewa chi- singular noun
(language) pfx + CHEWA]

chichinga /tʃi'tʃiŋgə/, n a dish
of shish kebab (in Ghana).
[? < Akan]

chigger, n the well-known insect
that sticks to the skin.
    Contrary to popular belief,
    chiggers do not burrow into
    the skin and stay there. They
    attack like ticks, usually in
    skin depressions at the base
    of hair....After they have fed,
    they back off and drop off.

Science News, 7/28/51, p 62
[< a West African language ~
Yoruba jigà jigger, Wolof jiga
insect or ~Tshiluba (n)jiga
sandflea]

chigoe /'tʃigou, -gə/, n = CHIGGER.

chijaga /tʃi'dʒagə/, n = CHIRUNDU.
The "chijaga" is worn with
colorful bandana head scarves
called "duku" and blouses with
national symbols and designs
called "malaya." P. Allen & A.
Segal, Traveler's Africa,
1973, p 730
[? < Chichewa chi- singular
noun pfx + jaga (root for) this
garment]

Chikabanga /tʃikə'baŋgə/, n =
CHILAPALAPA.
In the Rhodesian Copper Belt
nearly every white official or
technician speaks Chikabanga or
"Kitchen Kaffir," the dialect
which the 60 tribes in this
area use for inter-tribal con-
versations. Wall Street Journal, 8/19/60, p 4

chiko /'tʃi:kou/, n an Ethiopian
dish of pounded, dried barley
that is roasted, ground and
mixed with a spiced butter oil
to form a paste.
    Another flavorsome snack called
    chiko, good for breakfast, tea
    or cocktails, contains roasted
    barley and...can be stored in
    a cool place indefinitely. L.
    van der Post et al, African
    Cooking, 1970, p 40
[< Amharic]

chikungunya /,tʃikuŋ'gu:nyə/, n
a virus fever similar to dengue.
The viruses have been divided
into distinct families labeled
"A" and "B"; they crop up a-
round the world in a variety
of guises, e.g., Japanese "B"
in eastern Asia; Murray Valley
Fever in Australia; Chikungunya
in Africa; Omsk hemorrhagic

fever in Russia. <u>Time</u>, 10/5/59,
p 70
[said to be < the name of a small
town in East Africa where the fever was identified]

chikwemba /tʃi'kwembə/, <u>n</u> the traditional dress for men in Malawi,
consisting of a long cape or
cloak worn like a toga.
[< Chichewa <u>chi</u>- singular noun
pfx + -<u>kwemba</u> (root for) this
garment]

Chilapalapa /tʃi,lapə'lapə/, <u>n</u>
a pidgin language spoken in Zambia and Zimbabwe, based on Zulu,
Bemba, Afrikaans and English.
[< a Bantu language < <u>chi</u>-
singular noun (language) pfx +
<u>lapalapa</u> ? reduplicated form of
-<u>lapa</u> ~ Swahili -<u>apa</u> swear]

Chilolo /tʃi'loulou/, <u>n</u> =
CHILAPALAPA.

Chiluba /tʃi'lu:bə/, <u>n</u> a Bantu
language of Zaire, used widely
as a trade language. Also, <u>TSHI-</u>
<u>LUBA</u>.
[< Chiluba <u>chi</u>- singular noun
(language) pfx + <u>luba</u> (root for)
the people speaking it]

chimpanzee, <u>n</u> the well-known ape
of Africa.
[< a West African Bantu language
~ KiKongo, Tshiluba (<u>kivili</u>-)
<u>chimpenzi</u>, <u>kimpenzi</u> ape]

chimungu /tʃi'mungu/, <u>n</u> the bateleur eagle of southern Africa.
"It came to the water full of
fever and died miserably,"
Werner added. "Look at that
empty eye socket. A bateleur
eagle has been here and picked
out an eyeball. Natives call
him <u>chimungu</u>, the boss bird.
That's because he gets to the
carcass first and leads in the
vultures. The first thing he
eats is an eyeball." <u>National</u>
<u>Geographic</u>, 2/72, p 159
[< a southern Bantu language <

Bantu <u>chi</u>- singular noun pfx +
<u>mungu</u> God]

chimurenga /tʃimu'rengə/, <u>n</u> the
war of liberation formerly waged
in Zimbabwe; revolution.
The insurgency, which the
guerrillas call <u>chimurenga</u> is
now in its fifth year. It is
spreading like a malignancy.
"It's worse this week than
last," an off-duty "troopie"
(soldier) declared in a Salisbury bar, "and worse this year
than last." <u>Time</u>, 3/28/77, p 29
One large Portuguese language
registration book contained,
in English, several thousand
male names and listed their
age, occupations, education,
marital status, nationality
("Zimbabwean") and their <u>chi</u>-
<u>murenga</u> (revolutionary) names
– a vivid collection including
Hitler, Elvis, Crusader and
Killem, a brand name of a local insecticide. <u>The Times</u>,
8/30/76, p 3
White fears that Christmas and
Easter might be abolished were
based on the publication by
Zanu (PF) of a calendar for
1980 in which all religious
holidays were removed. Instead
the calendar marked a list of
non-religious days including
Chimurenga (Liberation Struggle) Day. <u>The Times</u>, 6/10/80,
p 9
[< Shona]

chinchin /'tʃin,tʃin/, <u>n</u> a Nigerian dish, a cake fried in peanut
oil, and formed into the shape
of a bow.
Later that afternoon as we were
going back from school I caught
you buying <u>chin-chin</u>, and when
I asked you you said it was
part of your own money, even
though you still had three
shillings in your hand. Have
you forgotten? I. Okpewho, <u>The</u>
<u>Victims</u>, 1970, p 90
[? < Ibo]

Chinyanja /tʃi'nyandʒə/, n the Bantu language of the Nyanja of Malawi, used as a national language.
[< Chinyanja <u>chi</u>- singular noun (language) pfx + -<u>nyanja</u>]

chiperone /tʃipər'ounei/, n <u>1</u> a heavy mist in Malawi that drifts west from Mozambique.
Tea is still mainly produced by large companies....It comes from estates on the southern slopes of the Shire Highlands and on the lower slopes of Mount Mulanje where rainfall is heavy, and the <u>chiperone</u> keeps the air moist during the dry season. R. Steel & E. Steel, <u>Africa</u>, 1974, p 184
<u>2</u> Also, <u>chiperoni</u>. a beer of Malawi.
The Bill seeks to empower the Minister of Trade and Industry to cancel licenses for the manufacture and supply of the so-called traditional beer, known as "chiperoni". Dr. Banda said the Bill was introduced on his instructions. <u>The Times</u>, 3/8/63, p 10
[def. 1 < the name of the district in Mozambique where the mist originates; def. 2 < its effect]

chipimbiri /tʃipim'bi:ri:/, n the black rhinoceros (in Zimbabwe).
The credit for "Operation Rhino" goes to the Rhodesian National Parks and Wildlife Management Department who mounted the project in 1970 and 1971 with the aim of capturing as many chipimbiri as possible in remote areas in north-west and north-east Rhodesia. <u>The Times</u>, 5/6/72, p 14
[? < Shona]

chiromila /tʃirou'mi:lə/, n a crescent-shaped fishing net used in Malawi, pulled between canoes.
Viewed on one of the windy days so frequent on Lake Nyasa, the manipulation of the <u>Chiromila</u> from apparently overcrowded, and most unstable, dugout canoes is an exciting spectacle. <u>The Times</u>, 7/30/64, p 12
[? < Chichewa]

chirundu /tʃi'rundu/, n a long, wraparound garment traditionally worn by Malawian women, often colorfully printed.
Almost as enticing as the hikes up the nearby mountain peaks are sorties into the market in Limbe, a bustling bazaar where cotton prints known as chirundu are sold. Skirts and shirts in large flowery designs and bright colors are displayed. <u>New York Times, Sec. 10</u>, 9/28/80, p 10
The ban on miniskirts is notorious but not really objectionable: the <u>chirundu</u>, a sort of colourful wrap-around maxiskirt, gives the streets of Blantyre a certain old-fashioned charm. <u>The Times</u>, 6/30/73, p 1
[? < Chichewa <u>chi</u>- singular noun pfx + -<u>rundu</u> (root for) this garment]

chitemene /tʃitə'meinei/, n a traditional method of crop cultivation and rotation in Zambia in which trees are cut to a height of about 3 feet and the branches and stump burned along with other trees. Various crops are then grown in the ashes and the land finally left fallow.
These soils have been cultivated with success for generations by the primitive technique of the <u>chitemene</u> garden. <u>Scientific American</u>, 11/60, p 130
[< Bemba <u>chi</u>- singular noun pfx + -<u>temene</u> ~ -<u>tem</u>- cut + <u>ene</u> verbal sfx]

chitenge /tʃi'teŋge/, n =

KITENGE (in Zambia).
There are several massive department stores that are interesting for browsing, with wares ranging from Polish china and Bulgarian feta-type cheese to Gilbey's gin and Indonesian batiks, from which Zambian women fashion chitenge, the national dress. R. Kane, Africa A to Z, 1961, p 405
[< a Bantu language of Zambia < chi- singular noun pfx + -tenge ~ KITENGE]

chiwara /tʃi:'warə/, n an antelope head piece sculpture of Mali, with geometric and abstract elements, used in ceremonial dances.
A man from Mali produced a replica of the chiwara antelope headdress, the national symbol of the new state of Mali (for, as he reminded me, Mali was a great West African empire in the fifteenth century...). Manchester Guardian, 8/19/79, p 20
[< Bambara] Also, TCHI-WARA.

Chuku /'tʃu:ku/, n the supreme deity among the Ibo.
We Freemen, of all colors of the spectrum, in the name of God, Ra, Jehovah, Anubis, Osiris, Tlaloc, Quetzalcoatl, Thoth, Ptah, Allah, Krishna, Chango, Chimeke, Chuku, Olisa-Bulu-Uwa, Imales, Orisasu, Odudua,...do exorcise and cast out the EVIL. Harper's, 3/68, p 96
[< Ibo chi-uku a great god < CHI + uku great]

cibalo /tʃi'balou/, n = CHIBARO.

Ciskei /'sis,kai/, n a homeland (region in South Africa set aside by the government for blacks) for the Xhosa, located to the south of TRANSKEI in the eastern Cape province.
In KwaZulu and the Ciskei, two so-called homelands or national states that have been established for the blacks under South Africa's apartheid policy...traditional subsistence farming had been hardest hit by the failure of the rains. The Government added substantial emergency relief to the Ciskei and offered it to KwaZulu, which declined it. New York Times, 11/23/80, p 22
[< Latin cis- this side + Kei name of a river forming the southern border of Transkei]

cola, n = KOLA.

columbin /kə'lʌmbin/, n a bitter, crystalline principle from the root calumba.
[alteration of CALUMBIN]

conga, n the popular Cuban dance of African origin; the narrow-headed drum used for rhythm in this dance.
You'd have thought all sixteen of them were doing the conga. And while I'm sorting them out there's this shifty-eyed wing-three creeping up offside. But I got him in the end. Punch, 12/16/59, p 587
Calypso time: One big Chicago music store reports sales of bongo and conga drums have leaped from near-zero to 15% of overall instrument volume. Wall Street Journal, 6/6/57, p 1
[< Spanish < Congo the region in Africa (now Zaire) named for the KONGO, a Bantu people living there]

Congo /'kaŋgou/, n a country in West Africa bordering on Gabon, Cameroon, Central African Republic, Zaire and Angola. Also, former name of Zaire.
[< KONGO]

cooter /'ku:tər/, n a turtle or tortoise of the southern United States; the Carolina box turtle.

They thought for a long time
it was a cooter, or some even
said a bear — but it turned out
to be a wild dog, who used to
kill calves. New Yorker, 8/29/
64, p 25
[< a West African language ~
Mandingo, Bambara kuta, ? ~ Tshiluba (n)kuda turtle]

coqui /'kok(w)i:/, n a type of
partridge or francolin found in
the African grasslands.
To the beat of conga drums and
the sounds of the coqui, the
jibaras washed clothes in a
nearby stream. New York Times,
9/2/67, p 12
[< Setswana, quail]

cossa-cossa /,kosə'kosə/, n a
Zairean dish of cooked crayfish.
Crayfish (cossa-cossa) is a
delectable specialty at Matadi,
and palm wine is called sambwa.
Walkers and budget travelers
can buy fish in a banana-leaf
platter. P. Allen & A. Segal,
Traveler's Africa, 1973, p 436
[< a Zairean language]

cramcram /'kræm,kræm/, n a wild
grass providing nutritional
grains, harvested in West Africa.
I met some of the former refugees in the marginal lands
between the river and the high
desert. They were Bellas, once
serfs to the Tuareg, but now
integrated into the tribes.
They were harvesting fonio and
cramcram. National Geographic,
8/75, p 177
We saw strange sights; we saw
naked women climbing mimosa
trees to crop the twig-tips
for cooking, we saw children
gathering the wild nettle called
cram-cram, we saw men attacking and pulverizing anthills
to recover the grains...My hand
grows too heavy to write as I
remember this misery. J. Updike, The Coup, 1978, p 39
[< a West African language,

? ~ Akan krãmãkrãmã wild]

cush /kuʃ/ or cushcush /'kuʃ-
,kuʃ/, n a dish of seasoned corn
meal dough fried, or baked and
served with meat.
There was calalu and there
were crab-backs, mutton with
pigeon peas, cush-cush, plantain, breadfruit, and christo-
phene. Atlantic, 9/57, p 91
[< a West African language ~
Hausa kusha thin peanut cake;
Efik kuskus couscous; ultimately
< Arabic kuskus couscous]

cusso or cussu /'ku:su:/, n
= KOSO.
[said to be < Amharic kussu,
but cf. etymology of KOSO]

D

D, abbreviation of DALASI.
More help will come from the
European Investment Bank,
which will finance 40 percent
of a D15 million project to
improve peanut processing, and
the United States, which has
approved an aid package valued
at D2.4 million. Collier's
Encyclopedia Yearbook, 1979,
p 277

dabo kolo /'dabou 'koulou/, n an
Ethiopian dish of roasted, pea-
nut-sized strips or bits of
wheat flour sometimes mixed with
BERBERE.
In Ethiopian cities, dabo kolo
is now often served at cocktail parties, but it tastes
best to me on its own, when
one is hungry and deprived of
other foods. L. van der Post
et al., African Cooking, 1970,
p 40
[< Amharic dabbo k'olo]

dacha /'daxə or 'dagə/, n = DAGGA.

daga /'dagə/, n = DAGGA².
The walls were of daga - mud
bricks, baked in the sun. The
Times, 7/14/64, p 12

dagaa /da'ga/, n a type of fresh
water sardine of eastern Africa,
resembling whitebait; AGAHUZA,
NDAGAA, NDAGALA.

Fishermen on Lake Tanganyika
ready their nets for dagaa....
They are best caught during
the dark of the moon, when
kerosene lamps draw the fish
to the surface. National Geographic, 4/75, p 506
[< Swahili, ? < Arabic] Also,
NDAGALA.

Dagachin or dagaci /dagə'tʃin/,
n a district commissioner in
Nigeria; formerly, a ruler in
the empires of central and western Africa.
The Dagachin's approval was
crucial and the stage, with
its sets and curtains - all
of which had a clear function
- was less of a cultural im-
position than performances
from other regions might have
been. The Times, 12/1/77, p XV
[? < Hausa or Kanuri]

dagga¹ or dacha /'daxə or 'dagə/,
n cannabis; marijuana; "pot"; or
the species of shrub (Leontis)
yielding it (in southern Africa).
Mr. Robert Randall may be the
US champion dagga smoker. The
National Organization for the
Reform of Marijuana (dagga)
Laws estimates that Mr. Randall
has smoked 10 kg of marijuana
in the past three years, at
the rate of 70 cigarettes a
week. It is all legal. Mr.

Randall's supplier is the US Government. Cape Times, 11/24/79, p 5

Rodney Kerr baked his own cakes for a buffet party in his flat. But the recipe he used for his gingerbread had an unusual ingredient - dagga. Rhodesia Herald, 2/16/73, p 6

[< Afrikaans dagga < Nama daxa-b the species of shrub]

dagga[2] or daga or dagha /ˈdagə/, n a mud, mortar, or cement of wetted and packed clay, used on walls and floors (in southern Africa).

The desire to stay still appears strong among most of them. Like many, he has been working the same farm since the end of World War II and began by living in a pole and dagga (mud-brick) hut located on the same spot as his spacious farmhouse sits today. "I'm quite prepared to be a Zimbabwean," says Travers. Manchester Guardian, 7/30/78, p 18

We all knew families like the Gordon-Forbeses, living like poor whites in pole and dagga huts or pigging it in Public Works Department road camps. London Sunday Times, 9/1/68, p 27

[< Afrikaans dagha mud mortar < Nguni (u)daka mud, clay ∿ Swahili -aka build using mortar]

Dahomey /dəˈhoumei/, n a kingdom of West Africa in Benin whose capital was at Abomey; the former name of BENIN.

[said to be < Fon Dã-ho-me, literally, in the belly of Dan, based upon the legend of a king whose land was gradually overrun by the Abomeyans and who then asked whether they wished to settle on his stomach]

daktari /dakˈtari:/, n a doctor (in eastern and central Africa).

When asked why I was digging in their grazing lands and filling plastic basins with dudus (insects), I replied, "Mimi ni daktari wa dudu - I'm a bug doctor." The Masai smiled in amusement at the crazy Mzungu (white man), no doubt wondering what a bug doctor actually did for a living. National Geographic, 4/78, p 545

[< Swahili < English doctor or German Doktor doctor]

dalasi /ˈdalasi:/, n a unit of currency in the Gambia, introduced in 1971, equal to 100 BUTUT.

The dalasi was revalued upward from 5 to 4 to £1 sterling on March 19. Britannica Book of the Year, 1974, p 328

[< DALASY]

dalasy /ˈdalasi:/, n a coin of Gambia formerly equal to four shillings.

In Gambia, most cash business is done in dirhems, or dalasies, as they are called - and in the vernacular a Gambian pound is a five-dirhem note. The Times, 11/16/66, p 20

[< Mandingo; believed to be ultimately < English dollar, dollars]

Damara /ˈdæmərə or dəˈmarə/, n a people of Namibia speaking NAMA; hence, Damaraland, earlier name of Namibia.

[< Nama damara feminine plural form of dama, literally, black people. The term damara was incorrectly applied both to the Nama and to the CATTLE DAMARA, the unrelated Bantu people HERERO]

dambo /ˈdæmbou/, n a small, grassy area, glade, or clearing of a floodplain, often near the headwaters of a stream.

Wherever the drainage is

sufficiently retarded to give
grey soils, seasonal water-
logging is common and grassy
'dambos' result on the valley
flats. W.H. Pearsall, in New
Biology, Vol. 17, 1954, p 13
[< Mang'unja dambo grass-covered
plain ~ Swahili (mw)amb(a)o area
near edge of sea]

dambonite /'dæmbə,nait/, n a
sweet, white crystalline substance derived from inositol,
occurring in a caoutchouc in
western Africa. Formula: $C_4H_6O_3$
[< a West African (Gabonese?)
language (n)dambo the vine
yielding caoutchouc + English
-ite chemical sfx]

dambose /'dæmbous/, n a crystal-
lizable sugar derived from dambonite.
[< dambonite + -ose suffix indicating sugar]

dandy or dandy fever, n = DENGUE
(in the West Indies).
[< an alteration (by folk etymology) of DENGUE]

danshiki /dan'ʃi:ki:/, n = DASHIKI.
On the streets women stroll
about in long, brightly colored African dress. And young
men wear danshikis and bubas,
colorful jacketlike African
shirts. New York Times, 3/12/68,
p 45
[< Yoruba]

dar /dar/, n a dwelling (in Ethiopia).
They dwell close-cooped in
their stinking dars, tall for-
tress-like keeps with slits
for windows, with the animals
stabled below the living ac-
commodation, and each house
is sited more for the purpose
of defence than to catch the
cooling breezes. The Times,
4/22/65, p 14
[? < Amharic dar edge, border,
outskirt]

dash /dæʃ/, n a bribe, tip, or
gratuity (in West Africa).
Genial Shad Tubman rules Liberia through his True Whig
Party and by the judicious
use of jobs and "dash" - the
local word for payoffs for
favors - to keep the important 20,000 Americo-Liberians
happy. Time, 1/17/64, p 27
And as for "dash," we are now
told that some tens of mil-
lions of dollars were poured
into ministerial pockets in
Nkrumah's Ghana. Atlantic,
10/66, p 83

--v t to give a bribe, tip,
gratuity (to); obtain by bribery.
A young Nigerian who had just
"dashed" (bribed) a police
official 20 guineas ($60) to
get a driving license huffed
"the price is unfair. It used
to be just 15 guineas." New
York Times, 9/1/68, p 4E
Each room would be furnished
with a box containing a little
china and glass "dashed" by
an employer or stolen by an
employer, a bed made out of
old packing-cases and a hurri-
cane lamp. G. Greene, Heart
of the Matter, 1948, p 19
[earlier dashee < a West African (Guinean) language; cf.
Portuguese das you give]

dashee /da'ʃi:/, n = DASH.

dashiki /da'ʃi:ki:/, n a loosely-
fitting, brightly colored or
patterned shirt-like garment,
usually with short sleeves.
In one picture, his wife is
smiling, a blue bandana
around her short afro....Be-
hind them, in a green dashiki,
...stands Banks himself. New
York Times (Mag. Sec.), 11/18/
79, p 74
Jesse Jackson...is a sharp
dresser - turtlenecks and
suede sport jackets, occa-
sionally a dashiki - but

wears high-top country boots
under his bellbottom trousers.
Harper's, 3/69, p 59
[< Yoruba danshiki, ? < Hausa
~Akan dán(ta) underclothing]

dattock /'dætək/, n the hard dark
mahogany-like wood of a tree
(Detarium senegalense) or the
tree itself.
[< Wolof detah]

daunha /'daunha/, n an animal-skin
blanket (in Zimbabwe).
Mr. P.K. Chiunye proudly dis-
plays two valuable garments
from bygone days. He holds a
(daunha) blanket made from two
different animal skins, more
than 100 years old, and (right)
a (gudza) blanket made from
tree bark. Rhodesia Herald,
1/8/79, p 3
[? < Shona]

dauw /dau/, n Burchell's zebra.
[< Afrikaans (obsolete) dauw;
(current) dou < a southern African language]

dawa /'dauwə/, n 1 medicine; magic
or anything having a magical effect (such as a charm, amulet,
talisman, potion, etc.).
Each [Hadza] carries a hide
pouch with shoulder strap containing scraps of skin and ten-
don; tobacco leaves and hemp;
...some rag-wrapped hornet-larva
medicine, or dawa, useful for
chest pain; and snakebite dawa,
of ingredients known only to a
few, which is used in trade
with other peoples. New Yorker,
9/30/72, p 62
There is now no doubt that the
stories of drugs, dawas, fetishes, and cannibalism have
not been exaggerated. Manchester Guardian, 1/14/65, p 5
Held in thrall by a powerful
black dawa (magic), the Simbas
were forbidden to steal from
the whites or even lay hands
on a white woman - whose touch,

they believed, was evil. Time,
7/26/68, p 69
2 an armed uprising and rebellion
in the former Belgian Congo (now
Zaire), similar to MAU-MAU.
Their organization is likely to
collapse when their supplies
and road transport disintegrates
but they will remain a latent
danger so long as "Dawa" in-
doctrination continues in the
bush. The Times, 11/30/64, p 10
[def. 1 < Swahili < Arabic dawa
remedy, medicine; def. 2 < def.
1, because its members drank a
potion at initiation rituals]

dayr /'daiər/, n the short rainy
season in Somalia from late September to early December.
[< Somali] See GU.

debe /'debei/, n a can or con-
tainer, originally a four-gallon
kerosene can.
The Hadza shaves the head of
the bereaved, who then strips
himself naked and presents to
the Hadza his clothes and all
belongings of the dead person
except money, which is not
thought of as polluted, and
also four debes of maize. P.
Matthiessen, Tree Where Man
Was Born, 1972, p 229
[< Swahili < Hindi]

debre /'debrə/, n a mountain
sanctuary (in Ethiopia).
[< Amharic debir, debr]

debtera /'debtərə/, n a layman
who serves the Ethiopian (Coptic)
church as a teacher, poet, musician, etc.
The debteras are a class of
non-priests unique to the
Ethiopian church. They are experts in reading and liturgi-
cal song and are administrators
of the church's traditional
wisdom. Once, when with aching
feet I wondered aloud why the
faithful must remove their
shoes before entering an

Ethiopian church, an elderly
debtera with the look of a Bib-
lical patriarch countered with
the question, "And would you
tread on the toes of angels
who crowd a church during services?" National Geographic,
12/70, p 877
[< Amharic dəbtəra]

defassa waterbuck /də'fæsə/,
n a large, wide-ranging greyish
brown waterbuck (Kobus defassa)
with white areas on the throat
and rump, found in swamps, riv-
erine forests, and open savannahs.
[said to be < Amharic defarsa]

dega /'degə/, n the highest zone
of the Ethiopian highlands, a-
bove 8,000 feet to some 14,000
feet. See WOINA-DEGA.
[< Amharic degə]

deiamba or diamba /di'æmbə/,
n marijuana (in western and central Africa).
[? < a Bantu language < di-
singular noun pfx + -amba ∿
JAMBA]

dejasmatch /də'dʒazmætʃ/, n
(formerly) the leader of the
political center in Ethiopia.
On the part of the Greats the
responsibility for protection
and food is likewise accepted.
The chief man (Shum) in a village reports to a higher official who may be a Fituari (a-
gent), or a soldier called
Kenzasmatch (leader of the
right wing), Grazmatch (leader
of the left wing), or Dedjaz-
match (leader of the center),
who in turn reports to the
Ras (King) commanding the province by order of the Emperor.
The leaders in Ethiopia lead
in a very personal sense,
whether as soldiers, chiefs,
or priests. National Geographic,
9/35, p 319
[< Amharic dəjjazmac]

demera /'deməra/, n a ceremonial
bonfire lit on a religious holiday (in Ethiopia).
Carrying crosses and incense,
they march through the streets
until they arrive at a huge
demera, or bonfire, standing
ready to be lit. All day long
men and boys have been adding
sticks and poles to the pile.
After circling it three times,
the clerics will bless it. L.
van der Post, et al., African
Cooking, 1970, p 49
[< Amharic damera]

dengue or dengue fever, n the
well-known infectious viral
disease.
[< Spanish dengue < an East
African language ∿ Swahili
(ki)dinga(popo) dengue;cf.
Giryama (ki)dhinghi(dyo) fever]

Dergue /dərg/, n the provisional
military ruling committee in
Ethiopia formed in 1974.
On some days, the Dergue –
the handful of soldiers who
overthrew a 3,000-year-old
empire without having really
planned to do so, seems to be
poised above a yawning chasm.
"The controls have gone dead,"
I was told some time ago by
an intellectual very close to
government circles. Manchester
Guardian, 8/1/76, p 13
Voting secretly, 108 members
of the then 120-man dergue
elected to execute 60 Ethiopians, including the council's own chairman, Lieut.
Gen. Aman Michael Andom, a
tough, independent 50-year-
old Eritrean who sought a policy of compromise with the
rebels in the northern province. New York Times, 6/3/76,
p 12
[< Amharic dərg committee∿ drg,
adərrəgə to do]

dia /'di:ə/, n compensation

usually in the form of camels
paid by a manslayer or his family,
clan, or tribe to the next of kin
of the deceased (in Somalia).
[< Somali < Arabic diyah]

dibatag /'dibətæg/, n Clark's
gazelle (Ammodorcas clarkei), a
small gazelle of northeastern
Africa.
  The superstitious tales of
  "primitive" natives have turned
  out to be soundly based often
  enough in the past, despite
  the repeated pooh-poohings of
  chairborne zoologists. What
  about the okapi, Dr. Heuvelmans
  asks, or the pygmy hippopotamus,
  the gerenuk, the dibatag, the
  grey ox of Cambodia, the giant
  panda or the Komodo dragon?
  Punch, 12/31/58, p 859
[said to be < Somali dabatag,
dibtag]

Defaqane or Defaquane /di:fə-
'kanei/, n a period of strife,
displacement and migrations of
black Africans from areas near
Natal and Swaziland to central
and southern Africa in the
eighteenth century, during the
reign of Chaka. Also, MFECANE.
  As a result of the Difaqana
  large tracts of the interior
  were depopulated, making it
  easier for the Voortrekkers to
  settle there. Flying Springbok,
  10/79, p 93
[< Nguni, literally, times of
trouble]

dika /'di:kə/, n a wild mango of
Africa; the food made from its
seeds.
[< Mpongwe (o)dika dika bread]

--dika bread, paste made from
ground and heated dika seeds.

dik-dik or dikdik /'dik,dik/, n
a small African antelope of the
genus Madoqua or Rhynchotragus
with a proboscis-like nose.
  There is a good deal of wildlife in the Ogaden. But except

for hundreds of dik-diks, a
tiny antelope, and the occa-
sional gazelle, I didn't see
much. Maclean's, 6/3/61, p 36
[< an East African language,
said to be < Swahili, literally,
quick-quick]

Dingaan's Day /diŋ'ganz/, n the
former name of a South African
holiday celebrated on December
16 to commemorate a victory of
the Boers over the Zulus and
their chief, Dingaan, in 1838
at Blood River (Ncome) in Natal;
now called Day of the Covenant.
  On the sixteenth of December
  the Union of South Africa cele-
  brates a day which is known as
  Dingaan's Day. Among the Dutch
  in the country it is commemo-
  rated by services of a religious character. S. Millin,
  South Africans, 1926, p 25

dinge /'diŋgi:/, n Also, dingy.
a derogatory, slang term for a
black person (in the United
States).
[? < a West African language,
? < Chiluba (mu)dingi rascal,
hypocrite (used jokingly among
Zaireans but unfriendly when
used by others)]

Dinka /diŋkə/, n a people of the
southern Sudan; their Nilo-
Saharan (Chari-Nile, Eastern
Sudanic) language, akin to NUER.
[< Dinka jieng people]

dioch /'daiak/, n Also, diock.
an African weaverbird (Quelea),
closely resembling various
finches.
  The red-billed dioch, a finch
  that is a "terrible pest in
  Africa," is widely stocked in
  pet stores in the United
  States. Science News, 1/7/67,
  p 26
[< an African language]

Djerma /di:'ərmə or 'dyərmə/, n
Also, Dyerma. a people of Niger;

44

their Nilo-Saharan (Songhai) language, akin to SONGHAI.

Djibouti /dʒi'buːtiː/, n a country
of northeast Africa bordering on
Ethiopia and Somalia; formerly,
Territory of Afars and Issas and
French Somaliland.
[< the name of its capital and
chief seaport]

djigga /'dʒigə/, n = CHIGOE.

Dogon /'dougan/, n a people of
Mali famous for their masks,
wood carvings, and cosmogony;
their Niger-Congo (Voltaic)
language.

doka /'doukə/, n a West African
tree (Isoberlinia) of the savanna
region; its fire-resistant wood.
[? < Fulani]

dolosse or dolos /də'los/, n 1
any of a group of concrete struc-
tures used as a breakwater in
coastal South Africa, shaped like
a tree trunk with four roots, to
diminish the force of tidal waves.
   Sand and gravel will be dumped
   on the seaward side of the
   caissons, then covered with a
   layer of stone to form a shelf
   facing the ocean. On top of
   the shelf, engineers will fit
   dolosse, huge cast-concrete
   pieces that look like the jacks
   of the children's game. Public
   Service engineers estimate
   that 69,000 dolosse, each weigh-
   ing anywhere from 6-1/2 to 42
   tons, will be needed. The dolosse will interlock with one
   another, providing thousands
   of spaces into which sea water
   can slosh, spending its energy.
   New York Times (Mag. Sec.),
   6/4/72, p 80
2 n pl animal bones, especially
metacarpal and metatarsal, or
knucklebones, used by diviners
(in southern Africa); the method
of divination using such bones.
[< Afrikaans; def. 1 < the

knucklebone shape of the struc-
tures that resembles def. 2;
def. 2 ? < seTswana (in)dawala
the bone(s) used in divination]

domodah /doumə'da/, n a West African dish of chicken or beef with
rice in groundnut stew and green
beans (in the Gambia and Senegal).
[? < Wolof]

donga /'dangə/, n a dry gully,
ravine or depression formed by
erosion and subject to flooding
in the rainy seasons.
   A donga was safely crossed. A
   Donga...would be called...in
   Scotland, a gully. Daily News
   (South Africa), 6/20/1879, p 5
   The club was one of those
   places one could never find
   again; I drove to it blindly,
   turning when Steven told me
   and following landmarks in-
   visible to me, down dirt tracks
   and through dongas, over the
   dark veld. New Yorker, 1/4/58,
   p 23
[< Afrikaans < Nguni donga
gully]

Dongola kid or leather /'dan-
gələ/, n leather from goatskin
or sheepskin specially tanned to
resemble kid. Also, Dongola process, the tanning process producing this leather.
[< Dongola northern province in
in Sudan, formerly an area co-
extensive with the kingdom of
Cush < the name of the Nilo-Saharan (Eastern Sudanic) language
of the Danagla a people of that
area]

dopkwe /'dapkwei/, n a cooperative work society in Benin for
men in which the beneficiary of
a group must provide food (but
not money) for the services of
his fellow workers.
   A Dahomean had recourse to a
   cooperative working group
   known as the dopkwe when his
   fields were "too extensive to

permit them to be hoed by his own labor and the labor of those whose services he has at his disposal." The Nupe used a larger cooperative unit called the egbe for agricultural production when, for various reasons, the extended family was insufficient. E. Skinner, Peoples & Cultures of Africa, 1973, p 209
The dopkwe includes men of various ages, although the young are the most active as these cooperative societies provide manual assistance to their members. H. Miner, The Primitive City of Timbuctoo, 1965, p 185
[? < Fon]

doro wat /'dorou 'wat/, n a highly spiced chicken WAT (stew) (in Ethiopia).
When Berhanu Wolde Emanuel, a civil servant in the Ethiopian city of Gondar, was about to marry Lishan Sefu (above), he made inquiries about the quality of her doro wat. L. van der Post et al., African Cooking, 1970, p 35
[< Amharic doro chicken + wət' stew]

dosinia /də'sini:ə/, n a lucinid bivalve mollusk (Dosinia orbicularis) with a rounded shell.
[< New Latin < dosin the Senegalese term for the mollusk + New Latin -ia (taxonomic suffix)]

drill /dril/, n a baboon (Mandrillus leucophaeus) of West Africa with a black face, smaller than the MANDRILL.
[< a West African language]

dudu /'du:du:/, n an insect (in eastern and central Africa); an insignificant, distasteful person or thing.
As we studied termite mounds, we frequently found ourselves surrounded by curious Masai

boys and their omnipresent cattle and goats. When asked why I was digging in their grazing lands and filling plastic basins with dudus (insects), I replied, "Mimi ni daktari wa dudu - I'm a bug doctor." The Masai smiled in amusement at the crazy Mzungu (white man), no doubt wondering what a bug doctor actually did for a living. National Geographic, 4/78, p 545
Insect pests are of more economic importance in the tropics, particularly in Africa, than in any other part of the world ...Development work is in progress on a new site for the centre's [International Centre of Insect Physiology and Ecology] headquarter's, to be known as "Duduville"...on land allocated to ICIPE by the Kenya government. Weekly Review (Nairobi), 5/18/79, p 37
"I have been in politics for 20 years and I cannot see how a bunch of handpicked men could dislodge me. For them to say that they have no confidence in me is tantamount to saying they have no confidence in the Kenya government....I don't want to go into any paper controversy with dudus because my intention is to preach peace, love and unity and I would very much plead to the people of Kajiado District and Narok to preach peace and unity." Weekly Review (Nairobi), 9/19/80, p 10
[< Swahili, literally, insect, pest]

duka /'du:kə/, n Also, dukah. a small general store or shop (in eastern and central Africa).
Turkana is far from here and full of naked men with spears, but my uncle Motibhai has a duka business there, and his sons, my cousins, adventure with lorries into that savage

land. Saturday Review, 6/1/68,
p 48
Gulu, capital of Acholi, is
over 100 miles from Kalisto's
village, along bumpy roads;
and the dukas, owned by Africans (no Asian tradesmen operate here), have little to sell.
The Times, 7/23/66, p 11
The life of the NFD was harsh-
ly simple. It was ruled by sun
and rain, by heat and cold, by
wet and dry. It revolved around
the dry-river beds, the Indian
dukah, the police post, and
the DC's boma. R. Ruark, Uhuru,
1962, p 9
[< Swahili < Arabic or Hindi
dukan]

dukawallah /ˌduːkəˈwalə/, n a
shopkeeper, especially an Indian
keeper of a DUKA (in eastern
Africa).
They [Indians] became the colony's 'Dukawallahs' (or shop-
keepers), running every kind
of establishment from the
smart shops in the capital to
tiny stores in dusty African
villages. Listener, 3/7/68,
p 294
The dukawallas made their money by working long hours, em-
ploying no help but their families, and accepting slim pro-
fit margins. Their industry
would have excited American
champions of the Protestant
ethic in the nineteenth century. But Africans had a different view. Atlantic, 12/72,
p 32
[< duka + -wallah Anglo-Indian
suffix meaning "one connected

with, associated with"]

duku /ˈduːkuː/, n a colorful
head scarf worn by women in
Malawi. See the quotation under
CHIJAGA.
[? < Chichewa]

duppy /ˈdəpiː/, n a ghost or
spirit brought back from the
dead by an OBEAHMAN in Jamaica.
"You saw the duppy, sah?" Lax-
ton asked in chattering ter-
ror. Manchester Guardian,
1/12/61, p 13
[< West Indian English ~ Bube
dupe ghost]

Dyula /diːˈuːlə/, n a people of
Ivory Coast, Upper Volta, and
nearby areas of West Africa;
their Niger-Congo (Mande) language used as a trade language
in Ivory Coast and Upper Volta.

dzimbahwe /(d)zimˈbawei or
zimˈbabwei/, n 1 pl the large
stone ruins used as dwellings
and compounds of the ZIMBABWE
civilization. 2 Dzimbahwe, the
official residence of the Prime
Minister of Zimbabwe.
Accompanied by a ululating
crowd of followers, Bishop
Abel Muzorewa rode in an ox-
drawn cart to the stately
white mansion - renamed from
Independence House to Dzimbahwe (House of Chiefs) - that
for fifteen years was occupied by Ian Douglas Smith.
Time, 7/16/79, p 38
[< Shona; cf. ZIMBABWE]

E

E, abbreviation of EMALANGENI.
Swaziland. Finance. Monetary
unit, Emalangeni: E1 = US$1.1980.
Budget (1979-1980): revenue,
E115 million; capital expenditures, E101 million. Collier's
Encyclopedia Yearbook, 1979,
p 539
University College of Swaziland.
Applications are invited for
the post of Lecturer in the Department of Mathematics...Salary
Scale: E5940-7860 pa (L1 sterling = L1.82). The British
Government may supplement salary. New Scientist, 7/12/79,
p 157
-- In the first quotation, the
abbreviation E is, strictly
speaking, improperly applied.
This is because emalangeni is a
plural noun; thus the expression
"E1" (one emalangeni") is anoma-
lous. The second quotation uses
both E and L (for LILANGENI)
correctly. See MALOTI for similar
problems.

eba /'eibə/, n a Nigerian dish of
boiled, prepared cassava.
As she stalked into the kitchen
once again she met the twins
rushing over their [poisoned]
eba with aggressive gusto.'Stop
nipping at the fish, you rogue!'
'What about the one you just
carried off in your morsel?'Nwa-
bunor nodded to herself. But
she was not satisfied yet. Her
main target was their mother.
I. Okpewho, The Victims, 1970,
p 200
[< Yoruba]

eboka /'eiboukə/, n = IBOGA(INE)
(among the Fang).
There is a deep satisfaction in
the membership borne of the
fact that they have danced all
night, achieved "one-hearted-
ness" and may look forward to
the fellowship of the communal
meal that comes immediately
after the cult practices. An
afterglow is brought to them
by eboka as well, for the drug
is not usually associated with
undesirable aftereffects. J.
Fernandez in R. Dorson (ed.),
African Folklore, 1972, p 343
[< Fon < Mpongwe IBOGA]

Ebola /i'boulə/, n, adj (of or
relating to) a tropical virus
causing high fever and internal
hemorrhaging, nearly always fatal, first isolated in Zaire and
the Sudan.
Ebola virus joins a growing
list of fatal hemorrhagic
fever viruses found in Africa,
of which Lassa fever and Mar-
burg disease (the so-called
green monkey disease) are the
most notorious. The Times,
3/21/77, p 17
Doctors must test each pint

48

collected to be sure it contains neither Ebola nor other viruses and at the same time has a sufficient amount of Ebola antibody to offer effective therapy. New York Times, 1/25/77, p 12
[< the name of a river in northern Zaire where it was discovered in 1976]

eddo or eddoe /'edou/, n the edible root of plants of the arum family or of the root of taro; taro.
Elephant's-Ear is a plant with large leaves shaped like an elephant's ear or shield. There are two common species. In the South Pacific, one type is eaten like potatoes. This type is also known as taro, eddo, poi, and dasheen. World Book Encyclopedia, Vol. 5, 1960, p 181
[< a West African language ∼ Akan (Twi) ode, Fanti odo yam]

eddy root, n = EDDO.
[Alteration (by folk etymology) of EDDO]

Edo /'edo/, n a people of southern Nigeria; their Niger-Congo (Kwa) language.
[< the local name of Benin city where many Edo live]

Efik /'efik/, n a people of Nigeria; their Niger-Congo (Benue-Cross) language.

efulefu /,efu;leifu/, n a useless, good-for-nothing man (among the Ibo).
None of his converts was a man whose word was heeded in the assembly of the people. None of them was a man of title. They were mostly the kind of people that were called efulefu, worthless, empty men. The imagery of an efulefu in the language of the clan was a man who sold his matchet and wore

the sheath to battle. C. Achebe, Things Fall Apart, 1958, p 130
[< Ibo]

egbe /'egbei/, n a cooperative work society of the Yoruba and Nupe.
Bascom reports cooperative societies, egbe, for the Yoruba (1944:65-66). It is noteworthy that upon the expansion of the monetary economy of the area, members of these societies ceased giving their labor when called upon. They paid for a laborer to do their work or contributed money directly. H. Miner, The Primitive City of Timbuctoo, 1965, p 185
[< Yoruba] See DOPKWE.

egusi /e'gu:si:/, n = AGUSHI (in Nigeria).
But Hughes ignored the anxiety in the doctor's voice and went on coolly: 'But if MacIntosh is not used to having local food, don't you think that that may have upset the poor chap?' Hayes cut in, a little annoyed. "I doubt it. I have had rice and stew and egusi soup and it hasn't affected me!" A. Ulasi, Many Thing You No Understand, 1970, p 137
[? < Yoruba]

Ekine /e'ki:nei/, n a secret society or cult of the Ijo of Nigeria.
On the face of it, Ekine serves many disparate ends. At a superficial glance, it appears as a religious institution, designed to solicit the help of the water spirits through invocations and dramatic representations of them by masquerades. A second glance suggests that these masquerades are recreational as much as religious in their intent. Yet again, many of the masquerades seem to be important status-symbols. And finally, Ekine

often appears as a significant
organ of government. R. Horton
in E. Skinner, Peoples and
Cultures of Africa, 1973, p 600
[< Ijo]

ekpwele /ek'pweilei/, n the monetary unit of Equatorial Guinea.
African place names were also
substituted for Spanish ones
in other areas, and the name
of the currency unit was changed
from the peseta to the ekpwele.
Collier's Encyclopedia Yearbook, 1973, p 253
[< a West African language ~
Fon]

ekuru /e'ku:ru:/, n a West African
dish of shrimp or small fish
mixed with mashed, steamed black-
eyed peas and fried vegetables
and pepper.
[< a West African language ~
Akan kòkúro or kokúro kind of
herring]

elongo /e'loŋgou/, n a Maasai
shield.
His father gave him the three
most important material things
in his life - arem, olalem and
elongo - spear, sword and
shield - which meant he was
ready to become one of the
strongest, most daring and
bravest men in the world:
ilmuran, the warriors of the
Masai. J. Hallet, Congo Kitabu,
1964, p 138
[< Maasai]

emabutfo /,eima'bu:tfou/, n pl
Swazi warriors.
The emabutfo - wearing toga-
like mahiya cloths around their
waists and feathers in their
hair, paid homage to the leader they call Ngwenyama, the
Lion, waving wooden knobkerries
and chanting ancient war cries.
The Times, 9/11/72, p V
[< siSwati ema- plural noun pfx
+ -butfo (root for) warrior]

emahiya /,eimə'hi:yə/, n = MAHIYA.

Five delegates from Swaziland,
one of the U.N.'s newest member nations, ...sauntered down
the aisle shortly before 3P.M.
wearing brilliant red emahiya
(knee-length off-the-shoulder
tunics). New Yorker, 9/27/69,
p 30
[< siSwati ema- plural noun pfx
+ hiya (root for) these clothes]

emakhulungwane /,eimɔxu'luŋgwa-
nei/, n pl Swazis who have become westernized, especially
when considered disdainful of
tribal customs or traditional
values.
[< siSwati ema- plural noun pfx
+ -khulu big, great (as from the
West); ~MAKULU + -ngwane ~
Swahili mwana child, son or
daughter, as in MWANANCHI citi-
zen]

emalangeni /,eiməlaŋ'geini:/,
n pl of LILANGENI (the unit of
currency in Swaziland).
The Umbuluzi dam scheme, which
would irrigate 8,000 ha, was
allotted a further 3 million
emalangeni. Britannica Book
of the Year, 1977, p 638
[< siSwati ema- plural noun pfx
+ -langeni (root for) money]

emasi /ei'masi:/, n = AMASI (in
Swaziland).
[< siSwati ema- mass noun pfx
+ -si (root for) milk]

emgalla /em'gælə/, n a wart
hog of southern Africa.
[< a southern African language]

Engai /eŋ'gai/, n the supreme
deity among the Maasai.
The Masai...would like to go
on living as their ancestors
have lived, following their
herds to new pasturage as the
tribal deity Engai, who dic-
tates when and where the rains
shall come, changes his godly
favors. Wall Street Journal,

8/28/61, p 6
[< Maasai, literally, heaven]

enjera /ən'dʒerə/, n = INJERA.
The most important export crop
is coffee and the most important grain crop for domestic
consumption is teff (Eragros-
tis abyssinica Link), a grass
with small seeds from which the
local unleavened bread enjera
is made. Other important crops
grown include wheat, barley,
maize, sorghum, oil seeds such
as nug. The Times, 7/22/72, p VI

enkang /en'kæŋ/, n a home village
or kraal of the Maasai.
Farther south, in the dry areas
of the Rift Valley and the lower land on either side, the
Masai, a Nilo-Hamitic people,
lead similar nomadic lives.
During the dry season, when the
grass is poor in the valleys,
they live on the higher slopes
where they have their semi-per-
manent enkangs. R. & E. Steel,
Africa, 1974, p 146
[< Maasai]

ensete /en'setei/, n a banana used
in Ethiopia to make flour for
unleavened bread or a highly nu-
tritive fermented starch.
[< Amharic insət]

Equatorial Guinea, n a country
in West Africa bordering on Gabon and Cameroon. See GUINEA.

erg /ərg/, n a desert region of
shifting sand; a sandy area.
Frantic patchwork with on-the-
spot materials heals the havoc
wrought by the Sahara's regs
and ergs - gravel-littered
plains and clogging dunes.
National Geographic, 11/67,
p 714
[< French, said to be < Amharic
aragăă rise, ascend or < Berber
'irj desert region]

eserine /'esəri:n/, n physostig-

mine, a poison derived from the
Calabar bean, formerly used in
West African ordeal trials.
Physostigmine (sometimes called
eserine), has in recent years
worked its way up to clinical
respectability. It can tempo-
rarily restore muscular strength
to an individual suffering from
the disease myasthenia gravis
and can relieve pressure within
the eyeball in the serious eye
disorder glaucoma. Scientific
American, 11/59/81
[< French eserine < a West African language eser the poison
+ -ine chemical suffix]

eta /'eitə/, n indigo and white
colored cloth made in Nigeria.
The classical clothes are
still made: red alari, fawn
sanyan and indigo and white
eta. But cotton spun and dyed
in Nigerian mills has replaced
the hand-spun cotton (unless
by special order) and weavers
make free use of metallic
thread, rayons and polymer
fibres. The Times, 12/1/77, p IX
[? < Yoruba]

etua /'etwə/, n a tropical African tree of the begonia family.
[< a West African language ~
Akan etwă a certain prickly plant]

Eunoto /eyu'noutou/, n a Maasai
ceremony in which warriors are
elevated to elder status.
After Eunoto, a man may marry.
But the ceremony also marks
the end of warrior comradeship.
...Throughout Eunoto, warriors
gather in small groups to deco-
rate themselves. Natural History, 8/80, p 50
One way of penetrating beyond
the popular image is to see
one of their Eunoto ceremonies,
when there may be several
thousand Masai, ...gathered at
a single mammoth-sized manyatta
village. The overall timing of
the ceremony depends upon the

moon. N. Myers, <u>Long African</u>
<u>Day</u>, 1972, p 56
[< Maasai]

Ewe /'eiwei/, n a people of Ghana
and Togo; their Niger-Congo
(Kwa) language.

F

fadama /fə'damə/, n a flood plain
with high water table.
Rivers flow across the plains
to the Niger in flat-floored
valleys; these are flooded in
the wet season, though in the
dry season the waters recede
and expose fertile alluvium.
Such areas are favourable for
cultivation and are known by
the Hausa as fadamas. R. & E.
Steel, Africa, 1974, p 95
[< a West African language, attested in Hausa and Fulani]

Falasha /fə'laʃə/, n an Ethiopian
sect that practices Judaism; a
member of this sect.
Allegations were made here
last week that the Israel government, the Jewish agency and
Jewish organizations around
the world are doing nothing to
get the Falashas out of Ethiopia, although hundreds, if not
thousands of them, are being
murdered or sold as slaves....
Today there are 28,000 Falashas
in Ethiopia and 300 in Israel.
The association fears that
there won't be any Jews left
in Ethiopia a few years from
now. Jerusalem Post, 1/7-13/79,
p 7
[< Amharic fəlasha literally,
exiled, immigrant or wanderer
~ falása he wandered, fəlasi
stranger]

Fanagalo or Fanakalo /fanə'ga-
lou/, n a pidgin language used
in the mines of South Africa,
based on Zulu, Afrikaans and
English.
"Mali," he says, putting his
drill down and wiping the
sweat from his brow with his
forearm. "Mali muhle!" In
Fanakalo, the hybrid language
of the mines, it means that
the money is good. New York
Times, 11/4/77, p D11
Most people with a reverence
for their own mother tongue
will sympathize with Professor
Jabavu's opinion of "Fanakalo"
the lingua franca of the mine
compounds of South Africa.
Cape Argus, 1/19/51, p 8
[< Nguni ifana nalo it is like
this or fana be like (~Luyia
-fuana resemble) + ka connective,
"of" + lo this, perhaps also
alteration of English vernacular]

Fang /faŋ/, n Also, Fan. a people
of Gabon, Equatorial Guinea and
Cameroon; their Bantu language.
Also known as PAHOUIN.
[< French Fan < Fang]

Fante /'fanti:/, n Also, Fanti.
a people of Ghana; their language, sometimes considered a
dialect of AKAN.

fanti or fantee /'fanti:/, n

go fanti, to 'go native'; to live
with or as if with the supposedly
more primitive local inhabitants
of an area; to act in an unre-
strained manner.
[< Akan FANTE the name of the
Fante people,

ferengi or ferenji /fə'rendʒi:/,
n a foreigner (in Ethiopia).
The four Danakil had decided
to get my camera bag. "If you
touch the ferengi or his belongings," Mahmud had declared,
"I promise you a lot of trouble." But they had chuckled.
National Geographic, 2/70, p 198
[< Amharic fərənj(i) < Arabic
< Frank a Frank or Crusader +
Arabic ethnic suffix -i]

fimbo /'fimbou/, n a whip made from
the dried and stretched penis of
a hippopotamus or water buffalo;
sjambok.
In 1955 flogging was completely
suppressed in the Congo - over
the indignant protests of many
traditional native chiefs -
while it remained a legal punishment in many countries of
the civilized world. I was
deeply relieved to see the end
of the fimbo, but as the native
crime rate peaked sharply in
every part of the Congo, I began to understand the practical
necessity which had driven
some government officials to
use it. J. Hallet, Congo Kitabu, 1964, p 35
[< a Bantu language < Swahili,
literally, stick]

Fingo /'fiŋgou/, n a people of
eastern South Africa; their
Bantu language.
[< Xhosa amamfengu, literally,
those looking for work < ama-
plural noun pfx + mfengu ~ fen-
guza seek work]

firiki /fə'riki:/, or firki /'firki:/, n a greyish, flat land in
the Chad basin, composed of a

clayey impervious soil, that
floods easily during rains.
[< a central African language,
? ~ Kanuri]

fisi /'fi:si:/, n hyena (in eastern
Africa).
Hyena eyes gleamed like fire-
flies from the roadside. Njovu
sensed my uneasiness and spoke
words of comfort. "Fisi is
harmless," he said. "Nothing
here will harm us." National
Geographic, 9/60, p 341
The game, seen within mere
yards of the vehicle, seemed
to personify their local names.
In Swahili, a lion is simba -
a word that rings with majesty and power; fisi captures
all the scavenging slyness of
the hyena, kifaru the ponder-
ous ferocity of the rhinoceros.
National Geographic, 11/62,
p 635
[< Swahili]

fituari /fi:tə'wari:/, n a general
of the vanguard (in Ethiopia).
See the quotation under DEJAS-
MATCH.
[< Amharic fitawrari < fit
face + wərrərə raid, invade]

Fon[1] /fan/, n a people of Benin
and Togo; their Niger-Congo
(Kwa) language akin to EWE, used
in southern Benin as a lingua
franca.

Fon[2] or Fong /fan or faŋ/, n (the
title of) a chief of the Bamileke of Cameroon.
There was a famous octogenari-
an called the Fon of Bikom
who lived in Cameroun with an
establishment of one hundred
wives....a United Nations
Mission climbed to the top of
a Camerounian mountain to
interview the Fon. Punch,
11/22/61, p 740
There were several more
speeches before the Fon
stepped to the microphone.

He walked slowly, as men over 70 are wont to do, but he stood tall and straight, and when he whisked a white handkerchief over his brow, it was with great flair. He wore a splendid robe of black and red checks. National Geographic, 7/74, p 143
[< Bamileke]

fonio /'founi:ou/, n a wild crab-grass (Digitaria) with nutrition-al seeds used as a cereal grain.
Some of the former refugees in the marginal lands between the river and the high desert were Bellas,...harvesting fonio and cramcram. National Geographic, 8/75, p 177
On the hillsides, where the thick forest has been felled and burned, mountain rice and fonio are the principal crops. Harper's, 12/61, p 70
[< a West African language]

fontomfrom /,fontəm'from/, n the talking drum(s) of the Ashanti, used to drum out proverbs, great news, etc. and occurring in sets of "male" and "female."
Bells, gongs, metal castanets and deep-throated fontomfroms took up the refrain, then fell to a deep hush as the palace gates swung open. Walking majestically, the new King - or Asantehene - led the procession. Time, 8/10/70, p 26
[< Akan fɔntomfrɔm largest kind of drum]

foo-foo or fou-fou /'fu:fu:/, n = FUFU.
The world was silent except for the shrill cry of insects, which was part of the night, and the sound of wooden mortar and pestle as Nwayieke pounded her foo-foo. Nwayieke lived four compounds away, and she was notorious for her late cooking. C. Achebe, Things Fall Apart, 1958, p 86

frenji /'frendʒi:/, n = FERENGI (in Somalia).
[< Somali; see FERENGI]

fufu /'fu:fu:/, n a West African dish made from boiled plantain, sorghum, yam, or cassava, form-ing a doughy paste and shaped into a ball.
A banana leaf at their feet serves as a plate. A servant brings a piece of meat, then three or four balls of fufu - yam or cassava paste - each of them as large as a two-pound loaf of bread. National Geographic, 8/59, p 239
With the durbar, the ban on drumming has been lifted and the taboo on eating "fufu" from the first day of the festival is also over. Ghanaian Times, 6/29/73, p 6
[< numerous West African languages: Ewe fúfú, Wolof fufu, Akan fufúu ~ fufu white, attested in Cuban Spanish fufú]

Fula /'fu:lə/, n Also, Ful. = FULANI.

Fulani /fə'lani:/, n 1 a breed of white West African cattle with wide-spanned horns and a large hump.
Every once in a while, we passed herds of Fulani cattle and their white-clad atten-dants, who were carrying long staves. New Yorker, 11/18/61, p 193
2 Also Fulbe. a people of Senegal, Gambia, Guinea, Guinea-Bissau, Sierra Leone, Liberia, Mali and Nigeria and other parts of West Africa; their Niger-Congo (West Atlantic) language spoken over a wide area of West Africa. Also known as FULFULDE, PEUL.
[def. 2 < the Hausa name for these people]

Fulfulde /fəl'fuldei/, n = FULANI.
[< Fulani]

fundi[1] /'fundi:/, n a skilled
mechanic, craftsman, expert, or
knowledgeable person.
>All over East Africa they
worked as fundis, possessed of
invaluable if rudimentary skills
as masons, carpenters, builders
and general fixers of things.
National Review, 10/13/72,
p 1124
>The stress on cooperative pro-
duction and on village involve-
ment - through the survey team,
training of local fundis, village meetings, etc. - provides
a basis by which the village
really can control both the
production and use of these
technologies...In practical
terms, we may find that this
group of fundis will contri-
bute considerably more towards
their community, for example
by building a school and a
village dispensary. New Scientist, 9/14/78, p 758
[< Swahili fundi ~ -funda teach
~ Nguni (um)fundi(si) teacher]

fundi[2], n a tropical grass (Dig-
taria) with nutritional seeds
resembling millet.
[< a West African language, ?
< Limba fandi ha grass]

funge /'fuŋgei/, n mealie-meal
porridge (in Angola).
>Other changes are on the way,
for there is hardly a man in
the interior who has not had
some experience of a Westernized
diet on plantations or in towns.
Funge is increasingly displaced
by bread, and the Portuguese
everywhere make excellent
bread. L. van der Post, et al,
African Cooking, 1970, p 116
[? < Kimbundu ~ Swahili fungu
portion; cf. POSHO food, or
portion of food]

funtumia /funtu'mi:ə/, n a genus
of trees of the begonia family
with yellowish flowers; a tree
of this genus.
[< a West African language Ewe
funtum the tree, Akan (o-)f(r)un-
tum rubber tree of this genus +
New Latin -ia]

G

galago /gə'leigou/, n the bush
baby; a small, furry, nocturnal
primate; the genus of such pri-
mates.
> Inside, he told me, were four
> live galagos taken from a nest
> in a hollow tree. National Geo-
> graphic, 8/56, p 285

[< New Latin, said to be < Wolof
golokh monkey]

galla /'galə/, n a derogatory term
for a white person, European, or
anyone considered a heathen (in
Somalia).
[< Somali, ? < GALLA, because
the Somali consider them bar-
barians < Arabic ghaliz wild,
rough; or < SHANGALLA]

Galla /'galə/, n a people of Ethiopia, Somalia and Kenya; their
Afroasiatic (Eastern Cushitic)
language. Also known as OROMO.
[? ultimately < Arabic ghaliz
wild, rough]

ganna /'ganə or xanə/, n a bush
or plant (Salsola) of South Africa, the ashes of which form a
strong caustic lye formerly used
in soap-making.
[< Khoikhoin kanna eland (because the animal feeds on this
plant), possibly from kannabos
this species] See KANNA.

Ganwa /'ganwə/, n a prince of the

Burundi royal family.
[< Kirundi]

gari[1] /'gari:/, n dried, grated
cassava or ground flour, sometimes fermented and made into a
thick porridge (in West Africa).
> The staple food of more than
> twenty million people in Cen-
> tral and West Africa is gari -
> a granular carbohydrate that
> swells in water to give a
> semi-stiff porridge. New Sci-
> entist, 1/28/65, p 218
> At a tea shop a poor Hausa man
> from the North told me that
> "gari" flour, the staple food,
> had gone from 7s a bag in Octo-
> ber to 12s and yams from 1s to
> 4s. Manchester Guardian, 2/17/66,
> p 7

[< a West African language, ? <
Yoruba]

--gari foto, a dish of gari meal
with eggs, tomatoes, and sometimes fish and onions.

gari[2], n a Hausa town; capital of
a village area.
> Larger settlements of the form
> of a gari would perhaps tend
> to grow up in such places. The
> introduction of the use of iron
> into Hausaland, presumably in
> the early part of the first
> millennium A.D., was probably
> a factor in the growth of such
> towns. A. Smith in J. Ajayi,

M. Crowder (eds), History of
West Africa I, 1971, p 186
[< Hausa gari, garuwa]

garra /'garə/, n a type of tie-dye
cloth, usually cotton or satin
(in Sierra Leone).
 The blue or brown "garra" -
 blue is indigo, brown is cola
 - is made in a kind of open-
 air workshop. The women sew the
 plain cotton or satin into varying folded patterns, dip it into huge vats of dye, and afterward beat the cloth in unison
 with a huge bludgeon till the
 cloth glows with a soft shine.
 S. Blumenthal, Bright Continent,
 1974, p 238
[< a West African language, ? <
Mande]

garri /'gari:/, n = GARI[1].
 Between December and January
 last year...a total of 427
 tons of yams, plantain and
 garri were also sold. Ghanaian
 Times, 3/3/73, p 5
 Two plowed caverns into the
 grass huts outside the Red
 Cross headquarters at Saint
 Stephen's School, where school-
 girl volunteers sat outside
 preparing garri for the evening
 meal. Time, 5/10/68, p 39

gasha /'gaʃə/, n a unit of land
measurement in Ethiopia.
 Traditional weights and measures vary considerably in the
 various provinces: the principal ones are: Frasilia = approximately 37-1/2 lb.; gasha
 ...is normally about 100 acres
 but can vary between 80 and
 300 acres depending on the
 quality of the land. Statesman's Year-Book 79/80, 1979,
 p 438
 Three police officers called
 on his widow who was in deep
 mourning to inform her that,
 under the agrarian reform laws
 proclaimed on March 4, 1975,
 the Government was confiscating

her land holdings (they a-
mounted to a few "gashas").
Manchester Guardian, 6/21/75,
p 13
[< Amharic gaʃʃa]

gavine or govini /gə'vini:/, n
an alcoholic drink made from
sugar cane (in southern Africa).
 The "Spirit of Natal" was in
 its early years known as gavine to caneworkers, mostly
 Indians. They distilled it
 from raw cane-sugar residue
 in illegal "stills" for self-
 satisfaction and sale in nearby African shebeens. (S. Africa)
 Star, 11/23/79, p not known
[< Zulu gavini]

Gazankulu /,gazaŋ'ku:lu:/, n
a homeland (region in South Africa set aside by the government
for blacks) for the Shangaan and
Tsonga, located in the northeastern Transvaal area.
[? < Shangaan or Tsonga, ? <
Gaza an earlier kingdom in nearby Mozambique + nkulu mountain,
high place]

gbo /gə'bou/, n a magic charm or
amulet worn for protection from
evil. It may be used for good or
evil.
 Among the Dahomeans of West
 Africa, for example, 18 kinds
 of gbo, or magical charms, have
 been recorded. Grolier Science
 Supplement, 1967, p 292
[< Fon gbo magic charm]

Geez or Ge'ez /gi:'ez or gei'ez/,
n an ancient Afroasiatic (Semitic)
language of Ethiopia, used in religious services of the Ethiopian Coptic Church. Also known as
Ethiopic.
[< Amharic ge'iz, literally,
(of) the free; cf. LESANA GEEZ]

gelada /gə'ladə/, n a baboon of
Ethiopia notable for the long
mane on the male's neck and
shoulders and for its tufted tail

Ramapithecus did not find itself overwhelmed by a super-
abundance of food. Instead, it
must have spent much of its
day searching for roots, seeds,
stems, nuts, tough fruits, and
insects, most of which had to
be pulverized between efficient
millstone teeth. This kind of
life-style is not unlike that
pursued by the hairy gelada
baboons that...spend their days
shuffling along on their
haunches, turning over stones
in search of roots, shoots and
insects, and they too pulverize
their food between flattened,
millstonelike molars. R. Leakey
& R. Lewin, People of the Lake,
1978, p 34
[? < Amharic, ? < Arabic qiladah
collar, mane]

gele /'gelei/, n a headdress worn
by women in West Africa.
    The most visible signs of the
    new black consciousness are
    Afro hairstyles, dashikis and
    geles. Time, 4/6/70, p 45
[? < Yoruba]

Gelede /gə'leidei/, n a cult of
Yoruba origin to appease witches.
    The Gelede is a dancing society
    headed by a priestess, but is
    otherwise a men-only affair.
    Harper's, 12/65, p 60
[< Yoruba]

gerenuk /'gerə,nuk/, n a rufous-
fawn colored, long-necked antelope (Litocranius walleri) of
eastern Africa.
    Among the many rare specimens
    landed was a fine young male
    gerenuk, or giraffe-necked
    antelope. The Times, 8/4/56,
    p 8
[< Somali garanug]

gesho /'geʃou/, n Also, geshu.
a plant whose green leaves are
used like hops to ferment TALLA
(beer) (in Ethiopia).
    Good beer, known as talla, is

brewed from barley and the
leaves of the geshu plant.
National Geographic, 9/35,
p 308
[< Amharic gešo]

ghaap or ghap or guapp /gap/,
n a South African flowering plant
(Stapelia or Trichocaulon) whose
spiny, edible stems quench thirst.
[< Nama guapp, u-gaap or ngaap]

Ghana /'ganə/, n the title of an
ancient king or emperor of Aoukar
(an early West African kingdom);
his kingdom or empire, which
lasted almost one thousand years;
hence, a country of West Africa
bordering on Ivory Coast, Upper
Volta and Togo, formerly known
as Gold Coast.
[< Soninke ghana, literally,
war chief, or < Malinke gana,
kana chief; later adapted by
the modern nation of Ghana because traditions claim that
early people of the ancient empire moved into the Asante re-
gion]

ghoen /gon or gən/, n a stone or
marble used in hopscotch-like
games (in southern Africa).
[< Khoikhoin]

gidigo /gə'di:gou/, n a musical
instrument of the Cameroons,
made of bamboo and calabash and
similar to the marimba.
    One foot feels the cool ivory
    of an elephant tusk, a reminder
    that his ancestors never trod
    bare ground but always veri-
    table roads of ivory. As they
    chant, the women play the gi-
    digo. National Geographic,
    8/59, p 244
[? < Bamilike]

giraffe, n the well-known long-
necked ruminant mammal.
[< Italian giraffa < Arabic
zirafah, zarafah said to be ultimately < an African language,
? < an Afroasiatic language

(∼ Egyptian s̲r̲)]

gnu /nuː/, n̲ the well-known large
    buffalo-like African antelope.
    [< Khoikhoin ng̲u̲]

gogga /'gogɔ or 'xoxɔ/, n̲ an in-
    sect (in South Africa).
        'Gogga'...stands alone to sig-
        nify the millions of creatures
        that crawl and creep and some-
        times fly, and it even includes
        that low grade of living things
        called vermin. M. Drennan,
        Gogga Brown, 1941, p 1
    [< Nama X̲o̲X̲o̲ insect or other
    small creature ∼ Sandawe /̲/̲o̲
    small creature]

Gola /'goulɔ/, n̲ a people of Sierra
    Leone and Liberia; their Niger-
    Congo (West Atlantic) language.

gombolola /,gambou'loulɔ/, n̲ a
    sub-county or territorial ad-
    ministrative unit in Uganda; a
    meeting of people at this level.
        The chairman of the chiefs
        selecting committee for Omoro
        County, West Acholi,...ad-
        dressed a rally in Lalogi and
        Koich gombolola headquarters.
        Voice of Uganda, 3/22/73, p 3
        Gombololas are being convened
        throughout Uganda this week-
        end so that ordinary citizens
        can advise the Government on
        the next steps in the coun-
        try's so-called economic war.
        The Times, 10/28/72, p 6
    [< Luganda]

gom-gom /'gomgom or 'xomxom/, n̲
    = GORAH.
    [< Khoikhoin]

goober /'guːbər/, n̲ peanut (in
    the United States, especially
    the South).
        She had set an earthen dish
        holding some unshelled pea-
        nuts. I took one, cracked it,
        and ate it. There is a sweet-
        ness, a docile pithy soul-
        quality of taste, to our

Kushian goobers that I have
        never met elsewhere. J. Updike,
        The Coup, 1978, p 134
    [< a West African Bangu lan-
    guage ∼ Kikongo, Tshiluba, Ki-
    mbundu (n̲)g̲u̲b̲a̲ peanut]

goofer or guffer /'gɑfər/, n̲ a
    witch doctor; a curse or spell.
    [< a West African language, ?
    ∼ Ewe g̲à̲f̲è̲ god's shrine, Mende
    (n̲)g̲a̲f̲a̲ spirit, ghost, Fon k̲a̲f̲o̲
    fetish, ? ∼ Tshiluba k̲u̲f̲u̲a̲ to
    die]

goombay /'guːmbei/, n̲ a form of
    calypso music of the Bahamas.
        Kick up your heels in the
        nightclubs that spill irre-
        sistible goombay music into
        the velvet darkness of every
        evening. New Yorker, 3/7/64,
        p 91
    [< a West African Bantu lan-
    guage ∼ Kikongo, Tshiluba
    (n̲)k̲u̲m̲b̲i̲ (ceremonial) drum]

gora or goura or gorah /'gorɔ
    or 'gurɔ/, n̲ a Khoikhoin musi-
    cal instrument similar to a
    Jew's harp, consisting of a bow
    with a string attached to a reed
    vibrated by the breath of the
    player. A calabash hanging from
    the string provides resonance.
    [< San k̲o̲/̲/̲a̲]

gorilla, n̲ the well-known ape from
    West Africa.
    [< New Latin < Greek, said to
    be < Gorillai̲ African tribe of
    hairy women]

goundou or goundhou /guːndu:/,
    n̲ a tumorous swelling on each
    side of the nose and on the
    nasal bones, occurring in tropi-
    cal areas.
    [◄ French < a West African lan-
    guage]

grazmatch /'grazmatʃ/, n̲ (former-
    ly) the leader of the left wing
    in Ethiopia. See the quotation
    under DEJASMATCH.

[< Amharic grazmac]

grigri or gree-gree or gris-
gris /'gri:,gri:/, n a voodoo
talisman, amulet, charm or incantation worn to protect oneself
against evil.
  Sorcerer and witch doctor, grigri and juju, are still an in-
  tegral part of the African pat-
  tern. Atlantic, 9/10/55, p 1
  "The God who made us all made
  us and turned his back. He is
  out of the picture, he does not
  want to be bothered. It is the
  little gods that make the con-
  nections, that bring love and
  food and relief from pain.
  They are in the gris-gris the
  leper wears around his neck."
  J. Updike, The Coup, 1978, p 108
  [(< French) < a West African
  language ～ Bulanda grigri, Akan
  gya- amulet]

griot /gri:'ou/, n a West African
bard, minstrel poet, or oral his-
torian who, as a member of a
hereditary caste, is charged with
the preservation of traditions,
genealogies, and important events
of his or her people.
  One massive illegal cache had
  been discovered and destroyed
  by the personal vigilance and
  action of Colonel Ellelou himself, in response to information provided by a female
  patriot, Kutunda Traore, a
  griot of the doughty Sara
  tribe. J. Updike, The Coup,
  1978, p 77
  By working backward through
  slave records, talking to linguists and finally interview-
  ing African griots, native
  oral historians, he [Alex Ha-
  ley] succeeded in tracing his
  slave ancestor, Kunta Kinte,
  back to a particular village.
  Newsweek, 8/5/74, p 75
  Despite Haley's much-touted
  labors of research, the dimensions of the several plagiar-
  ism lawsuits brought against

him, and of one settlement,
indicate that there were at
times some more than modest
confusion in his mind as to
his sources; also, a 1977 chal-
lenge by a reporter of the
London Sunday Times to the
plausibility of Haley's griot-
obtained information about his
remote African ancestor Kunta
Kinte has cast at least a little doubt on the factual, or
detective-story, basis of his
adventure. New Yorker, 3/26/79,
p 114
[< French < a West African language ～ Wolof gewel oral histori-
an]

Griqua /'gri:kwə/, n a person of
mixed Khoikhoin, San, and white
descent (in southern Africa).
  Griquas one could call them,
  or Bastards, it was more or
  less the same thing. They were
  a nation descended from the
  association of white men with
  Hottentot women. S. Willin,
  The South Africans, 1926, p 35
  [< Afrikaans Griekwa < Khoikhoin,
  ? < grigriqua name of a certain
  Khoikhoin tribe]

grugru /'gru:gru:/, n a tropical
spiny palm (Acrocomia); hence,
grugru grub, edible grub of a
South American weevil that feeds
on grugru.
  [< American (Puerto Rican)
  Spanish grugru, said to be < Yao
  grugru basket made of grugru]

gu /gu:/, n Also, goo. the rainy
season in Somalia from March to
June.
  [< Somali] See DAYR.

guarri /'gwari:/, n a tree or
shrub (Euclea) of southern Africa; the sweet-tasting fruit of
this tree or shrub.
  [< Khoikhoin gwarri]

guarriboom /'gwari:,bu:m/, n =
GUARRI.

[< Afrikaans < Khoikhoin gwarri
+ Afrikaans -boom tree]

guban /'gu:ban/, n the hot, northern coastal plain(s) of Somalia.
The Somali word for coastal
plain is "guban," which means
"burned." New York Times,
4/1/67, p 10
[< Somali]

gudza /'gu:dzə/, n a blanket made
of tree bark (in Zimbabwe). See
the quotation under DAUNHA.
[? < Shona]

Guelede /gə'leidei/, n = GELEDE.

guereza /gə'reizə/, n a black,
reddish colored monkey (Colobus)
with long white hair fringes on
the body sides and tail.
[< Amharic gureza]

Guinea /'ginei or 'gini:/, n 1
a country in West Africa bordering on Guinea-Bissau, Senegal,
Mali, Ivory Coast, Liberia and
Sierra Leone. 2 Guinea-Bissau.
a country in West Africa bordering on Guinea and Senegal.
3 Gulf of Guinea, a gulf of the
Atlantic ocean in the region of
Equatorial Guinea, Gabon and
Cameroon. 4 guinea, an English
gold coin, supposedly first
struck with gold from the Guinea
region. - Used attributively in
such terms as guinea fowl, guinea
gold, guinea pig, etc.
[< Portuguese, said to be < the
name of an eighth-century kingdom of the upper Niger river
called Ghinea, Genni or Jenne]

Gullah /'gʌlə/, n a black people
of the coast and islands of
South Carolina, Georgia and part
of Florida; their language, a
creolized English with strong
African lexical and syntactic
influence.
[? < ANGOLA, or ? < GOLA]

gumba /'gumbə/, n a water jar,
usually of clay (in Ethiopia).
An indispensable article of
household furniture in every
Ethiopian home is the gumba.
Daily, the women fill the vessels at the nearest spring or
water hole and cover the tops
with green leaves, then carry
them home on their backs, held
by a strap around the forehead,
in the Bible-time manner. National Geographic, 9/35, p 298
[< Amharic gəmbo or gənbo]

gumbo /'gəmbou/, n the okra plant
or its pods; a soup dish containing gumbo.
A gumbo is a Creole soup that
contains stock, meat, vegetables with peppers, okra and
sometimes ham. New York Times,
5/24/67, p 24
Crawdaddy, Vanderbilt Ave. at
45th St. - Doc Cheatham and
his trio (see page 118, this
issue) are here Mondays through
Fridays from six to eleven.
Jambalaya, crawfish pie, and
seafood gumbo. Closed Satur-
days. New Yorker, 2/5/79, p 6
[< Louisiana French < a Bantu
language ~ Tshiluba kingumbo,
tshingombo okra]

gumbo-limbo, n a tropical African tree (Bursera) yielding a
sweet-smelling resin used in
making varnish.
We identified the umbrella-
shaped rain tree with its
pink flowers and pods tasting
of licorice; and - most obvi-
ous because of its smooth and
copper-colored bark - the tree
with a name you can taste on
your tongue, the gumbo limbo,
or turpentine tree. Harper's,
12/60, p 53
[< GUMBO + limbo, ? < Kikongo
(e)dimbu bird lime]

gumbotil /'gəmbou,til/, n a dark,
sticky clay from a glacial till.
[< GUMBO + till glacial drift]

gungo pea /'guŋgou/, n Congo pea. Begin perhaps with pepperpot soup, made from a spinach-like vegetable called callaloo, or soup, made with gungo peas, meat stock and scallions. The Times, 4/17/76, p 5
[? alteration of Congo]

Gur /gər/, n a group of Niger-Congo languages including Dagomba, Mossi, Bariba and Gurma.
[? < Gurma]

gwacha /'gwatʃə/, n variant of KWACHA[2] (as a political slogan in Zambia).
European administrators stopped tribal wars in the nineteenth century, but as colonialism recedes before uhuru, gwacha, independence, or any other name given "Africa for the Africans," men feel free to take up their spears to settle old scores. Atlantic, 1/61, p 45
[< a Bantu language, literally, it is dawning, shining, ? < Bemba < gw- infinitive pfx or locative, "impersonal" subject pfx + -acha dawn, shine ~ Swahili -cha dawn]

gursha /'gərʃə/, n bribe, gratuity, or bonus (in Ethiopia).
[< Amharic, perhaps gərš obsolete coin or < gursʼa gift from superior put in recipient's mouth as sign of favor ~ gorrəš take a mouthful]

H

hadada /hə'dɛədə/, n a large
brownish-green ibis (Hagedashia).
There were also baby hippo like
small suitcases, ten waterbuck,
tern flying around, two saddle-
back storks and a Hadada ibis.
London Sunday Times, 12/31/67,
p 26
[? < a Southern African language]

hadithi /ha'di:θi:/, n sg and pl
a tale, or story among the Swahili.
All poems composed for public
performance are called mashairi,
but there are several kinds of
these: nyimbo, which are songs
of one sort or another, hadithi,
which are tales, and best known,
perhaps, utendi, the heroic
poems about the deeds and lives
of famous men and great events.
All these styles are very old.
B. Davidson, History of East &
Central Africa, 1969, p 136
[< Swahili < Arabic ḥadit tale]

hagi /'hagi:/, n = BAO (in Benin).

Hadza /'hadzə/, n a people of
northern Tanzania; their Khoisan
language.

hamba /'hambə/, intj Go away!
Shove off! (in southern Africa).
"I don't care what you've come
for, just get on your feet and
hamba out of my yard, go on,

quickly, OUT!" Atlantic,
1/68, p 57
[< Nguni < (uku)hamba (to) go]

harambee /haram'bei/, n a national slogan and rallying cry of
Kenya meaning "Pull together";
a fund-raising event, project,
etc., especially for national
development.
When he finished, the white
farmers roared Kenyatta's
battle cry of "Harambee!", a
Swahili expression meaning
"Let's all push together – get
up and go." Not all were won
over. Time, 8/23/63, p 24
The Reverend Stanley Wanjohi,
of Nyeri C.P.K. Church, said
the harambee will start at
10:30 a.m. and appealed to
wananchi to turn up in large
numbers and donate generously.
Standard (Nairobi), 11/30/79,
p 2
[< Swahili]

harmattan /harmə'tan/, n hot,
scorching wind from the Sahara
that blows over much of West
and Central Africa.
For the last few million years
the Sahara has been like the
centre of a galaxy, spiralling
dust out to the surrounding
hemisphere: south in the harmattan to West Africa in win-
ter; west across the Atlantic

to the Caribbean and even Florida, in the summer; north to
give the pluies de bou in Europe; and north east to the
Levant, especially on the tails
of the khamsin in the spring
months. Geographical Magazine,
6/79, p 658
[< numerous West African languages, cf. Akan haramata, ?
ultimately < Arabic harām evil
thing]

Hausa /'hausə or 'hauzə/, n a
people of West and Central Africa, chiefly of Nigeria and Niger;
their Afroasiatic (Chad) language, used widely as a trade
language and as an official language of Nigeria.

Herero /he'reirou/, n a people of
Namibia and Botswana; their
Bantu languge.
[said to be imitative of the
sound of their spears in flight]
Also incorrectly called CATTLE
DAMARA.

herola /hə'roulə/, n = HIROLA.

hincty or hinkty /'hinkti:/,
adj (in Afro-American slang)
snobbish; conceited; (a) white
(person).
    "None of these stores hire
    colored, but the help are the
    hinctiest and now they done
    gone and killed that child."
    L. Meriwether, Daddy Was a
    Number Runner, 1970, p 147
    We were in this hincty little
    town in Georgia doing this
    flick about this rural pot-
    head... New Yorker, 7/19/69,
    p 20
[? < a West or Central African
language ∼Chiluba mpingi one
who curses, damns ∼Swahili
mping(ani) one who obstructs <
-pinga obstruct, block]

hirola /hə'roulə/, n Hunter's
hartebeest (Damaliscus hunteri),
a small yellowish-brown antelope.

[< Oromo]

hlonipa /'hlounipa/, n a Nguni
system of showing reverence or
respect to certain persons or
objects, including the use of a
specialized vocabulary for women
toward male in-laws, avoidance
of contact, gestures of respect,
refraining from mentioning revered peoples and animals, etc.
Also used attributively and as
a verb.
    To the Zulu woman, for instance,
    her husband's name is hlonipa;
    so are those of his parents.
    ...The name of the king is
    sacred and powerful and fraught
    with danger, and therefore
    hlonipa to all. Funk & Wag-
    nall's Standard Dictionary of
    Folklore, Mythology and Legend,
    Vol. I, 1949, p 499
    The ones who hlonipha - avoid
    respect, will eat in the hut.
    Times of Swaziland, 7/20/73, p 5
[< Nguni (uku)hlonipha (to)
respect or reverence]

hogon /'hougoun/, n a village
wise man, elder, or priest among
the Dogon of Mali whose behavior
and dress in certain rituals symbolizes the myth of creation.
    Confined to the village by
    tradition, Kire, hogon of
    Yenndouma, received visitors
    in the narrow entrance to his
    compound. When men came with
    problems, Kire would chase
    away the curious women and
    children, tuck his tiny frame
    into a recess in the passage-
    way, and listen. National
    Geographic, 3/69, p 440
[< Dogon]

hoodoo /'hu:du:/, n a jinx; bad
luck; VOODOO.
    So many managers foundered
    there that it became known as
    a hoodoo house. New Yorker,
    4/9/55, p 44
    From the moment the overture
    struck up, in fact, it was

evident that a hoodoo was pur-
suing the show. New York Times,
11/26/55, p 49
[< a West African language, ?
< Hausa huduba rouse resentment
against, or ? < VOODOO]

hopo /'houpou/, n a trap for game
formed by two rows of hedges
forming a V with a pit at the
apex into which the animal is
driven.
[< a southern or central Bantu
language, ? < Swahili bopo pit,
mud hole, act of pressing in]

Hottentot /'hatən,tat/, n a term
(often derogatory) used by the
early European settlers of
South Africa for the KHOIKHOIN,
and formerly for the XHOSA,
people and their language.
[< Afrikaans, in imitation of
the click sounds found in the
language(s) of these people]

hungan /'huŋgan/, n a priest of
the VODUN cult in Haiti.
Often the peasants turn to voo-
dooism to alleviate their misery. They seek out the voodoo
priest or priestess, the hungan or the mambo, for cures.
Science News Letter, 5/11/63,
p 299
[< Fon hun vodun deity + ga
chief]

Hutu /'hu:tu:/, n Also, Bahutu.
a people of Burundi and Rwanda
who speak the Bantu language of
KIRUNDI or KINYARWANDA, respectively.

I

ibeji /i'beidʒi:/, n one of a
pair of sculpted figures representing the spirits of twins
born among the Yoruba; the cult
of Africa and Latin America cen-
tering on these twins or their
sculpted figures.

Yoruba mothers have told me
the secrets of their ibejis.
It seems that when twins are
born, the local witch doctor
sculptures two statuettes about
a foot high representing the
two children. The mother safe-
guards these figurines, or
ibejis. If one twin dies, its
ibeji is returned to the diviner, in whose care it has
oracular powers. National Geographic, 8/59, p 224
[< Yoruba] See OGBANJE.

ibiharag(w)e /,ibiha'rag(w)ei/,
n a Burundi dish of lima, pinto,
or kidney beans or black-eyed
peas sauteed in hot oil with
onions, garlic and chili peppers;
MAHARAGWE.
[? < Kirundi ibi- plural noun
pfx + -haragwe (root for) the
bean(s), ? < Swahili maharagwe]

Ibo /i'bou/, n Also, Igbo. a people
of southern Nigeria; their Niger-
Congo (Kwa) language, a national
language of Nigeria.

iboga /i'bougə/, n a species of

bush (Tabernanthe iboga) with
yellowish or pinkish-white flowers, an orange-like fruit, and
roots that produce an alkaloid
narcotic used for cult rituals
of the BWITI, among others; the
narcotic itself. Called EBOKA
among the Fan.

According to one medical report the President [Macias
Nguema of Equatorial Guinea]
is partly deaf, although he
doesn't use a hearing aid. He
never drinks alcohol but takes
a drug called iboga and smokes
bhang, the local hashish.
Daily News (Durban, South Africa), 2/14/79, p 13
[< Mpongwe]

ibogaine /'i:bou,gein/, n a
colorless, crystalline compound
producing hallucinatory effects,
derived from the roots, leaves,
and bark of IBOGA.

There was no doubt about it:
The Man from Maine had turned
to massive doses of Ibogaine
as a last resort....He had developed a tendency to roll his
eyes wildly during TV inter-
views...his thought patterns
had become strangely fragmented,
and not even his closest advisers could predict when he
might suddenly spiral off into
babbling rages, or neo-coma-
tose funks....There he was -

67

far gone in a bad Ibogaine
frenzy - suddenly shoved out
in a rainstorm to face a sullen
crowd....Those in a position to
know have flatly refused to
comment on rumors concerning
the Senator's disastrous ex-
periments with Ibogaine. H.
Thompson, Fear & Loathing: On
the Campaign Trail '72, 1972,
p 152
[< IBOGA + -ine chemical suffix]

Ifa /'i:fə/, n a divination cult
of West African origin in which
prophetic verses are matched to
patterns of throws of palm nuts
and interpreted by a BABALAWO.
Ifa is an African system of
divination based on a set of
numerical patterns and the
chanted interpretation which
they provoke from the initiated practitioner. Atlantic,
10/73, p 130
For diagnostic purposes Chief
Obafemi makes use of Ifa, the
cult of the god of fate and
the local name for a kind of
divination. Harper's, 12/65, p 58
[< Yoruba Ifa a god of fate said
to be < Ife a town in Nigeria]

ikhetho /i'keiθou/, n the family
of the groom in a Zulu wedding.
"The loss of a woman," Tayson
said as we sat on the ikhetho
side, "is a serious thing to
a family, for the women grow
the crops and raise the children. To make good such a loss,
the groom has to pay lobolo.
It has always been paid in cattle, usually 11 head, but it
may be more, depending upon
the woman." National Geographic,
12/71, p 756
[< Zulu]

ilmuran /ilmə'ræn/, n pl Maasai
warriors; MURAN.
Then his father gave him the
three most important material
things in his life - arem, olalem and elongo - spear, sword

and shield - which meant he
was ready to become one of the
strongest, most daring and
bravest men in the world: ilmuran. J. Hallet, Congo Kitabu,
1964, p 138
"Young are the warriors, and
we feed them the best of our
meat. Healthy, they will protect our herds from enemies
and famine..." These words,
sung by senior warriors to
their younger comrades, express something of the significance and the almost magical
powers attributed to the title
ilmoran. Natural History, 8/80,
p 43
[< Maasai il- plural noun pfx
+ muran warrior]

Imbokodvo /imbou'koudvou/, n a
pro-royalist political party in
Swaziland.
The Imbokodvo National Movement...now rules in the Swaziland legislative council. New
York Times, 4/19/67, p 8
The Chief organized his own
political party, Imbokoduo, to
fight the elections. This co-
alition of tribal tradition-
ists and white segregational-
ists won an overwhelming victory in the election. M. Benson
in C. Legum (ed), Africa, Handbook to the Continent, 1966,
p 320
[< siSwati, literally, grind-
stone]

imbongi /əm'baŋgi:/, n a praise
singer for a Zulu chief; a
fawning sycophant.
Reminders of the 20th century
were rarely absent from the
rites. Prince Gabheni, the
Swazi king's son, and K.H.
Dlamini, a government minister
(below, left), arrived in pin-
striped suits, and when im-
bongis - praise singers - announced the entrance of the
bride, a band joined in with
a number from Broadway's The

Sound of Music. National Geographic, 1/78, p 48
[⪡ Zulu im- singular noun pfx
+ -bongi ∿ bonga praise, extol,
laud] Also, MBONGI.

imfe /'imfei/, n a South African
sorghum (Dochna); IMPHEE.
[⪡ Nguni imfe sweet cane]

imojo /i'moudʒou/, n a Ghanaian
dish of shrimp and other fish
simmered in water and spices and
served with a sauce of vegetables,
fish stock, and spices.
> Every day, the fishermen have
to paddle their dugouts through
a savage surf to get to their
most productive fishing ground.
But their catches include some
of the finest fish of Africa
and fish imojo depends for its
success on the freshness of
the catch. L. van der Post et
al., African Cooking, 1970,
p 76
[⪡ a West African language]

impala /im'pæələ/, n the well-
known South African antelope.
> There are elephants and buffa-
lo by the thousands in the
valley, zebra, eland, kudu,
puku, roan, impala, waterbuck,
rhinoceros, hippopotamus and
many other species. Scientific
American, 11/60, p 130
[⪡ Zulu impala ∿ seTswana phala
∿ Swahili paa]

imphee /'imfei or -fi:/, n = IMFE.

impi /'impi:/, n a Zulu regiment
(originally organized by the
chieftain Chaka); any armed
band.
> Experienced Boers warned
Frere's military commander,
Lord Chelmsford, of the amazing
mobility of the Zulu impi, but
to no avail. Manchester Guardian, 7/4/63, p 10
> We were recalling the titles
of the chapters: "Pendulum of
Doom," "Death Dials a Number,"

when suddenly I noticed the
girl I had rescued advancing
toward us with an impi of six
armed men. Atlantic, 11/63, p 99
[⪡ Nguni impi regiment, military ∿ Luyia tsimbia army]

impoof or impufu /im'pu:f(u:)/,
n an African eland, Tauratragus
oryx.
[⪡ Zulu impofu ∿ mpofu tawny
∿ Swahili mpofu or pofu eland]

impoon /im'pu:n/, n a small antelope, Sylvicapra grimmia, of
southern Africa; grey duiker.
[⪡ Zulu impunzi]

Incwala /in'tʃwalə/, n a national
holiday of Swaziland marking the
harvesting held in December or
January and celebrating unity
and kingship.
[⪡ siSwati, said to mean feast
of first fruits, ? ⪡ TJWALA]

indaba /'indabə/, n a tribal con-
ference in southern Africa; con-
ference, parley; concern, problem.
> It was on the second occasion
that the famous indaba took
place between Rhodes and the
Matabele chiefs. N. Davitt,
Spell of South Africa, 1938,
p 70
> At another village, Mr. Flet-
cher's portable radio was a
centre of attraction to children....At one indaba the party encountered rigid opposition
to the education of women.
The Times, 9/2/55, p 6
> Other expedients are being
tried, including the "indaba"
or national convention which
began on Monday, which give
vent to feelings but are un-
likely to result in action.
Manchester Guardian, 11/3/60,
p 8
[⪡ Nguni, literally, matter,
affair; conference]

indlovukati /in,dlouvə'kati:/,
n = NDLOVUKAZI.

The Paramount Chief - Ngwenyama, or Lion - has a mystical
bond with his people, and his
personality is linked with
their health and the fertility
of the soil. The Queen Mother
- Indlovukati, Lady Elephant
- has a particularly important
role. M. Benson in C. Legum
(ed), Africa, Handbook to the
Continent, 1966, p 319

induna /in'du:nə/ or indvuna /in-
'dvu:nə/, n a top adviser to a
chief among the Zulu; senior
councillor among the Swazi; a
man, especially a black African,
in authority.
An elderly induna emerged from
a hut, rendered the palms-to-
gether salute of respect, and
inquired as to our business.
After a moment he led us into
the simple but spotless living
room of the house of Prince
Israel Mcwayizeni, son of
Solomon, son of Dinuzulu,
acting paramount chief of the
Zulu nation. National Geographic, 12/71, p 738
It was a few days after this
last occurrence that Ignosi
held his great "indaba" (council), and was formally recognized as king by the "indunas"
(head men) of Kukuanaland. The
spectacle was an imposing one,
including, as it did, a great
review of troops. H. Haggard,
King Solomon's Mines, 1885,
p 180
[ᐸ Nguni]

ingubu /iŋ'gu:bu:/, n clothing;
second-hand garments; a blanket
(of animal skin or any material)
(in southern Africa).
[ᐸ Nguni ingubu clothing, skin
of an animal ᔕ Swahili nguo
clothing]

injera /in'dʒerə/, n Also, indgeria. thin, unleavened, pan-
cake-like sourbread of Ethiopia.
Wat is a kind of curried stew
made of lamb, beef or chicken
and liberally seasoned with
red pepper and other spices.
The injera is served with the
wat - usually for dipping.
Time, 6/14/63, p 18
Women are modest; they work
steadily, yet not too hard.
Flour they make from teff,
baking thin loaves of bread
called indgeria; they weave
cloth of good quality into
the distinctive native robe
called a chamma. National Geographic, 9/35, p 308
Air hostesses did everything
they could to make every min-
ute of our stay on the air-
liner quite enjoyable. We obtained service whenever we
wanted it, injera wot [sic]
one of the most popular Ethiopian dishes. Voice of Uganda,
3/10/73, p 2
[ᐸ Amharic injəra]

Inkhata or Inkatha /iŋ'katə or
iŋ'kaθə/, n a political movement among the Zulu for equali-
ty for all; originally a cultural and social organization
founded by the Zulu King Solomon aimed at preserving Zulu
heritage.
The fierceness of Inkatha's
reaction to what it perceived
as an attack was reflected in
a speech by Oscar Dhlomo,
KwaZulu's Minister of Education, who...warned that Inkatha was "now prepared to shed
blood when it comes to dealing
with those people who make it
their hobby to discredit and
abuse Chief Buthelezi's stature as our leader." New York
Times, 11/30/80, p 18
Zulu Chief Buthelezi, whose
broad-based Inkatha (Ring)
movement gives him some claim
to a national leadership role,
is broadly criticized by
young militant blacks for his
commitment to working peace-
fully within the system. Time,

6/15/81, p 45
In KwaZulu the chief minister,
Gatsha Buthelezi, in January
extended his Inkatha organization into an alliance with members of other black homelands
as well as Coloured people and
Indians. Compton's Yearbook,
1979, p 303
[< Zulu inkhata tribal emblem
(a mystical coil) of solidarity]

inkhululeko /iŋxulu'leikou/, n
Also, inkululeko. independence
(in Southern Africa).
  King Sobhuza plans to move into
  a relatively modern palace
  costing $48,000 and keep Swazi-
  land moving forward after "inkhululeko". New York Times,
  9/6/68, p 8
  But for Paramount Chief Kaizer
  Matanzima, Transkei's imperi-
  ous Prime Minister, it was the
  fulfilment of a long-standing
  dream that he would one day
  lead four million Xhosa-speak-
  ing people to inkululeku - to
  freedom and independence. The
  Times, 10/26/78, p 13
[< siSwati and Xhosa] See UHURU.

inkosi /iŋ'kousi:/, n title of a
Zulu leader or chief; term of
respect (in Southern Africa).
  It is true, inkosi, that they
  have been teaching these things
  for many years. A. Paton, Cry
  the Beloved Country, 1948, p 227
  "Why do you ask whither we go?
  What is it to thee?" I answered,
  suspiciously...."It is this, O
  white men, that if indeed you
  travel so far I would travel
  with you." There was a certain
  assumption of dignity in the
  man's mode of speech, and especially in his use of the words
  "O white men," instead of "O
  Inkosis" (chiefs), which struck
  me. H. Haggard, King Solomon's
  Mines, 1885, p 38
[< Zulu inkosi king, paramount
chief ~ Karanga (Shona) (a-)hosi,
Gogo (mu)gosi, Sotho kxosi (with

similar meanings)]

inkosikazi /,iŋkousi'kazi:/, n
a term of respect for a woman,
especially a married woman (in
Southern Africa).
[< Zulu INKOSI + -kazi ~ Haya
-kazi ~ Luyia -xasi woman]

insangu /in'sæŋgu:/, n Also,
intsangu. marijuana (in Swaziland).
  intsangu [Africa] cannabis.
  R. Lingeman, Drugs from A to
  Z: A Dictionary, 1969, p 116
  Fines of up to R1 000 and
  prison sentences of three years,
  the maximum penalty, were imposed last year for the cultivation and possession of Insangu....Police confiscated
  and destroyed 7,447 kgms of the
  drug. Times of Swaziland, 6/8/73,
  p 18
[< Zulu insangu cannibis]

intombi /in'tambi:/, n a girl or
unmarried woman (in Southern
Africa).
[< Zulu, Xhosa]

inyala /in'yælɔ/, n the harnessed
antelope (Tragelaphus angasi)
with long, slightly twisted horns,
with a white stripe down the
back, found in southern Africa.
[< Zulu inxala ~ Luyia (in)zala
antelope ~ (axa)yala small ante-
lope]

inyanga /in'yaŋgɔ/, n medicine
man, herbalist, or water doctor
among the Zulu.
  The itinerant combination of
  sangoma and inyanga - diviner
  and medicine man - diagnoses
  ailments through communication
  with spirits. Then he prescribes
  from his grab bag of herbs and
  potions. National Geographic,
  12/71, p 758
[< Nguni inyanga doctor ~ Swahili (m)ganga doctor]

inyenzi /in'yenzi:/, n (pl) acti-

vists among Batutsi refugees
from Rwanda seeking to overthrow
the Bahutu rule; an organization
of these refugees.
> But the Watutsi tribesmen
> vowed revenge. Bands of night-
> time raiders called inyenzi be-
> gan attacking Behutu villages.
> Time, 1/24/64, p 21
> Among the hard-core exiles a
> secret terrorist organization
> known as the Inyenzi was
> formed. This became the focus
> of counterrevolutionary activi-
> ty directed at overthrowing the
> Rwanda government and restoring
> the monarchy. Atlantic, 6/64,
> p 28

[‹ Kinyarwanda or Kirundi, literally, cockroaches]

ipiti /i'pi:ti:/, n a very small
South African antelope, the blue
duiker (Cephalophus monticola).
[‹ Zulu impiti]

Iraqw /i'rak/, n a people of
northern Tanzania; their Afroasiatic (Cushitic) language.

irimbako /i'rimbəkou/, n Hadza
name for the MARIMBA.
> The Muslim custom of eating
> only with the right hand comes
> up from the coast by way of
> the part-Arab Swahili, once
> the agents of the trade in s
> slaves and ivory; so does the
> marimba, called irimbako by
> the Hadza. New Yorker, 9/30/72,
> p 70

[‹ Hadza ‹ a Bantu language
irimba marimba + -ko Hadza neuter
suffix]

irio /iri:'ou/, n a Kikuyu dish
of ground maize porridge mixed
with green vegetables or seeds
(in Kenya).
> At the Panafric, the menu is
> at once French-accented and
> Kenyan, with the local speci-
> alties including the ground-
> beef dish called sukuma wiki,

served with saffron rice and
irio - a corn and peas melange.
R. Kane, Africa A to Z, 1961,
p 191
[‹ Kikuyu]

iroko /i'roukou/, n a tree (Chlorophora) sacred to the Yoruba
and yielding a teak-like hardwood; the wood; ODUM.
> We have had trouble with cer-
> tain metals and plastics and
> modern fittings, but the good
> stout hull, framed with English
> oak, [is] planked with iroko.
> The Times, 7/18/55, p 9
> Even the calmness looked un-
> canny and unreal. Out in the
> distance an iroko tree rose
> tall, superior and awesomely
> alone, like a raped priestess.
> Around her at a reverent radius
> a few houses stood, stolid and
> sombre. I. Okpewho, The Victims,
> 1970, p 62
[‹ Yoruba iroko]

isangoma /i'saŋgouma/, n = SAN-
GOMA.
> The isangoma walked ahead, a
> slight old man wearing a mon-
> key-fur cap and carrying a
> thin blackened wand. Harper's,
> 8/61, p 62
[‹ Zulu]

isano oil /ə'sanou/, n an oil
extracted from the nuts of an
equatorial tree (Ongokea Olaca-
ceae) of Africa, used in fire-
resistant paints.
[isano said to be ‹ an African
language of the Zaire (Congo)
river and to mean the tree that
yields it]

isanusi /,isa'nu:si:/, n an Nguni
witch doctor, usually a woman
who can determine if another is
a witch.
> "And what came they for, the
> white ones, the terrible ones,
> the skilled in magic and all
> learning, the strong, the

unswerving? What is that bright stone upon thy forehead, O king? Whose hands made the iron garments upon thy breast, O king? Ye know not, but I know. I the old one, I the wise one, I the Isanusi!" H. Haggard, King Solomon's Mines, 1885, p 110
[< Nguni is(i)- singular noun pfx + -anuse or -anusi ~ (uku)nuka smell ~ Swahili nuka give off a smell, nusa smell out]

isokite /'i:soukait/, n a whitish or pinkish phosphate, flouride of magnesium and calcium. Formula: CaMgPO$_4$F
[< Isoka small town in Zambia where it was gathered (? < soko market (in certain Bantu languages) + -ite mineral suffix]

Issa /'i:sa/, n Also, Isaq or Isha(a)k. a people of Djibouti, Ethiopia and Somalia, a subgroup of the SOMALI; hence, Territory of Afars and Issas, former name of DJIBOUTI.
[< Somali, ? < Issachar son of Jacob and Leah (in the Bible); one of the twelve tribes of Israel]

iwa /'i:wə/, n a rubbing board and a piece of wood that is rolled back and forth along the board, used as a means of divination by the Azande. It answers when the piece of wood sticks or does not move.
[< Azande]

izibongo /,i:zi'baŋgou/, n a praise song among the Zulu, sung by an MBONGI.
After Tayson had sung the izibongo, the prince came out of his mud-brick hut and announced that a young girl of the kraal, a granddaughter, had died. National Geographic, 12/71, p 757
[< Nguni izi- plural noun pfx + -bongo ~ bonga praise, extol]

izicaza /,i:zi'tʃazə/, n a person from the boondocks; a yokel or country bumpkin (in southern Africa).
The hostel inmates, irrespective of tribe, tend to form an alien and often alienated group within the wider community, said an expert on the township....This latent tension is reflected in the Zulu term izicaza...[that] expresses the contempt that city people feel for less sophisticated rural folk. New York Times, 8/27/76, p A2
[< Zulu] See SHENZI.

J

jako /'dʒækou/, n a common, gray
parrot of Africa.
[< an African language]

jamba /'dʒæmbə/, n marijuana
(in western and central Africa).
[? < a Bantu language < j(i)-
singular noun pfx + -amba ~ DI-
AMBA]

jambo /'dʒambou/, n a greeting in
Swahili; "hello."
   Whenever I stopped by the road
   for lunch an African would appear from the ground and say
   pleasantly, "Jambo, Mama," and
   ask the basic questions: where
   have you come from, where are
   you going, how many children
   have you. Atlantic, 2/66, p 71
   [Princess] Margaret asked and
   got a school holiday for them.
   Pleased natives promptly dubbed
   her the "Jambo" Princess, which
   in Swahili means "happy to meet
   you." Newsweek, 10/8/56, p 44
   [< Swahili, literally, thing,
   concern, matter < hujambo you are
   without a concern, trouble]

jamhuri /dʒam'huri:/, n a republic (in eastern Africa).
   The celebration of Tanganyika's
   becoming a jamhuri in December,
   1962, was much like the independence celebration a year
   earlier. New Yorker, 10/23/71,
   p 54

[< Swahili, a meeting, a republic < Arabic jamhuriya republic; ~ UJAMAA]

jazz , n (v, adj) the well-known
form of music.
   [? < an African language, ? <
   Chiluba jaja cause to dance,
   make dance]

jazzbo /'dʒæzbou/, n a fancily-
dressed black man.
   R.L. Duffus...travels a well-
   remembered section of the
   California coastline to judge
   whether a new highway should
   nip the edges of a jazzbo mo-
   tel (Jimmy's Place) or eclipse
   a vaguely suspect old folks'
   home. New York Times, 11/11/66,
   p 45
   [? < a West African language,
   ? < Chiluba (ku)jabo (they)
   dance]

jebena /dʒə'benə/, n a pot, kettle,
or small jug for coffee (in
Ethiopia).
   At its peak of refinement,
   Ethiopian coffee is served
   unsweetened, after being spiced,
   boiled and reboiled into a concentrated richness that smells
   faintly of cloves. At left below a serving woman fills cup
   with coffee from the typical
   black jebena. L. van der Post
   et al., African Cooking, 1970,

p 43
[< Amharic jəbəna]

jembe /'dʒembei/, n an adze-like
hoe with a blade like a shovel,
used for farming, digging, etc.,
in East Africa.
>Jusuf Shee and Omar Harjii
denied...that on Nov. 24 at
Waa in Kwale District, they
were found in possession of
143 pangas and 171 jembes which
had not been cleared by the
customs people. Standard (Nairobi), 11/30/79, p 9
Edible oils: situation in the
edible oil industry group is
not clear so far. Hoes and
jembes: importation should not
be allowed. Glass Bottles:
some importation should be allowed as there appears to be
no local production. Voice of
Uganda, 2/23/73, p 1
[< Swahili]

jigger /'dʒigər/, n = CHIGGER.
>As he limped away the children
trotted mockingly round him
part of the way. He looked
like a discomfited scrounger
with jiggers in his feet. I.
Okpewho, The Victims, 1970,
p 97
Tiptoeing to the door so as
not to waken Harris, he felt
the little sting of a jigger
under his toe-nail. In the
morning, he must get his boy
to scoop it out. G. Greene,
Heart of the Matter, 1948,
p 147

jiko /'dʒi:kou/, n a charcoal-
burning stove often made of
scrap metal (in eastern Africa).
>Agunga adds some of the hair
to a piece of dried bat...which
he places on the glowing charcoal of his small jiko (charcoal stove). When the mixture
has burned down, he pours the
ashes onto a piece of paper.
New York Times (Mag. Sec.),

10/19/80, p 81
Contrast this slow progress,
again, with the success of the
"jiko", a little inefficient
charcoal-burning stove...that
sells for 8 shillings and is
found in every poor urban home.
New Scientist, 11/20/80, p 522
[< Swahili, originally, fireplace, hearth, kitchen < ji-
singular noun pfx + -ko (root
for) this fireplace]

jikungu /dʒi'kuŋgu:/, n a tropical African plant (Telfairia
pedata) with edible seeds yielding oil.
[< Shambala zikungu, nkungu
plural of lukungu ~ Swahili
kungu < earlier ji-kungu (the
ji- pfx was lost in Swahili except in a few words like JIKO);
plural, makungu nut(s) from the
tree mkungu]

jilaal or jilal /dʒi'lal/, n
the hot, dry season in Somalia,
from late December or January
to March.
[< Somali]

jird /dʒɜrd/, n a gerbil of
northern Africa.
>The needs of less common lab-
oratory species, such as ham-
sters, cotton rats, jirds (ro-
dents found in desert areas),
ferrets and a number of others,
are not so easily met. New
Scientist, 10/23/58, p 1103
[< Berber agherda]

joala /dʒou'alə/, n beer made
from maize in Lesotho.
[< seSutu jo- singular noun
pfx + -ala ~Luyia (ama)lwa
beer]

jocko /'dʒakou/, n a chimpanzee;
any monkey.
[< French < a West African language ~Akan (Fanti) (ɔ)doku
monkey; Efik idiok monkey]

jogoo /dʒou'gou/, n a rooster, the symbol of the Kenya African National Union (KANU) the country's ruling party.

> The Duke turned to Mr. Kenyatta and asked what the silver badge on his lapel was. Mr. Kenyatta replied: "That is a jogoo (cockerel)" -- the symbol of Mr. Kenyatta's party which has now become part of the national crest. The Times, 12/11/63, p 9

[< Swahili]

Jollof rice /'dʒoləf/, n a West African dish, a stew of fish, chicken or beef, tomatoes, onions, rice, and chili peppers; said to be ultimately of Sierra Leonean origin.

> On the day of his death the family drew out ₤2,000 for immediate expenses, the streets round the house were closed, crates of beer and whisky and quantities of jollof rice and fufu were placed round about, and the band from one of the night-clubs was engaged to play highlife until dawn. Manchester Guardian, 10/29/59, p 5
> The area [Covent Garden] is cosmopolitan, too. It has London's only African restaurant ...where groundnut stews are eaten with Jollof rice and plantains. The Times, 6/19/80, p 24

[Jollof < a West African language; probably alteration of WOLOF]

juju /'dʒu:dʒu:/, n a fetish, magic charm, amulet, spell, incantation, or evil spirit.

> Amulets - Koranic phrases, often inauthentic, in little bark or leather cylinders - were littered here and there, and empty bowls in which...a soul had been captured. My soul, perhaps. How often, I wondered, had my death been rendered in mime, and the king's escape been effected via the fragile fabrications of juju? J. Updike, The Coup, 1978, p 25
> 'Eh?' Okafor cried. 'But I hear juju no take to white man.' 'This one take! I make sure it take,' Chukwuka assured them. 'If ADO cross water and go back for him own country, the juju go leave him. But if he go and come back again or if he stay for here, the thing go stay thick with him!' A. Ulasi, Many Thing You No Understand, 1970, p 124
> Kofi Gbede also maintained that a woman gave the papers cut to the size of cedi notes to him to perform "juju" for her to trace certain persons who had duped her. Ghanaian Times, 5/4/73, p 1

[< Hausa dʒudʒu fetish, evil spirit]

juke or jook /dʒu:k/, n a brothel or cheap roadside inn; music played in such a place; hence, juke box, coin-operated automatic record-playing machine.

> A Saturday night jook is a simple uninhibited orgy of drinking, dancing, singing, gambling, love-play, and, occasionally, knife-play, in the pines outside. A. Cook, One Man's America, 1952, p 124

--v to dance, especially to the music of a juke box; feint, jerk or move suddenly.

> He outlined specific Cleveland plays, instructing the defense when to key and when to juke. Newsweek, 12/22/58, p 80

[< Gullah juke, joog wicked a West African language ~ Bambara dzugu wicked, Wolof dzug to live wickedly; cf. Jamaican English juk to have sexual intercourse with a woman, ? < Fulani jukka poke]

jumbe /'dʒumbei/, n a chief or headman, especially on Zanzibar.

> Northern Zanzibar and the small island of Tumbatu were

governed by a chief called the
Sheha, usually a man but occa-
sionally a woman. He lived on
Tumbatu, and his people bore
the same name. The rest of Zanzibar was ruled by another chief,
called the Jumbe or the Mwenyi
Mkuu, whose people were the
Hadimu. B. Davidson, A History
of East and Central Africa,
1969, p 156

[< Swahili]

jumby or jumbie /'dʒumbi:/, n
a spirit, ghost, or demon in
certain cults, beliefs, or folklore of African origin.
[< a West African language, ?
∼ Kikongo zumbi fetish, spirit,
? < Mandingo dyumbo one wearing
a pompom as an amulet]

K

K, abbreviation of KWACHA[1], KWACHA[2], KWANZA, MAKUTA.

> University of Malawi, Lecturer in Agricultural Entomology. Salary Scale: K3500-6600 per annum (₤1 sterling = K1.62). If no British Government supplement is available, the University may pay an addition of between K1320-K1656 per annum (taxable in Malawi). New Scientist, 2/15/79, p 516
> Zambia. Finance. Monetary unit, kwacha. K1 = US$1.31. Budget (1979): expenditures, K849.4 million; revenues, K583.9 million. Collier's Encyclopedia Yearbook, 1979, p620
> Paper money now in circulation consists of 10 Zaire, 5 Zaire, and 1 Zaire notes, as well as 50K (Makuta), 20K and 10K notes. The coins are 5K, 1K and 10 Sengi. The Times, 12/6/72, p III
> The kwanza was issued at par with the Angolan escudo. The late 1977 dollar exchange rate was $1 = K31.55/K1 = $0.03169. G. Kurian, Encyclopedia of the Third World (Vol. 1), 1979, p 59

kaama /'kamə/, n = CAAMA[2].

Kabaka /kə'bakə/, n title of the king of the Baganda of Uganda.
> The Kabaka of Buganda is a frail, 29-year-old African king named Mutesa II. His 900,000 subjects in his cotton-rich kingdom on Lake Victoria make Buganda the key province of the British protectorate. Newsweek, 12/14/53, p 46

[< Luganda]

--Kabakaship, n: "As you have married an English girl, neither your children nor your grandchildren can be recognized as being in the direct line of succession to the Katakaship." Time, 3/30/59, p 32

--Kabaka Yekka, n: Sarah took me to the family burial ground....
> "This is my Maama Kezia, who died ten years ago. She was a very political lady. She used to take me to the rallies of the Kabaka Yekka - the King Only - party." National Geographic, 7/80, p 83
> One interesting factor about the link-up is the ideological differences of the two leaders. Museveni is a radical leftist and Lule is a conservative. The only major common factor is their opposition to Obote. The link-up will definitely boost a rather insignificant party, which opponents have enjoyed dismissing as marking time, into a major factor that will play a decisive role in determining the Ugandan elections when they are held. Lule commands the support of many Baganda who were formally loyal

to the Kabaka Yekka. That alone
would deal a major blow to the
DP's chances of winning despite
its recent success in broadening
its appeal. Weekly Review (Nairobi), 9/19/80, p 5

kabela or **kabella** /kə'belə/, n
= KEBELE.
Hannah, a former student, is
now, at 19, secretary to one
of the local revolutionary
councils called "Kabellas"
which govern Addis Ababa and
among her duties is the training of women members of the
Kabella defence squad. Manchester Guardian, 2/19/78, p 6
The unions are in the process
of being "restructured" in the
new popular organisations set
up by the revolutionaries (kabella, district committees,
women's committees and so on).
Manchester Guardian, 8/1/76,
p 13

kaffir /ka'fiːr/, n an offensive,
derogatory term for a black person (in southern Africa).
Yet, in their own eyes, the
Faasens are not bigots. Unlike
others, they do not call their
hands "kaffir" or "munt." They
encourage religious services
and they give clothing and food
to the workers and their children. New York Times (Mag. Sec.),
7/11/76, p 37
[< Afrikaans, formerly a Xhosa
person or the Xhosa languages
Zulu, ? < khafula person of uncivilized manners < Arabic kafir
heathen, person of uncivilized
manners]

kaffir beer, n beer made from
corn or sorghum in South Africa,
said to contain some vitamins
and have medicinal properties.
Also called: UTSHUALA.
They have great joy in their
kaffir beer, which is made of
corn, and when brewed is a
nauseous grey mixture. B. Hicks,

The Cape as I Found It, 1900,
p 153

kaffirboom /ka'fiːrbuːm/, n a
coral tree (Erythrina caffra)
with red flowers and soft wood.
The kaffir-booms, with their
magnificent scarlet flowers,
look gorgeous when growing, as
they habitually do, among the
boulders. A. Balfour, Twelve
Hundred Miles in a Wagon, 1895,
p 170
[< Afrikaans < KAFFIR + -boom
tree]

Kafuan /kə'fuːən/, adj of or relating to a Lower Pleistocene
culture of eastern and central
Africa characterized by pebble
tools roughly chipped on one
side only. See the quotation
under TUMBIAN.
[< Kafu a river in Uganda near
which artifacts of this culture
were discovered + English -an]

kaikai /'kai,kai/, n a potent alcoholic liquor distilled from
the fermented sap of the raphia
palm (in West Africa).
[They] sang 'Land of Hope and
Glory' with me. Then I made a
short speech in dialect about
the King and they'd disperse
and trot home to the jungle for
a spot of kaikai. Punch, 8/4/65,
p 149
King Edumu, bobbing with the
aftereffects of his interroga-
tion...was led forth in white
robes by some soldiers who, it
was clear from their carriage
and aura, had greeted this day
with tumblers of kaikai. The
meagre throng, at least half
of them children given a school
holiday, attempted a cheer. J.
Updike, The Coup, 1978, p 79
[< a West African language∿
Ijaw kaikai this drink (also,
headache)]

Kakwa /'kakwə/, n a people of
northern Uganda and southern

Sudan, also known as <u>Bari</u>; their
Nilo-Saharan (Eastern Sudanic)
language.

Kalabari /ˌkælə'bari:/, <u>n</u> a people
of Nigeria, closely related to
the IJAW.

kalabule /ka:'la:bu:lei/, <u>n</u> illegal profiteering or other illicit
business practices (bribe-taking,
black-market transactions) in
Ghana.
> Also over the week-end Mohammed
> Ibrahim, 35, was arrested at
> Kaneshie for selling above the
> control price. He was alleged
> to have sold a pair of foreign
> shoes for ₵155 instead of ₵40.
> Mr. Kugblenu had earlier as-
> sured the public that the police
> had intensified their activi-
> ties to stamp out the re-emer-
> gence of 'kalabule'. He also
> admitted that the police were
> overstretched since they could
> not reach everywhere every time,
> and therefore welcomed the for-
> mation of vigilante groups as
> a step in the right direction.
> <u>Ghanaian Times</u>, 1/23/80, p 1
> [? < a Nigerian language; not
> thought to be < Akan, Ewe, or
> Hausa]

kalimba /kə'li:mbə/, <u>n</u> a type of
thumb piano.
> Munro has purchased instruments
> which require little musical
> ability or background. The in-
> struments, which include a
> slitlog (an African drum), a
> kalimba (a wooden box with met-
> al strips which are plucked)
> and a bow harp, allow the pa-
> tients to improvise spontane-
> ously. <u>Maclean's</u>, 2/26/79, p 51
> Among those played are the
> mbira, timbila, kalimba, guitar-
> lute, Lozi drums, tampura drone,
> bamboo pipe, Japanese koto zith-
> er, and double respiratory lin-
> guaphone. <u>Time</u>, 3/18/66, p 69
> [< a Bantu language ∼ Bemba <u>aka-</u>
> <u>limba</u> zanza < ka- singular noun

pfx + <u>limba</u> ∼ (ma)<u>rimba</u> ∼ Swahili
<u>imba</u> sing]

Kalunga /ka'luŋgə/, <u>n</u> the god of
the sea in the Bahia (Brazil) pantheon; the supreme being among
certain peoples of Angola and
Zaire.
[? < Kikongo or Kimbundu, said
to mean ocean]

Kamasian /kə'meiʃən/, <u>adj</u> of or
relating to a major pluvial (period of increased rainfall) in
Africa.
> Olduvai Gorge is a cut some 25
> miles long. Displacements of
> the earth's crust have disturbed
> the sequence of the strata, but
> we can trace five main deposits
> ...laid down in a shallow lake
> at a time when the climate of
> East Africa was appreciably wet-
> ter than today - a time called
> the Kamasian Pluvial period.
> Then came a much drier period,
> drier even than today. <u>Scien-</u>
> <u>tific American</u>, 1/54, p 68
> [< <u>Kamasia</u> Hills, area in the
> Rift Valley Region of Kenya where
> evidence for such a period was
> found + English -<u>an</u>]

kamassi /kə'masi:/, <u>n</u> a tree of
Southern Africa (<u>Gonioma</u>); its
yellow, hard wood.
[< Afrikaans < Xhosa <u>kamamasane</u>]

Kamba /'kambə/, <u>n</u> a people of central Kenya; their Bantu language.
[< Kamba, said to mean traveler]

kanaga /'kanəgə/, <u>n</u> a mask of the
Dogon topped by a short pole to
which two parallel pieces are
fastened crosswise, creating the
image of outstretched arms or
wings.
> Half a dozen <u>kanaga</u> dancers,
> men in masks topped by the out-
> stretched arms of Amma, swung
> into line in front of me. Now
> they began a series of great
> swooping arcs. Three, four times
> they circled, swept down to

touch the ground with Amma's creating hands, and then soared up again. National Geographic, 3/69, p 442
[< Dogon]

kanga or khanga /kæŋgə/, n a wraparound cloth, usually brightly colored and patterned, worn as a skirt or shawl.
This year, at Dior and Vivier, it's fetishes and masks, Bou Bous, kangas, javas, and coconut bark. London Sunday Times, 1/29/67, p 53
Khadejha cut out a bright place for herself in fashion by creating exciting designs in colorful African, kanga-cotton fabrics. New York Times, 10/1/66, p 20
[< Swahili]

kani /'kani/, n a chief or wizard among certain peoples in the Congo.
Along the banks of the muddy Alima River a kani's orders are not taken lightly. Time, 4/9/56, p 70
[< a West African language ~ Mboshi kani chieftain]

Kanjera or Kanjeran /kan'dʒerə or kan'dʒerən/, adj 1 of or relating to the remains, artifacts, or culture of an extinct East African man, Kanjera Man, of the Middle Pleistocene. 2 of or relating to a major pluvial (period of increased rainfall) in Africa.
The long dry period, during which the lake disappeared... was followed by another wet spell called the Kanjeran Pluvial. Scientific American, 1/54, p 68
[< Kanjira region in Kenya where evidence for these discoveries were found + English -an]

kantiba /kən'ti:bə/, n a mayor in Ethiopia.
[< Amharic kəntiba < kətəna town, city]

Kanuri /kə'nuri:/, n a people of Nigeria and Niger; their Nilo-Saharan (Saharan) language.

kanzu or khanzu /'kanzu:/, n a full-length robe of white cotton or linen for men in East Africa.
He was a cheerful, willing boy, who, as he stood behind Bill that evening, alert and elegant in his white shoulder-to-heel kanzu and crimson sash and tarboosh, made a very attractive figure. Harper's, 9/60, p 61
At the Coast Vice-President Mwai Kibaki also attended a traditional ceremony in Lamu at which he was given a traditional Muslim "kanzu". Weekly Review (Nairobi), 2/16/79, p 16
[< Swahili < Arabic kasa to clothe]

kapenta /kə'pentə/, n a perch-like lake fish of eastern and southern Africa, Engraulicypris, served fried or stewed and, when dried, exported.
[? < a (Zambian) Bantu language]

kapitula /kapi'tu:lə/, n European-style tropical shorts.
One evening when we were rather preoccupied, I became aware of a tremendous racket. I rose, jumped into my kapitula and rushed outside to look for the trouble. J. Hallet, Congo Kitabu, 1964, p 51
[< Swahili, variant of kaputula ~Nyanja (ku)butula (to) cut off]

karai /kə'rai/, n a kind of earthpan in Uganda, measuring from 13 to 19 inches in diameter.
A temporary ban on the following items has been imposed until further notice. The reason is that most of them are produced locally and some appear to be of a luxury nature: Radios and radiograms. Gramophones and tape recorders. Passenger cars. Matches....cooking utensils, sufurias and karais.

Voice of Uganda, 2/23/73, p 1
[? < Luganda]

Karamojong /ˌkærə'moudʒəŋ/, n
Also, Karamojo. a people of northeastern Uganda; their Nilo-Saharan (Eastern Sudanic) language.

karamu /kə'ramu:/, n a feast celebrated on the sixth night of
KWANZA.
Nearly every Kwanzaa celebration
has a karamu, or feast, on New
Year's Eve. *Wall Street Journal*,
12/24/75, p 6
[< Swahili, generous feast, ban-
quet, festive entertainment, ?~
Arabic karama generosity, noble-
heartedness]

karani /kə'rani:/, n a clerk;
scribe.
The first Bakuba I met were my
new karani and pishi. Francois
Ndugulu, an earnest young evolue
who planned to become a lawyer
and perhaps even a judge of the
local native tribunal, read and
studied incessantly. J. Hallet,
Congo Kitabu, 1964, p 44
[< Swahili < Arabic or Persian]

kareba or **kareeba** /kə'reibə or
kə'ri:bə/, n a short-sleeved
shirt for men worn over matching
trousers (from Jamaica).
He [Michael Manley] was wearing
a blue Kareba suit, the open-
necked, loose-fitting African
garb he popularized in Jamaica
in line with third-world fashion.
New York Times (Mag. Sec.),
7/25/76, p 32
The guests sauntered from booth
to booth viewing paintings by
Jamaican artists, photography
by Jamaicans, asking questions
about land development in Jamaica, and about travel, from
the many persons who manned the
several travel booths. They saw
the latest kareebas and...canned
and bottled Jamaican manufactured
items. *Kingston Week-end Star*,

9/28/73, p 6
[< an African language]

karite or **kariti** /'kærəti:/, n
= SHEA TREE.
Mali. Trade. Chief imports are
foodstuffs, automobiles, petrol,
building material, sugar, salt,
beer. Chief exports are ground-
nuts, karite, gum, dried fish
and skins. *Statesman's Year-
Book*, 1979, p 831
[< a West African language ~
Wolof karite kariti]

karoo /kə'ru:/, n = KARROO.
He is a dachshund reared in
the Karoo and unaccustomed to
our wild city ways. *Cape Times*
(Mag. Sec.), 4/4/59, p 5

kaross /kə'ros/, n a blanket or
cloak-like garment of animal
hides, often with the hair left
on, worn as traditional clothing
by men and women in southern Africa.
There was his iron bed, with
its clean pillowcase and big
jackal-fur kaross. *New Yorker*,
5/23/59, p 36
Sale. Bargains include...One
only, Springbok Kaross - Was
$210 - Now $125,00. (Rhodesia)
Herald, 1/8/79, p 3
[< Afrikaans < Khoikhoin caros
skin blanket]

karroo /kə'ru:/, n Also, **karo**,
karoo. dry, barren, arid land of
extensive plateaus, with a clayey soil in South Africa.
But there were no trees, no
water, hardly a blade of living
grass or a leaf on the stunted
Karroo. *Harper's*, 2/56, p 61
[< Afrikaans < Khoikhoin karusa
dry ~ karo, garo desert]

kashata /kə'ʃatə/, n a dessert or
confectionery of East Africa made
of grated coconut, finely chopped
peanuts, sugar and cinnamon and
shaped into small balls.

[< Swahili < Arabic]

kasolite /'kæsə,lait/, n a yellow-ocher mineral, a hydrous uranium lead silicate. Formula: Pb(UO$_2$)Si-O$_4$H$_2$O
[< Kasolo locality in Katanga (Shaba) province (?< Mbundu kasolo a honeyguide (bird)) + English -ite]

katemfe /kə'temfei/, n the fruit of a tropical West African plant (Thaumatcoccus danielli) that yields a protein, thaumatin, used as a natural sweetener.
 The two sweet berries, "katem-fe" (Thaumatcoccus danielli) and "the serendipity berry" (Dioscoreophyllum cumminsii), whose active components "thau-matin" and "monellin" have been isolated and investigated in the US, are raising little interest even though they are about 3000 times as sweet as sugar and seemingly biologically inert. New Scientist, 11/14/74, p 467
[< a West African language]

katikiro /kati'ki:rou/, n the prime minister in the Baganda kingdom of KABAKA.
 The Katikiro (Prime Minister) of Buganda who disappeared at the same time as the Kabaka when troops stormed the royal palace on May 24, emerged from hiding in Nairobi today. The Times, 7/11/66, p 1
[< Luganda]

Kawaida /kə'wai:dʒ/, n a set of principles or doctrines of the US organization (an Afro-ameri-can black-consciousness move-ment).
 Maulana Ron Karenga is pri-marily known for...Kawaida ("a doctrine of social change and cultural revolution which contains the Nguzo Saba - the Seven Principles of Blackness").

First World, 5+6/77, p 50
[< Swahili, literally, regula-tive principle, fundamental cus-tom < Arabic]

kebele /kə'bele/, n a self-gov-erning neighborhood association in urban areas of Ethiopia, re-vived by the Dergue after the overthrow of Haile Selassie.
 Each kebele is headed by a fifteen-man policy committee, which names a chairman, who, in turn, names subcommittees responsible for such matters as public safety, youth, and women's affairs. There is sup-posed to be a kebele for every town of more than two thousand people. In the larger cities, every neighborhood of five hun-dred families or more is or-ganized into a kebele. New Yorker, 7/31/78, p 48
 Anyone putting up for the night - friends or relatives - come from a zone falling within the jurisdiction of another kebele must promptly report the fact to his own kebele officials. All absences from demonstra-tions, community work and "pol-itical training" classes are carefully noted down, and are likely to bring a severe repri-mand - at first. Manchester Guardian, 2/26/78, p 11
[< Amharic k'əbəle neighborhood organization for organizing funerals]

keftanya /kef'tanyə/, n a higher administrative unit of the KE-BELEs in Ethiopia.
 The higher kebele, or keftan-ya, oversees anywhere from six to twelve kebeles. The higher kebeles elect a coun-cil, which, in turn, elects a mayor and a deputy mayor to run the city. New Yorker, 7/31/78, p 48
[< Amharic kəffitənna higher]

kehla /'keihlə/, n Also, keshla.
a headring made of resin, worn
by married or elder Zulu men and
regarded as a sign of status; a
man wearing such a headring.
> If you rush into conversation
at once a Zulu is apt to think
you are a person of little dignity or consideration. I observed, however, that he was a
"Keshla" (ringed man), that is,
that he wore on his head the
black ring, made of a species
of gum polished with fat and
worked in with the hair, usually assumed by Zulus on at-
taining a certain age or dignity. H. Haggard, King Solomon's
Mines, 1885, p 37
[< Nguni khehla headring]

Kei apple /kai/, n a thorny, bushy
tree or shrub (Dovyalis caffra)
of South Africa; its yellow, sour
fruit, used in jams or jellies,
also called Dingaan's apricot.
[Kei   river in South Africa <
Khoikhoin kei water(s)]

keitloa /'kaitlouə/, n a black
rhinoceros of southern Africa
having two horns of nearly equal
length, considered to be a distinct species.
[< seTswana khetlwa]

kelele /kei'leilei/, n noise; dis-
turbance.
> "When I make a great kelele, I
am cheered to the echo." Time,
2/16/58, p 27
[< Swahili]

kelewele /kele'wele/, n a Ghanaian
dish of fried plantains with pepper, ginger, and other spices.
[< a West African language]

kenkey /'kenkei/, n a Ghanaian
dish of bread or balls of fermented cornmeal dough.
> Mr. D.D. Lartey, district ad-
ministrative officer for Winne-
ba, has distributed 70 bags of

corn to kenkey and porridge
sellers in the district. Ghanaian Times, 3/1/73, p 7
> For other Americans, however,
Ghana holds a case of culture
shock. Its relatively Spartan
hotels disappoint some tourists and the spicy native diet
upsets some U.S. stomachs. "The
only thing I can't hack is the
food," admits Mrs. Eleanor
Charles of Spring Valley, N.Y.,
who hopes to start a program to
bring U.S. ghetto youngsters to
Ghana. "I love the people here,
but fu-fu and kenkey just aren't
my style." Newsweek, 9/4/72, p 49
[< a West African language]

kente /'kentei/, n Also, kenty.
a brightly-colored textile material of Ghana, often consisting
of small, handwoven squares of
heavy silk with careful embroi-
dery; a cloak, robe, or garment
made of this cloth.
> In Accra this week, jubilant
Ghana citizens, standing on
the site where Europeans had
built trading forts back in
the seventeenth century, donned
their gaudiest hand-woven kente
togas and festooned their homes
with red, gold, and green bunt-
ing. Newsweek, 3/10/58, p 49
> We no longer giggle loutishly
or stare with gauche, parochial
disapproval at a sari or kenty
cloth. Listener, 1/2/64, p 25
[< Akan kente]

Kenya /'kenyə or 'kiːnyə/, n a
country in East Africa bordering
on Uganda, Sudan, Ethiopia, Somalia and Tanzania.
[< Kikuyu, ? < kenyá gourd or <
Kere-Nyaga Kikuyu name of Mt.
Kenya, said to mean "mountain of
whiteness" or "white stripes"]

Kenyapithecus /,kenyə'piθəkəs/,
n an extinct man-like ape of the
Miocene period whose remains and
artifacts were discovered near

Lake Victoria.
During the subsequent ten years, fossil hunters found many specimens of what looked to be an early hominid, but because people were usually unable to compare their specimens with the Yale material [Ramapithecus], there was a wondrous blossoming of names to describe what was basically the same type of animal: Graecopithecus, Rudapithecus, and Kenyapithecus all were coined but are now dropped in favor of Rama's ape. R. Leakey and R. Lewin, People of the Lake, 1978, p 29
[< Kenya + Greek pithekos ape]

kenyte or kenyite /'kenait or 'kenyait/, n a type of alkali-trachyte containing olivine, found in surface flows on Mt. Kenya.
[< Kenya + -ite mineral suffix]

kenzasmatch /kenzəs'matʃ/, n (formerly) the leader of the right wing in Ethiopia. See the quotation under DEJASMATCH.
[< Amharic gennazmac]

kevazingo /kevə'ziŋgou/, n a BUBINGA (Copaifera) tree of Africa; its hard wood, used in veneers.
Kevazingo was preferred not only for its texture and promising match for the color scheme of the auditorium, but also for its adaptability to the purpose of acoustical paneling. Saturday Review, 9/17/66, p 48
[< a West African language]

kgotla /'xoutlə/, n a tribal court or meeting place in Botswana and southern Africa.
In the center of the town we have the office and the square of kgotla, the Chief's court, where meetings are held and policy discussed and where cases are heard and judged by Tswana law and custom under the shelter of dark branches. Harper's, 9/66, p 91
[< seTswana or seSuto (le)kgotla meeting place ~ Swahili kuta meet (with)] See BARAZA, KUTA, LIBANDLA, PITSO.

khanga /'kæŋgə/, n = KANGA.
Department stores are selling authentic khangas from East Africa. These border-printed, boldly designed cotton fabrics, which are usually about 48 by 58 inches, are to be wrapped as skirts or halters over bathing suits, as head scarves or even tied as totes. New York Times (Mag. Sec.), 4/11/76, p 98
The main products are khanga, those wildly colorful sheets of cotton women wrap around themselves. They buy them in pairs, using the second sheet for head cover, or as a sling for hauling the baby around. You see them everywhere, in the markets, in the fields, those little heads peering out so sweetly. National Geographic, 4/75, p 486

khanzu or khansu /'kanzu:/, n = KANZU.
A barefoot waiter, clad in the voluminous white khanzu, and scarlet fez commonly worn by East African servants, dozed upright against a wall. New Yorker, 7/31/54, p 16

khaya /'kayə/, n a type of African tree (Meliaceae) closely resembling mahogany; its wood.
[< New Latin < Wolof khaye this tree]

Khoikhoin /koi'koin/, n Also, Khoikhoi. a people of southern Africa including the NAMA, Korana and others; their Khoisan language, including NAMA, !Kora, and others.
[< Khoikhoin khoi(i) man +

khoin men, said also to mean 'men of men']

Khoisan /'koi,san/, adj of or relating to a language family of
Africa comprising the KHOIKHOIN
(Hottentot), SAN (Bushman), and
certain languages of northern
Tanzania which are distinguished
by their use of click sounds as
phonemes.
[coined by I. Schapera < Khoi
name of the Khoikhoin for themselves + San name used by the
Khoikhoin for the San peoples]

khotla /'xoutlɔ/, n = KGOTLA (in
LeSotho).
[< seSutu; see KGOTLA]

khotso /'koutsou or 'xoutsou/,
n a greeting or salutation of
the Basotho; literally, peace
(a word appearing on Lesotho's
national emblem).
[< seSutu]

kia /kya/, n a hut, or a small
room or rooms, used as servant's
quarters in South Africa.
But the law is designed for the
convenience of Europeans; thus,
employers who want to house African labour on their farms,
mines, or in "kias" in the
grounds of their urban homes
are permitted to do so. London
Sunday Times, 7/23/76, p 9
[< Zulu khaya place of abode]

kiama /ki'amɔ/, n a council of
elders among the Kikuyu of Kenya; a political organization.
The Kiama administers justice
and the members are in a state
of brotherhood and absolute
purity among themselves so that
impartial judgment could be
ably effected. The Oba and his
Igbimo administer absolute justice under a honest condition
among the Yorubas. J. Sofola,
African Culture and African
Personality, 1973, p 9

On Jan. 16, 1958 the Kenya
government proscribed a secret
Kikuyu society known as Kiama
Kia Muingi (Party of the People) which is stated to have
similar aims to Mau Mau. New
International Yearbook, 1958,
p 248
[< Kikuyu ki- singular noun pfx
+ -ama organization ~ Swahili
(ch)-ama club, organization,
party]

kiboko /ki'boukou/, n a heavy,
strong whip made of hippopotamus
hide, formerly used for punishment.
The report includes accounts
of what went on during late
1975 and early 1976 in Naguru
Prison in Kampala, run by President Amin's Public Safety
Unit. Flogging with the kiboko,
once used by slavers, was standard. Manchester Guardian, 5/29/
77, p 3
Old Schweitzer treats them like
Wogs and cures them if he has
to kill them to do it. The
Come-to-Jesus ones, the reform-
ers and the changers, I think
that basically the African
hates them worse than he hates
the old hard-handed kiboko colonial who beats him when he's
bad and pats him on the head
when he's good. R. Ruark, Uhuru,
1962, p 91
I stretched him upon the
ground, dragged him to the
fire and, with the kiboko,
sobered him completely. The
Times, 10/31/70, p 20
[< Swahili, literally, hippopotamus < ki- singular noun pfx
+ -boko (root for) hippopotamus]

kibunzi /ki'bu:nzi:/, n an ear of
corn, used as a symbol of each
child in a family celebrating
KWANZA (Afro-American festival).
See the quotation under KWANZAA.
[< Swahili, literally, cob of
corn; also, the end of the year

< ki- singular noun pfx + bunzi
cob of corn]

kierie, kierri or kirri /'ki:ri:/,
n a hard, strong stick with a large
knob at one end, used as a weapon
in South Africa.
> He stooped low to pick up his
> cane, a kierie of dark African
> wood, which had fallen on the
> floor when he picked up his
> gloves. New York Times, 12/10/55,
> p 55
> I don't believe in enforcing
> discipline with a sjambok in
> one hand and a kierie in the
> other. Cape Times, 4/11/59, p 1

[< Afrikaans < Khoikhoin kirri
stick]

Kihindi /ki:'hindi:/, n a form of
Swahili spoken by Indians in Africa.
[< Swahili ki- singular noun
(language) pfx + hindi < mhindi a
person from India, ? < Hindi a
major language of India, or a
person speaking it]

kikoi or kikoy /ki'koi/, n a
white or striped cloth of East
Africa worn around the waist, with
a patterned design and an end
fringe, similar to a KANGA.
> What do other stylish women
> wear? Cheryl Tiegs wraps her-
> self up in one of her African
> "kikoys": a saronglike piece
> of handwoven, fringed cotton
> that comes in bright patterns.
> Tiegs either winds this under
> her arms like a strapless dress,
> or ties it around her waist.
> New York Times (Mag. Sec.),
> 4/13/80, p 94

[< Swahili ki- singular noun pfx
+ -koi (root for) this cloth, ?
< Kikuyu]

Kikongo /ki'koŋgou/, n the Bantu
language of the KONGO, also known
as KONGO or CONGO, spoken in Zaire, Angola and the Congo.
[< Kikongo ki- singular noun

(language) pfx + Kongo]

kikuyu /ki'ku:yu:/, n a hardy,
coarse grass (Pennisetum clandes-
tinum) with nutritional grains.
> The anti-kwashiorkor formula
> called Incaparina...contains
> 55 percent grain, 38 percent
> oilseed meal, 3 percent dried
> torula yeast, 3 percent kikuyu
> leaf meal and 1 percent calcium
> carbonate. Science News Letter,
> 1/4/64, p 11

[? < KIKUYU or ? < a southern
African Bantu language < ki-
singular noun pfx + -kuyu ~ Swahili mkuyu fig-mulberry tree]

Kikuyu, n a people of south-central
Kenya; their Bantu language, also
known as Gikuyu.
[< Swahili; the self-designation
for the Kikuyu language is Gikuyu]

Kimbanguism /kim'bæŋguizəm/, n
a messianic cult or sect with aspects of Christianity originating
in the Belgian Congo (now Zaire);
Eglise de Jesus-Christ sur la
Terre par le Prophete Simon Kimbangu.
> A French official remarked in
> 1885, "we have destroyed the
> past and nothing has taken its
> place." They also include the
> nativist African cults that
> multiplied during the early
> years of this century: Kitawala
> and Kimbangu, the "Antonians,"
> and the Epikilipikili prophetic
> sect in the Congo. New Yorker,
> 12/18/78, p 57

[< Simon Kimbangu Kongo tribesman (died 1950) who founded it
in 1921 + -ism]

--Kimbanguist, n

Kimbundu /kim'bundu/, n the Bantu
language of the Mbundu people of
Angola; MBUNDU.
[< Kimbundu ki- singular noun
(language) pfx + mbundu]

kinara /ki'narə/, n a candle

holder for seven candles, used in celebrating KWANZA (Afro-American festival). See the quotation under KWANZAA.
[< Swahili ki- singular noun pfx + nara ~ nuru light < Arabic]

Kingwana /kiŋ'gwanə/, n a form of Swahili spoken in eastern and southern Zaire.

kino /'ki:nou/, n a dark reddish brown or black juice used in medicine, tanning, and dyeing; the tree yielding it.
[< New Latin kino < a West African language ~ Mandingo keno, kano]

Kinyarwanda /,kinyar'wandə/, n a Bantu language of Rwanda spoken by the Hutu and Tutsi.
[< Kinyarwanda ki- singular noun (language) pfx + -nya- associative morpheme + RWANDA]

kipande /ki'pandei/, n an identification card carried by black Kenyans in colonial times.
The Kipande system was officially introduced in Kenya in 1921. Every male African above sixteen years of age had to be registered, finger-printed, and issued with a registration certificate - Kipande. Kipande was different from the passport, the birth certificate, the identity cards in Britain, or social security numbers in the United States of America. In Kenya a policeman could stop an African on the road or in the street and demand that he produce his Kipande - regardless of whether the African concerned was as wise as Socrates, as holy as St. Francis, or as piratical as Sir Francis Drake. R. Gatheru, Child of Two Worlds, 1965, p 90
[< Swahili < ki- singular noun pfx + -pande (root for) card, small bit of anything]

kirri /'ki:ri:/, n = KIERIE.
Effective in a hand-to-hand struggle is the kirri, a club of ironwood or horn with a knob the size of a man's fist on the end. National Geographic, 6/35, p 745

Kirundi /ki'rundi:/, n a Bantu language of the Rundi spoken in Burundi.
[< Kirundi ki- singular noun (language) pfx + RUNDI]

kisambila /,kisam'bi:l /, n = BAZIMO.
[< a Bantu language]

Kisetla /ki'set(ə)lə/, n a pidgin language, a form of Swahili, formerly used between Europeans and Africans, with a simplified grammatical structure.
[< Swahili ki- singular noun pfx + setla < English settler]

Kissi /'kisi:/, n a people of Guinea, Sierra Leone and Liberia; their Niger-Congo (West Atlantic) language.

Kiswahili /,kiswa'hi:li:/, n = SWAHILI.
[<. Swahili ki- singular noun (language) pfx + SWAHILI]

Kitawala /,kita'walə/, n the name of the Watchtower religious movement in central Africa, especially in Zaire. See the quotation under KIMBANGUISM.
[< a central African Bantu language, ? < Chiluba or Kikongo, said to mean tower; cf. Swahili kitawa devout life (in a religious way)]

kitchen kaffir, n a pidgin language spoken in southern Africa, based on Xhosa, Zulu, Afrikaans and English.
His greatest regret, after thirty years in Africa, was that he had not taken the

advice given him when he came, not to try to learn the languages, since there are so many of them, but to use the pidgin form called Kitchen Kaffir. Harper's, 5/53, p 47

kitenge /ki'teŋgei/, n a brightly-colored, patterned cloth worn as a wraparound skirt or shawl, and often printed with political slogans on the borders.
 Women and girls were so committed to minis that when those dresses were banned they immediately saw an alternative in the kitenge (popularly known as lesu) and began tying them around their legs. Voice of Uganda, 3/14/73, p 6
 [< Swahili ki- singular noun pfx + -tenge < (ki)tengele stripe, band of color]

kithitu /ki'θi:tu/, n a death-binding oath (in East Africa).
 Mr. Paul Ngei...said that he was popular enough in Kangundo and did not need any oaths or to intimidate anyone in order to win elections....Ngei said that at the time the kithitu oath was administered in 1964, he was not qualified by age to take part in any oathing. Weekly Review (Nairobi), 3/6/81, p 17
 [? < Kikuyu]

Kiunguja /kiuŋ'gu:dʒə/, n a form of Swahili spoken in Zanzibar and considered the standard form of the language.
 [< Swahili ki- singular noun (language) pfx + Unguja Zanzibar]

kiva /'ki:va/, n a trough between dunes in the Kalahari desert.
 [? < Nama]

kob /kob/, n a bright reddish-brown antelope (Adenota) with a white ring around the eye.
 As large numbers of grass-eaters including buffalo, kob,

water buck and elephants share the grazing with them, the Park authorities face considerable erosion problems - not to mention hippo starvation. New Scientist, 6/14/62, p 588
 [< a West African language ~ Fulani koba, Wolof koba roan antelope]

kobo /'koubou/, n a unit of money in Nigeria; 1/100th of a NAIRA.
 The new currency being introduced by the Central Bank of Nigeria consists of naira and kobo. Kobo are coins and naira are notes. The origin of the names has not been fully explained, but naira is said to have been derived from the word Nigeria; and kobo was the popular name for the old penny pieces. The Times, 10/9/72, p VIII
 [< a Nigerian language < English copper penny]

koboko /kou'boukou/, n a heavy, strong whip used in Nigeria.
 The road traffic edict under which cars with odd and even number registration plates are allowed on the roads on alternate days has also helped to alleviate it. For those who can afford a second car (and they are not few) the edict enforced by civil and military police armed with kobokos has not proved too onerous. The Times, 12/1/77, p 8
 A large number of the springy whips known in Nigeria as Koboko have been ordered and soldiers will be assigned to administer beatings, some reports said. Col. P.C. Tarfa, chairman of the traffic committee, warned ...that violators would be dealt with severely for using unroadworthy vehicles or for parking on highways. New York Times, 9/26/77, p 2
 [? < Yoruba]

koko /'koukou/, n coco, an araceous plant such as the taro with starchy, edible roots grown widely in West Africa.
[< a West African language ∼ Akan kóokó koko]

kokoon or kokong /kə'ku:n or kə'kaŋ/, n a large antelope (Taurina); the bridled gnu.
[< seTswana kgokon or khokong]

kombe /kam'bei or kom'bei/, n a juice from the seeds of a climbing plant (Strophanthus kombe) that yields strophanthin, used to poison the tips of arrows.
[< Mang'anja]

'komfo /'kamfou/, n a person who is possessed by the spirit of an African diviner (in Surinam).
[< Akan ɔkɔmfó priest]

kondo /'kondou/, n a gang of armed thugs in Uganda and East Africa; thuggery.
We chased the setting sun toward Kampala with growing fear that darkness would catch us still out in the countryside, prey to the human wolves called kondos - the thieves who come at night. National Geographic, 7/80, p 74
"I have had friends killed for a radio," said Hermann Marcksheffell, a West German engineer, and he went on to tell a story about a friend of his, a Polish chemistry professor: "Kondos shot through the glass from his veranda and hit him in both legs. Then he was shot twice in the arm and then through the stomach. His wife had a butcher knife and she was screaming for them to take anything but do not kill her husband." New York Times (Mag. Sec.) 11/16/80, p 79
In Uganda, President Idi ("Big Daddy") Amin has ordered roadblocks of troops and police to check on tax receipts and de-

creed that evaders - those lacking receipts - will be treated as kondos, or armed robbers, and shot on sight. Time, 4/24/72, p 37
[< Swahili, literally, war, strife, difficulty]

--kondoism, n: Tourist arrivals will be maintained in spite of the discouraging reports of military skirmishes on the Tanzanian border in the south and Sudanese border in the north, and in spite of kondoism (armed robbery) in the towns and countryside. The Times, 1/25/72, p VII
"Kondoism has become a cult rather like thugee in India used to be, there is some mysticism attached to this violence," said one diplomat who had talked to the families of several victims killed with deliberation. Manchester Guardian, 9/9/79, p 6

Kongo /'koŋgou/, n a people of Zaire, Congo and Angola; their Bantu language, also known as KIKONGO.
[< Kikongo < the name of a kingdom of the 1400's to the 1700's in present-day Zaire, Angola and Congo whose king was called Mani-Kongo; said to be < kongo mountain; cf. Kongolo traditional Luba ancestor]

kongoni /kaŋ'gouni:/, n Coke's hartebeest (Alcelaphus buselaphus cokii), a long-faced, humped antelope with a whitish rump of southern Kenya and Tanzania.
Giraffes were running beneath us, as well as herds of zebras, topis, kongonis, Grant's gazelles, oribis, buffaloes and ostriches - all of them catching the sunlight in different ways. New Yorker, 9/6/58, p 74
[< Swahili]

konyagi /kou'nyagi:/, n an alcoholic drink somewhat like gin,

distilled from cashew nuts in East
Africa.
  It was odd to recognize the
  familiar taste of the finished
  product [cashews] so far from
  any cocktail party. (Tanzanians
  also distill from cashews a delicious "brandy," if one is to
  respect the ambitious deriva-
  tion of its Swahili name, konyagi.) Atlantic, 5/73, p 16
[< Swahili < English cognac]

konze /'konzei/, n Lichtenstein's
hartebeest (Alcelaphus lichten-
steinii), a rufous-tawny antelope
with flattened horns curved in
and black markings on the legs.
[< Makonde nkonzhe]

koolokamba or kulukamba /ˌku:-
lǝ'kambǝ/, n a chimpanzee (Pan
koolokamba or troglodytes) of
West Africa with a dark face.
[< a West African language said
to be < a language on the Gabon
River]

kora /'korǝ/, n a harp of West Africa with a calabash resonator
and twenty-one strings.
  Only in those areas that were
  closely in contact with the
  Ghana empire does one find the
  casted bards and the kora. C.
  Bird in R. Dorson (ed.), African Folklore, 1972, p 292
[< a West African language ∽
Akan kora calabash vessel made
by scooping out one half]

Kordofanian /ˌkordǝ'feini:ǝn/,
adj of or relating to a group of
languages spoken in the Nuba hills
of the Sudan, thought to consti-
tute a coordinate branch with the
Niger-Congo languages within a
still larger language family.
[< Nubian kurta men]

kori or kori bustard /'kori:/,
n a large, buff, black, and grayish bird (Ardeotis kori) with
three-toed feet and a long neck,
found from Ethiopia to East and
South Africa.
  Bird life – you will see the
  brilliant blue wingspan of the
  lilac-breasted roller; the kori
  bustard (heaviest flying bird
  in the world); jewel-coloured
  kingfishers and bee-eaters; the
  distinctive secretary bird. In
  the Clouds (South African Air-
  ways), 11/79, p 58
  When two female kori bustards
  – South African birds related
  to the crane – were shipped
  recently from Amsterdam to the
  Los Angeles zoo the forwarders
  did not even bother to insure
  them, even though the pair were
  worth about Ƚ400. The Times,
  12/3/70, p VI
[said to be < seTswana]

korin /'korin/, n a small gazelle
(Gazella rufifrons) found in West
Africa from Senegal to the Sudan.
[? < a West African language]

korrigum /'kori,gǝm/, n an ante-
lope (Damaliscus korrigum) of
West Africa; topi.
[< Kanuri kargum]

kosin /'kous n/, n a yellowish-
brown powder derived from the
flowers of the KOSO and used as
an anthelmintic.
[< KOSO + -in chemical suffix]

koso or kosso /'kousou/, n a
tree (Hagenia abyssinica) of
Ethiopia whose dried flowers are
used to make a medicine against
tapeworm.
[< Oromo kosso]

Kpelle /kǝ'pelei/, n a people of
Liberia and Guinea; their Niger-
Congo (Mande) language.

kra /kra/, n a spiritual double
that, according to the Ashanti,
visits the tomb after death;
the human soul (among people in
the Guianas); divine power.
  To employ West African terms,
  a goddess or god is an abstrac-

91

tion unless she or he has a
sunsum as well as a kra. Atlantic, 6/61, p 43
[< Akan kra soul; thought to
be ~Egyptian ka]

kremt /kremt/, n the long rainy
season in Ethiopia from June to
September.
[? < Amharic]

Krontihene or krontehene
/,kronti'heinei/, n a sub-chief
in Ghana.
Nana Simpeh Wiredu, Krontihene
of Abone, Nana Kwaku Amanfo...
were introduced to the council
members. Ghanaian Times, 3/1/73,
p 7
Whenever Nana, as chief, is re-
quired to take part in a tribal
religious ceremony, he has his
krontehene, or headman, act in
his place. New Yorker, 1/8/55,
p 23
[< Akan kronti of undetermined
meaning + -hene chief]

Kru /kru:/, n Also, Krou. a people
of Liberia and the Ivory Coast;
their Niger-Congo (Kwa) language.

Kwa /kwa/, n a group of Niger-
Congo languages including Akan,
Ewe, Yoruba and Ibo.

Kuanzisha /,kuan'zi:ʃə/, n a holiday celebrated by members or followers of the Afro-American US
organization, commemorating its
founding on Sept. 7 (1965).
Kwanzaa isn't the only holiday
he has inaugurated....Three
others are: May 19, Kuzaliwa
(birth), marking the birthday
of Malcolm X; August 11, Uhuru
(Liberation) Day, commemorating
the Watts "uprising" in Los
Angeles in 1965; and September
7, Kuanzisha (founding), to
note Mr. Karenga's 1965 founding of the US Organization.
Wall Street Journal, 12/24/75,
p 6
[< Swahili, literally, insti-

tuting, starting < ku- infinitive
pfx + -anz (root for) begin (~
KWANZA) + -isha causative suffix]

kudu /'ku:du:/, n Also, koedoe or
koodoo. a large, majestic grey
or fawn antelope (Tragelaphus
strepsiceros or strepsiceros im-
berbis) with wide-spreading,
curling horns and narrow, white
stripes.
[< Afrikaans koedoe < Xhosa
iqudu or iquda < Nama kudu-b or
kudu-s]

kugoma /ku'goumə/, n a planned
campaign of resistance to British
rule in Tanzania prior to independence, consisting of strikes,
civil disobedience, and other
actions.
This wide threat to peace and
good government was known in
Swahili as kugoma; and between
the middle of 1958 and the
second quarter of 1959 the Tanganyika air was crammed with
ominous forecasts of what would
happen when the promise of kugoma became reality. The Times,
4/9/65, p 15
[< Swahili, literally, showing
fight, being firm in demanding
one's rights < ku- infinitive
pfx + goma refuse]

kujitegemea /ku:,dʒi:tegə'meiə/,
n self-reliance, a slogan and
policy of Tanzania.
For Nyerere, the ujamaa idea
goes hand in hand with kujitegemea (self-reliance) often
translated as self-sufficiency.
Manchester Guardian, 11/9/80,
p 14
[< Swahili, literally, to lean
or rely on oneself < ku- infinitive pfx + -ji- reflexive pro-
noun pfx + -tegemea (root for)
lean or rely on]

kujur /'ku:dʒur/, n a witch doctor or diviner among the Nuba.
"You've got to cure my hurt
back. Our kujurs laid hot irons

against my neck, but it did no
good. When you fix me, I will
bring you a cow in payment." I
told the man that he needed hospital treatment. National Geographic, 11/66, p 688
The most important influence
over the tribe is held by the
kujur, or holy man. His main
job is rain making. The position carries with it much responsibility, and lack of success can result in the direst
punishment. In time of drought
the kujur used to be led out of
the village to a newly dug grave.
With sincere apology he was
asked to step into it. Having
done so, he was asked if he was
comfortable. National Geographic, 2/51, p 272
[< Nuba]

kukama, kokama, or kookaam
/ku:'kamə/, n an antelope of
southern Africa.
[< seTswana]

Kuke /k(y)u:k/, n = KYUKE.
One helpful farmer lined up his
Kukes and told them to speak to
me freely. The farmer is a good
bwana, they said, but that isn't
the point. The land was always
ours; now we are hired laborers.
Time, 11/10/52, p 40

kuku /'ku:ku:/, n a fowl (in South
Africa); chicken (in East Africa).
[< Nguni (n)kuku, Swahili kuku]

kukumakranka /,ku:ku:m 'krank /,
n a small, perennial plant (Geth-
ryllis) of Southern Africa; the
Cape flower.
[< Khoikhoin]

kumi /'ku:mi:/, n a Somali ten-cent
coin.
[< Somali ∿ Swahili kumi ten]

!Kung or Kung /!kuŋ/, n a people
of Angola whose self-designation
is Dzu/twasi or Zhu/twasi; their

Khoisan language
[< !Kung, literally, they]

kungena /kuŋ'geinə/, v.t. to marry
a deceased brother's wife (an
obligation among the Swazi).
When a man ngena's [sic] his
brother's widow and cohabits
with her, children are born
not to him but to the deceased
man. Times of Swaziland, 7/13/
73, p 9
[< siSwati, literally, to enter
< ku- infinitive pfx + -ngena
enter ∿ Swahili -ingia enter]

kungu /'kuŋgu:/, n a small gnat
(Chaoborus edulis) of East Africa, used in making a kind of cake
kungu cake.
Replying to a suggestion that
the native name of the flies,
kungu, might account for the
origin of the regional name
Congo, Mr McCrae said the word
merely meant "mist" in Swahili.
New Scientist, 7/7/66, p 8
He is a reflective observer,
and the sights to which he calls
our attention - the mile-high
mushroom swarms of kungu flies
on Lake Nyasa. New Yorker, 4/4/
64, p 192
[< Chinyanja (n)kungu this gnat]

kuomboka /,kuom'boukə/, n a festival in Zambia originally celebrating the annual rise of the
Zambezi river, now a national
holiday in late February.
In a spectacular day of African
pageantry, President Kenneth
Kaunda donned his black and purple toga, and Sir Mwanawina Le-
wanika, the Litunga of Barotseland, his 58-year-old British
admiral's uniform to set the
seal on the former feudal kingdom's integration into Zambia.
This was at Barotseland's annual
kuomboka ceremony, which this
year had a special political
significance for Zambia. The
Times, 4/2/65, p 11

[< Lozi, literally, to get out
of the water]

kusimanse /kusi'manse/, n a small,
dark-brown mongoose-like animal
(Crossarchus obscurus) of West
Africa.
[< a West African (Liberian)
language]

kuta /'ku:tə/, n = KGOTLA.
[< a southern Bantu language ~
Swahili (m)kuta(no) meeting ~
-kuta meet]

Kuzaliwa /kuza'li:wə/, n a holiday
celebrated by members or followers
of the Afro-American US organization, commemorating the birth of
Malcolm X on May 19.
   US, a black nationalist group,
   was promoting the holiday as
   the first annual observance of
   kuzaliwa. New York Times, 5/21/
   67, p 46
   We had the children stay away
   from school this year on Kuzaliwa, and in one school here
   almost 100 percent of the children didn't go that day, and
   the principal had to dismiss
   classes. Atlantic, 3/68, p 71
[< Swahili, literally, to be
born < ku- infinitive pfx + -za-
liwa be born < -zaa bear offspring]

kwacha[1] /'kwat∫ə/, n a unit of currency in Malawi, introduced in
1971.
   The United Kingdom granted Malawi 2.3 million kwachas (£1
   million) toward construction
   of an army barracks for the 2nd
   Battalion Malawi Rifles to be
   established at Lilongwe, site
   of the new capital city. Britannica Book of the Year, 1973,
   p 442
[< Chichewa, literally, it dawns
< kw- locative pfx + -acha dawn
~ Chinyanja -acha dawn, Swahili
(ku)cha to dawn]

kwacha[2], n a unit of currency in
Zambia, equal to 100 NGWEE; a

political slogan or rallying cry
for independence.
   Although during this same period real per capita income
   rose by 66 per cent to about
   197 kwacha, or US $281, one of
   the highest in Africa, its uneven distribution aggravated
   many of the country's diffi-
   culties. Manchester Guardian,
   5/1/71, p 7
   The Zambian Government gives
   thousands of kwacha a year to
   the African liberation movement, through a fund set up by
   the Organization of African
   Unity (OAU). Cape Times (Mag.
   Sec.), 3/24/73, p 1
   Four years and two months from
   the day it finally won kwacha
   - freedom - Zambia last week
   held its first parliamentary
   election as a sovereign state.
   Time, 12/27/68, p 28
[< Chinyanja, literally, it
dawns, to dawn, dawning < kw-
infinitive pfx + -acha dawn ~
Chichewa -acha dawn, Swahili
(ku)cha to dawn]

Kwandebele /,kwaəndə'belei/, n
a homeland (region in South Africa set aside by the government
for blacks) for the Ndebele, located in the Transvaal.
   Mr Botha will hold separate
   meetings with each homeland
   leader. The leaders whom he
   will meet are...Mr Simon Sko-
   sana, leader of the Kwandebele;
   and Mr E. J. Mabuza, the Swazi
   homeland leader. Star (Johannesburg), 1/26/80, p 3
[< Nguni kwa- (< ku- locative
pfx "in" or "at" + -a connective
morpheme) + NDEBELE]

kwanga /'kwangə/, n manioc bread
in Zaire.
   ...mountains of mango, of pine-
   apple, of kwanga. Manchester
   Guardian, 8/7/71, p 17
[< Lingala]

Kwanza /'kwanzə/, n a holiday

celebrated by members or followers of the Afro-American US organization, a festival celebrated
on the six days preceding New
Year's Day.
   Although Africans themselves
don't celebrate Kwanza, it has
been growing in popularity in
black communities here since
the early 60s, when it was developed by Los Angeles black
leader Maulana Ron Karenga,
founder of the organization US.
New York Post, 12/31/73, p 7
Seven pupils were then chosen
to light candles that had been
placed on the mkeka. The Kwanza
lasts seven days, and each day
a candle is lighted in the observance. It officially started
yesterday. New York Times, 12/
24/71, p 28
[< Swahili, literally, beginning
< ku- infinitive pfx + -anza be-
gin]

kwanza, n a unit of currency in
   Angola, equal to 100 LWEI.
   On January 8 the Finance Min-
istry announced the introduction of a new currency, the
kwanza. Collier's Encyclopedia
Yearbook, 1977, p 122
[< Kwanza large river in Angola,
but ? ⌣ Swahili kwanza beginning]

Kwanzaa /'kwanzə/, n = KWANZA.
   Symbols of Kwanzaa are supple-
menting or replacing traditional holly and evergreen decora-
tions in more and more inner
city homes and meeting places.
...A straw mat (mkeka) in Swahili represents tradition. An
ear of corn (kibunzi) represents each child in a family,
and through them symbolizes
immortality of the race. A
candle holder (kinara) represents the African forebears
of U.S. blacks. The kinara
holds seven candles, one for
each day and principle of
Kwanzaa....As for how kwanza
became Kwanzaa, Mr. Karenga

says he deliberately changed
the spelling, and for good
reason. At the very first observance, he explains, seven
children wanted to present a
short pageant, and each wanted
to represent one day, one principle and one letter of the
holiday. "We showed where our
priorities are," Mr. Karenga
says, "by placing people before
formality and adding one letter." Wall Street Journal,
12/24/75, p 1
"I created Kwanzaa," laughed
M. Ron Karenga like a teen-
ager who's just divulged a
deeply held, precious secret.
"People think it's African.
But it's not. I wanted to give
black people a holiday of their
own. So I came up with Kwanzaa.
I said it was African because
you know black people in this
country wouldn't celebrate it
if they knew it was American.
Also, I put it around Christmas
because I knew that's when a
lot of bloods (blacks) would
be partying!" Washington Post,
5/9/78, p B1
[coined by Maulana Ron Karenga,
founder of the US organization,
to "distinguish the Afro-American
nature of the celebration from a
purely African one," i.e., from
KWANZA]

kwashiokor, n the well-known
   disease caused by protein deficiency.
   "An infant here is weaned abruptly. One day -- generally
when the mother realizes that
she is again pregnant-- he must
join the rest of the family at
the matoke bowl. Well, matoke
is all carbohydrate and the
child falls ill with a disease
called kwashiokor. Without
treatment he may die. My job is
to show mothers simple sources
of protein-- peanuts, beans, or
even fried termites-- they can
include in their menus." Nat-

ional Geographic, 11/71, p 715
[said to be < a West African language, ? < Akan, literally, red
boy; cf. kɔɔ red, ɛkorɔ red skin
rash; ? < Akan Kwassi name for a
boy born on Sunday (cf. QUASSIA)
+ kɔɔ or ɛkorɔ]

KwaZulu /kwa'zu:lu:/, n a homeland
(region in South Africa set aside
by the government for blacks) for
the Zulu, located in eastern Natal and Zululand.
Under the Government's Bantustan programme, a large part
of the province is scheduled
as the KwaZulu "homeland", the
traditional home of the nation's
five million Zulus. Under the
present distribution of land
cities such as Durban and Pie-
termaritzburg and the port of
Richard's Bay are virtually
white enclaves surrounded by
large tracts of Zululand. The
Times, 5/27/77, p 9
His [Kaiser Matanzima] tactics
in choosing to take Transkei
into a kind of independence
were vigorously criticized by
other prominent homeland leaders such as the KwaZulu spokesman, Chief Gatswa Buthelezi,
and by radical nationalists
and white liberals. Britannica
Book of the Year, 1977, p 44
[< Zulu kwa- (ku- locative pfx
"in" or "at," + -a "connective"
morpheme) + ZULU]

kwedini or **kwedin** /kwei'din(i:)/,
n a young, uncircumcised Xhosa
boy; a black boy in South Africa.
[< Xhosa (in)kwenkwendini voca-
tive form of (in)kwenkwe boy;
ndini ∿Swahili -ni 2nd person
plural in commands]

kwela /'kweilə/, n a popular,
jazz-like music and dancing of
southern Africa, with the penny
whistle as the main instrument.
The kwela music, the rhythm
of Africa, throbbed out loudly

from every Bantu shop I
passed. Cape Times (Mag. Sec.),
3/24/73, p 4
This time the Princess will
have to distinguish tactfully
between the Emirs and the Sar-
daunas, the Onis and the Sena-
tors, the Hausas and the Yorubas, and to conserve enough
energy so that when night falls
she can dance the kwela, mambo,
or high-life with any or all
of them. Manchester Guardian,
4/7/60, p 6
[< Nguni khwela climb on, mount
∿Swahili -kwea go up, mount]

kwisha /'kwi:ʃə/, adj finished;
over; no more, ended (in East
Africa).
In Kampala, where food is
kwisha, water is kwisha and
gasoline is kwisha, Kampala
is all but kwisha....The other
morning, at the Apolo Hotel,
the grandest hotel in the region when it was opened in
1965, coffee was kwisha. That
night, beer was kwisha. All day,
water was kwisha. New York
Times, 4/20/80, p not recorded
[< Swahili (an irregular verb)
to be finished, come to an end
< kw- infinitive pfx + -isha
(root for) be finished]

kwolla /'kwolə/, n Also, kolla.
the hot, lowland areas in Ethiopia.
Cotton is grown in the south-
west and on irrigated land below Asmara in the former Italian colony of Eritrea and in
the Awash valley below the
Koka Dam, 100 km (60 miles)
from Addis Ababa. Cotton could
be cultivated on the kwolla,
but the people are reluctant
to settle in unhealthy areas.
R. & E. Steel, Africa, 1974,
p 131
[< Amharic qwəlla or qolla]

Kyabazinga /,kyabə'zingə/, n the
title of the king of the Basoga

(a Bantu people) of eastern Uganda.
[< Lusoga (the language of the Basoga)]

--Kyabazingaship, n: The petty kingdoms amalgamated into the district of Busoga have continued their competition, so the dispute over the Kyabazingaship (kingship) demonstrated. N. Kasfir in V. Olorunsola Politics of Cultural Sub-Nationalism in Africa, 1972, p 68

kyeame /kye'ama or tʃe'ame/, n a spokesman or interlocutor for the chief of the Fante.
    Tradition requires that a chief should never address the public directly, nor be spoken to except through the kyeama. The latter should be well-versed in customary law, and have a broad knowledge of proverbs to illustrate and emphasize his statements. J. Christensen in E. Skinner, Peoples and Cultures of Africa, 1973, p 512
[< Akan (ɔ)kyeámé speaker, reporter]

kyekyema /kyei'kyeima or tʃei'tʃeima/, n a divorce or dismissal of a wife by a man (in Ghana).
    The trouble would start brewing when you show the least signs of financial interest in the man's pocket. Very soon you would be on your way out. The more you persisted to stay the more speedily your "kyekyema" would be. Ghanaian Times, 4/23/73, p 4
[< Akan nkyekyem act of dividing]

Kyuke /kyu:k/, n a derogatory term for a Kikuyu.
    The men, he noticed, had changed even more than the women and seemed to be changing that much more each year. You had to go really deep into the bush up past the Kinangop, maybe, to see the old-time Kyukes, away up in the hills where the hut consolidation schemes hadn't taken full effect and the Kikuyu still lived in little isolated patches of mud-and-wattle beehives instead of in bloody great villages. R. Ruark, Uhuru, 1962, p 63
    But others present understood that Independence had to come. As one such man remarked to me after a game warden had decried the "bloody Kyukes," "the end of the game," and all the rest, "Those old boys oughtn't to take on like that - after all, they had the best of it." P. Matthiessen, The Tree Where Man Was Born, 1972, p 39

L

L, abbreviation of LILANGENI.
University College of Swazi-
land. Applications are invited
for the post of Lecturer in the
Department of Mathematics...
Salary Scale: E5940-7860 pa
(L1 sterling = L1.82). The
British Government may supple-
ment salary. New Scientist,
7/12/79, p 157

laibon /'leibən or 'laibən/, n
chief priest or medicine man
among the Maasai.
The Maasai are thought to have
reached Nakuru and the Ngong
Hills near Nairobi in the seventeenth century, and their
heaven-born first laibon or
medicine man was found as a
youth in the Ngong at a time
thought to have been about
1640. P. Matthiessen, Tree
Where Man Was Born, 1972, p 113
[< Maasai]

lapa /'lapə/, n a courtyard formed
by a number of houses of the
Ndebele in southern Africa.
These houses stand in family
clusters inside the low walls
of a courtyard, a lapa as we
say. Harper's, 9/66, p 88
[< Ndebele, literally, court-
yard]

lappa /'lapə/, n Also, lapa. a
brightly colored or patterned
cloth from West Africa, worn as
a shawl or skirt, often measuring 2 yds. x 2 yds. or 2 yds. x
1 yd.; a measure of this cloth.
The maternal image is enhanced
by her ample figure and by the
matching lappa (skirts) and
turbans that she prefers to
the businesslike suits worn
by most other women delegates
at the U.N. Time, 9/26/69, p 27
Mr. ADO, Mr. Oduta say him no
fit tell because this be first
baby. And him wife no take
clothes come out for him face.
But him catch her one day when
she put pillow for front of
belly and wrap lappa around.
A. Ulasi, Many Thing You No
Understand, 1970, p 100
The women sew the plain cotton
or satin into varying folded
patterns, dip it into huge
vats of dye, and afterward
beat the cloth in unison with
a huge bludgeon till the cloth
glows with a soft shine. A
2-yard piece (or 2-1/2 yards
if the cloth is narrow width)
or lappa (the equivalent of
the two-meter pagne in Franco-
phone Africa) is enough for a
dress up to size 14, and sells
for about $2.50 (cotton) to
$5.00 (satin). S. Blumenthal,
Bright Continent, 1974, p 238
[< Hausa]

98

Lassa fever /'læsə/, n a highly
contagious viral disease causing
a high fever, internal hemorrhage
and heart infection.
> A brownish-gray mouse common
> in African forests, fields and
> villages is the chief animal
> reservoir of Lassa fever virus,
> the cause of one of the most
> lethal human diseases known.
> Science News, 3/3/79, p 136
[< Lassa village in eastern Nigeria where it was discovered]

Lebowa /lə'bouwə/, n a homeland
(region in South Africa set aside
by the government for blacks) for
the Ndebele and Pedi, located in
the northern Transvaal.

lechwe /'letʃwe/, n a small
African antelope (Kobus lechwe)
related to the waterbuck, inhab-
iting marshy areas.
> Startled lechwes churn marsh
> waters in Northern Rhodesia.
> Before World War II some 250-
> 000 red lechwes roamed the
> flood plain of the Kafue River;
> today fewer than 30,000 remain.
> National Geographic, 9/60,p 398
[< a (southern) Bantu language∼
seSutu letsa lechwe]

Legba /'legbə/, n a deity, or the
devil, in the voodoo cult, known
as a trickster.
> The voodoo loa of remote Afri-
> can memory-- Maitresse Erzulie,
> Papa Legba and the snake-god
> Damballa-- are still highly
> serviceable in such workaday
> matters as appeasing the dead
> and assuring sucessful births.
> Time, 2/22/54, p 41
[?< Ewe]

lela /'leilə/,n = BAO (in central
Africa).
> Several pairs of men squatted
> on either side of carved wood-
> en boards and nimbly dropped
> bean-sized pebbles into a ser-
> ies of saucer-shaped hollows.
> They were playing lela, the

most popular game in Black
Africa, which, according to
Kuba tradition, had been invented over three hundred
years ago by their greatest
king, Shamba Bolongongo. J.
Hallet, Congo Kitabu, 1964,
p 46
[< a Bantu language]

Lesana Geez /lə'sanə gi:'ez/, n
= GEEZ.
[< Amharic lesanə ge'iz said
to mean tongue (or language) of
the free]

Lesana Negus /... nei'gus/, n =
AMHARIC.
[< Amharic lesanə negus, literally, tongue (or language)
of the king]

Lesotho /lə'soutou/, n a country
in southern Africa entirely surrounded by South Africa; formerly Basutoland.
[< seSutu le- singular noun
pfx + SOTHO]

lesu /'leisu:/, n Also, leso. a
handkerchief of printed calico,
worn as a scarf, or combined
with others to form a KANGA.
See the quotation under KITENGE.
[< Swahili leso < Portuguese
lenco handkerchief or English
lace]

letsema or letsima /let'seimə/,
n a system of obligatory labor
among the Sotho in which men
work in the chief's fields or
gardens.
[< seSotho le- singular noun
pfx + -tsema (root for) this
system]

Libandla or Libandhla /li'band-
lə/, n a tribal court or meeting
place in Swaziland; traditional
council to the king.
> It [Swaziland] has a parlia-
> mentary system of government
> but...the Libandla, made up
> of chiefs and elders, still

plays a major role in the nation's affairs. There is also a second royal council, the Liqoqo, consisting of a few members of the Royal Family and chosen advisers which must also approve policy. The Times, 9/11/72, p V
The Libandla, the King's Council, is open to all Swazi men or their traditional representatives; and the King gives effect to the consensus the Libandla establishes. The system has, indeed, been described as a classic example of rule by consultation and consent, said the South African Broadcasting Service. Times of Swaziland, 4/20/73, p 1
[< siSwati, literally, council < li- singular noun pfx + -band-la ~ Swahili -bandika be attached to a person]

Lifa /'li:fə/, n a community fund among the Swazi, used to raise money to buy back land from Europeans, etc.
Since 1946 the Swazi, in an unprecedented national effort, steadily paid levies to the Lifa, a tribal fund...which finances measures to reduce over-stocking. M. Benson in C. Legum (ed.), Africa, A Handbook to the Continent, 1966, p 319
[< siSwati~Swahili lipa pay]

Lifaquane /,lifə'kanei/, n = DIFAQANE.
[< seSutu]

likembe /li'kembei/, n a thumb piano among the Luba of Zaire.
The Club Zaire, a favorite of those of the Luba tribe, featured a band from the Kasai. They were country boys, lean and tout, in white shirts and ties that stood out amid a sea of city sport shirts. They played flutes, whistles, and the likembe - an instrument

consisting of a sound box and eight or ten metal spokes plucked by the thumbs - while their leader, Kabala, performed the hip dance. National Geographic, 3/73, p 423
[< Chiluba]

likuta /li'ku:tə/, n a unit of currency in Zaire, equal to 1/100th of a ZAIRE. Pl.: MAKUTA. The Zaire is divided into 100 Makuta and the Likuta (the singular of Makuta) in turn consists of 100 Sengi   Paper money now in circulation consists of 10 Zaire, 5 Zaire and 1 Zaire notes, as well as 50K (Makuta), 20K and 10K notes. The coins are 5K, 1K and 10 Sengi. The Times, 12/6/72, p III
[< a Bantu language < li- singular noun pfx + -kuta said to mean stone in Nupe, but probably abstracted from (MA)CUTA < Kikongo nkuta cloth]

lilangeni /,lilan'geini:/, n a unit of currency in Swaziland. Pl.: EMALANGENI.
As Swaziland is part of the Rand Monetary Area, visitors do not even have to change money. South African rand and the local currency, the lilangeni (plural emalangeni) which is pegged to the rand, are used interchangeably. The Times, 9/6/78, p I
[< siSwati li- singular noun pfx + -langeni (root for) money]

Limba /'limbə/, n a people of Sierra Leone; their Niger-Congo (West Atlantic) language.

limba /'limbə/, n a tall West African tree (Terminalia superba); its straight-grained wood used in plywood and veneers.
African mahoganies and cedars, limba and parasol trees, ebony, teak and a host of others that have no familiar names...they

grow to enormous dimensions, some towering up to 160 feet. J. Hallet, Congo Kitabu, 1964, p 88
[< a West African language]

limbo /'limbou/, n 1 = LIMBA.
The Belgian Congo has been particularly successful in exploiting the uses of one of its commoner veneer woods, namely, Terminalia superba, or limbo. This tree, which grows well in the very accessible Mayumbe region of the lower Congo, yields a straight-grained wood with a blonde finish. G. Kimble, Tropical Africa I, 1960, p 192
2 the popular dance in which performers must pass under a wooden stick or bar held horizontally a few inches from the ground without using the hands.
If the youngsters think it will impress the adults they'll do the twist and the limbo, and tell them anything they think they want to hear. Maclean's, 7/6/63, p 18
[def. 1 < a central or West African language, ? ⋠ a Bantu language ∼ Swahili mlimbolimbo type of euphorbia; def. 2 < def. 1 or < Jamaican English (ca)limbe stick dance]

Lingala /liŋ'galə/, n a Bantu language spoken in Zaire.
[< Lingala li- singular noun pfx + NGALA]

lipute /li'pu:tei/, n = KITENGE (in Zaire).
The postponed but upcoming World Heavyweight Championship fight had its impact on Zaire fashion trends: "liputes" ankle length skirts, have shown up with African prints of boxing gloves and the fighting images of the two contenders. The image of George Foreman decorates the derriere of the lady at right. Border at ankle carries picture of Zaire flag

with a hand holding a torch. Nigerian Observer, 10/1/74, p 95
[< a Bantu language, ? < Lingala]

liqoqo /li'koukou/, n an advisory council to the king in Swaziland, consisting of chiefs and headmen. See LIBANDLA.
Even in the old National Council we had working committees, notably Liqoqo (freely translated, the Inner Council)... Those were, and are still, the working bodies for the execution of the day to day business of state. Times of Swaziland, 7/6/73, p 8
[< siSwati li- singular noun pfx + -qoqo (root for) this council]

liretlo or liretla /li'retlə/, n ritual murder among the Sotho. Lepotane takes a reluctant part in a tribal ceremony that involves human sacrifice. This ceremony, which is known as liretlo, is called for whenever certain parts of a human body are needed by the medicine man for use in his tonic mixtures. New Yorker, 7/26/58, p 73
[< seSutu]

Lisa /'li:sə/, n a deity of the Fon of Benin, the male aspect of the androgynous god of creation, associated with the sun. See MAWU.
[< Fon]

lisente /li'senti:/, n a unit of currency in Lesotho, equal to 1/100th of a LOTI.
[< seSutu, ? < li- singular noun pfx + sente < English cent]

litunga /li'tungə/, n the paramount chief of the Lozi of Zambia. On one such mound the litunga's capital, Lealui, was established; but the litunge also had another capital, Mongu, on the eastern hills. Once a year he was taken in a great cere-

monial canoe from Lealui to
Mongu, and then back again when
the floods went down. This ceremony is still observed, although
nowadays, of course, the journey
during the dry season can be
made in a few minutes by car.
B. Davidson, History of East
and Central Africa, 1969, p 236
What probably would be accepted,
however, is recognition of the
position of the Litunga and
his family, rather in the way
that the Asantehene is still
recognized in Ashanti. The
Times, 7/22/63, p 9
[< Lozi]

loa[1] /'louə/, n a filarial worm
(Filaria loa) that infects the
subcutaneous tissues and eyes of
man producing allergic reactions.
[< a West African language ?
of Angola ~ Kikongo lowa, loba
eye worm]

loa[2], n a spirit or god of a
Haitian voodoo cult.
> The drums beat, the dancing
becomes more and more frenzied,
some participants climb trees,
and soon one of them falls into
a stupor and is then considered
to have been 'mounted' by a
loa. Words issued by that person are then the voice of the
loa. Saturday Review, 3/11/61,
p 76
In traditional voodoo religion,
power comes from the spirits,
loa, that enter into a person's
body when he is in a trance.
Science News, 5/11/63, p 299
[< Haitian Creole lwa < a West
African language, ? < Loango an
older kingdom on the west coast
north of the Congo river]

lobola /lə'boulə/, n bride price;
money or cattle paid to the
bride's parents (in southern
Africa).
> African bridegrooms do not
buy their brides; the lobola
(rapidly disappearing these

days) is a guarantee against
decent [sic] treatment and is
refundable if the bride goes
back home. Polygamy is the ex-
ception to-day rather than the
rule and bears no status or
prestige. Cape Times (Mag. Sec.).
3/3/73, p 8
The bride's father for his
part received 200 head of cattle from the bridegroom's family. Lobola - bride price -
consoles the father for the
loss of his daughter and also
legalizes the marriage and
legitimates the children. National Geographic, 1/78, p 48
[< Nguni (uku)lobola to pay or
give dowry]

Lomé Convention /lo'mei/, n an
international trade agreement
between the European Community
and numerous developing countries
in Africa, the Caribbean and the
Pacific, allowing trade prefer-
ences and export price supports
for certain raw materials from
the Third World.
> The European Community has
increased its financial and
technical aid to "non-associ-
ated" developing countries by
57 per cent in the 1979 budget.
These countries, not helped by
the Lomé convention where aid
is linked to trade agreements,
will now receive about Ł74
million. New Scientist, 4/5/79,
p 41
[< Lomé capital of Togo where
the original agreement was signed
in February, 1975]

loti /'louti:/, n a unit of currency in Lesotho, equal to 100
LISENTE. Pl.: MALOTI.
> Lesotho announced that it would
mint its own currency, the
loti (plural, maloti), equal
to one South African rand. The
loti, however, will supplement-
rather than replace the South
African rand. Collier's Encyclopedia Yearbook, 1980, p 464

Lozi /'louzi:/, n̲ a people of Zambia; their Bantu language. Also
known as BAROTSE.
[< (Ba)rotse]

Lucumi /'lu:k mi:/, n̲ a secret
society of magic and witchcraft
in Cuba of African origin; a
member of this society; the language used by its members, said
to be derived from Yoruba.
    He remembers items of witch-
    craft, Congolese and Lucumi
    magic, how to make a devil and
    keep it in a bottle. The Times,
    4/20/68, p 22
[< a West African language]

Luganda /lu:'gandə or lu:'gænðə/,
n̲ the Bantu language of the Baganda.
[< Luganda lu- singular noun
pfx + -ganda (root for) these
people]

Lukiko /lu'ki:kou/, n̲ a parliament
or council of the Baganda.
    Mr. Kintu is a saza chief, and
    his wife is the daughter of
    Sir Aplo Kagwa, who was Kati-
    kiro from 1889 to 1926. The
    new Katikiro was chairman of
    the Lukiko drafting committee
    which went to draw up new Bu-
    ganda agreements in London.
    The Times, 8/25/55, p 6
    After a riotous two-day dis-
    cussion in the Buganda Lukiko
    ...the little kingdom of
    1,000,000 people declared it-
    self independent of British
    protection. Manchester Guardian,
    1/5/61, p 2
[< Luganda lu- singular noun pfx
+ kiko (root for) this council]

Luo /'lu:ou/, n̲ Also, Lwoo. a people
of Kenya, Tanzania and Uganda;
their Nilo-Saharan (Chari-Nile,

Eastern Sudanic) language.

lusaka /lu:'sakə/, n̲ a type of
dense bush vegetation in Zambia
(for which the country's capital
is named).
[? < Chibemba]

lusendvo /lu'sendvou/, n̲ a council of kindsmen among the Swazi;
the extended family.
    The responsibility for choosing
    the new king lies with the
    lusendvo and all the indications
    are that here, as in other
    areas of Swazi life, the old
    customs will prove the safest
    and smoothest path to the fu-
    ture. The Times, 10/14/76, p I
    The extended family (lusendvo)
    is of special significance.
    For instance, in Swazi Custom,
    it is accepted that a newly
    wedded woman joins, by virtue
    of her marriage, not only her
    husband, but also the husband's
    extended family. Times of
    Swaziland, 6/1/73, p 7
[< siSwati]

lusuku /lu'su:ku:/, n̲ a garden
plot of 1 or 2 acres in Uganda,
often a banana garden in which
the homestead is set.
[< Luganda]

Luyia or Luhya /'lu:y /, n̲ a
people of southwestern Kenya;
their Bantu language.
[< Luyia oluluyia < olu- singular noun pfx + (o)luyia people]

lwei /lə'wei/, n̲ a unit of currency in Angola, equal to 1/100th
of a KWANZA.
    The currency is the kwanza di-
    vided into lwei. Statesman's
    Yearbook, 1979, p 85
[< an Angolan language]

M

M, abbreviation of MALOTI.
   Lesotho. Finance. Monetary unit,
   maloti, M1 = $U.S. 1.1980.
   Collier's Encyclopedia Yearbook, 1979, p 340

maalam /'malǝm/, n a learned man,
   scribe, teacher, or diviner
   among the Hausa. Also MALAM.
   We also remembered to get
   Hausa charms from a maalam who
   lived near our village, because we knew that even though
   white magic was very strong,
   black magic was even stronger
   if it wasn't badly used. Atlantic, 5/68, p 90
   [< Hausa malam(i)]

maandazi /maǝn'dazi:/, n a cookie
   or deep fried bread or cake in
   East Africa.
   [< Swahili, literally, pastries,
   confectionery < ma- plural noun
   pfx + -andazi < -andaa prepare
   (cakes, food)]

maas /mas/, n = AMASI.
   [< Zulu amasi]

Maasai or Masai /'ma,sai/, n a
   people of Kenya and Tanzania;
   their Nilo-Saharan (Chari-Nile,
   Eastern Sudanic) language, also
   known as Maa.

mabati /mǝ'bati:/, n pl sheets of
   corrugated tin, used as roofing
(in eastern Africa).
   Because of the hard work farmers have put in their shambas
   the yields have been very high.
   ...Because of this what used
   to be a geography of grass
   thatched houses with smoke
   oozing out (a mark of poverty)
   has been replaced by a whole
   geography of mabati and stone
   houses. Weekly Review (Nairobi),
   4/27/79, p 32
   [< Swahili < ma- plural noun
   pfx + bati tin < Arabic]

mabele or mabela /ma'belǝ/, n
   millet, sorghum, or meal made
   from it.
   The women pound mabele, the
   millet which is the staple
   food, in tall wooden mortars
   using a well-balanced five-
   foot wooden pestle. Harper's,
   9/66, p 88
   [< Nguni amabele ∼ Luyia ama-
   beele millet]

macaque /mǝ'kak/ or macaco
   /mǝ'keikou/, n the well-known
   monkey of Asia and northern Africa, including the rhesus.
   [(< French) < Portuguese macaco
   < a West African language, ? <
   an Angolan or Congolese language,
   ? < Fiot or Vili ma- plural noun
   pfx + kako (root for) this monkey;
   ? < reduction of Kako(ngo) former
   kingdom in this area, or ? <

Luango ma-ncanca monkeys]

macumba /mə'ku:mbə/, n a Brazilian
fetish cult of African origin,
combining elements of voodoo and
Christianity.
  In that other African-dominated
  culture, Brazil...most Roman
  Catholics practise macumba, and
  one can see affluent white busi-
  nessmen laying out food, wine
  and candles on the pavement to
  propitiate the African "spirit
  of the crossing." Manchester
  Guardian, 1/30/71, p 18
  Iemanja...is one of the pantheon
  worshipped by the various devotees of the pagan cults [of
  Brazil] known as Umbanda, Quimbanda, Candomble, or - to its
  detractors - as Macumba. Time,
  1/10/72, p 44
  [< Portuguese, ? < a West African Bantu language (? Mbundu), ?
  < Jamaican English macoo a voodoo god who causes zombies to
  climb trees backwards (in African cults) < an African language]

macuta /mə'ku:tə/, n an old West
African unit of currency, con-
sisting originally of a piece of
cloth, and later as a coin of
various denominations in former
Portuguese colonies and other
West African countries.
  [< Portuguese < Kimbundu mukuta
  ~ Kikongo nkuta cloth] See MAKUTA.

Madaraka Day /,madə'rakə/, n a
holiday in Kenya held on June 1
to commemorate the introduction
of self-rule in 1963.
  It was Madaraka Day, the anni-
  versary of the attainment of
  internal self-government for
  Kenya two years ago. New York
  Times, 6/2/65, p 5
  Mrs. Kiano was the only woman
  who received an award at Madaraka Day, when she was made
  an Elder of the Burning Spear
  (second class). Weekly Review
  (Nairobi), 6/8/79, p 17

[< Swahili, literally, arrangements, responsibilities < ma-
plural noun pfx + daraka arrange-
ment, duty < Arabic]

madoqua /mə'doukwə/, n a tiny
antelope (Neotragus saltianus)
or Ethiopia, the size of a rab-
bit; the royal antelope.
  [< Amharic medaqqwa]

mafe /mə'fei/, n a Senegalese
dish of beef or chicken, tomatoes, onions, peppers, cassava,
squash and other vegetables
fried in oil and mixed with peanut butter.
  [? < Wolof]

mafura or mafurra /mə'fu:rə/, n
a tree (Trichilia) of eastern
Africa whose seeds yield an oil
resembling cocoa butter.
  [< a Bantu language ~ Sotho mafura, Swahili mafuta, Luyia ama-
  fuura, fat, oil]

mafuta /mə'fu:tə/, n a fat person;
hence, among some peoples, a
wealthy person (in southern and
eastern Africa).
  The economy began to get in
  serious trouble when Amin introduced his Mafuta Mingi
  (Wealth for Everyone) program.
  The implication was that there
  would be enough for all ordi-
  nary Ugandans once the Asian
  merchants who then dominated
  the economy were thrown out of
  the country. Time, 4/30/79, p 46
  [< Swahili, Nguni, and other
  Bantu languages, literally, fat
  or oil (from fat) ~MAFURA,
  which see]

magadi /mə'gadi:/, n a soda lake
(in eastern AFrica); soda.
  Many wildebeest, streaming
  toward the Highlands, crossed
  the south end of Lake Lagarja,
  the headwaters of the Olduvai
  stream that cut the famous
  gorge; like almost all lakes

of this volcanic region, it is a shallow magadi, or soda lake, of natron. New Yorker, 9/16/72, p 40

[< Swahili, soda]

magadiite /mə'gadi,ait/, n a mineral substance composed chiefly of magadi.

Unlike the magadiite bed (8), which is probably a lake-wide chemical precipitate, the chert-series rocks must have originated from hot-spring areas similar to the ones of the areas of the gel deposits. Science, 7/12/68, p 163

[< MAGADI + -ite mineral suffix]

magendo /mə'gendou/, n the black market, or any illegal or illicit activities or transactions (in eastern Africa).

To send fleets of State Research Bureau cars to girls' institutions for the weekend pleasures of these nefarious men was normal practice. The disinclination to work except by engaging in magendo was a respectable practice! Weekly Review (Nairobi), 4/20/79, p 10 Economic recovery, necessary as it is, will count for little if spiritual recovery does not accompany it. "Magendo" - rampant corruption - and ethnic animosities remain. New York Times, 5/1/79, p A8 On the magendo, 70 Uganda shillings equal one dollar. This does not help the bulk of the 13 million Ugandans, however, because most of them do not have access to foreign exchange. ...One day a Ugandan soldier with a lean look was offering to sell an AK-47, the Soviet-made automatic rifle, for 500 shillings at the magendo rate. That means he was asking $8 for one of the world's most ubiquitous killers - which explains why everyone who wants a weapon has one. New York

Times (Mag. Sec.), 11/16/80, p 82 Virtually everyone in Uganda must purchase essential commodities on the black market, which potentially makes the entire population guilty of magendo. Time, 5/4/81, p 42

[(< Swahili) < Kikuyu ma- plural/mass noun pfx + gendo ∿ -genda trade in the black market; cf. Haya omugenda mistress, girlfriend; perhaps also < Luganda]

Magosian /mə'gouʃən/, adj of or relating to a late Middle Stone Age and Late Stone Age culture of Africa (ca. 10,000-6000 B.C.), characterized by the use of microliths and small blades.

Rose Cottage Cave, near Ladybrand in the Orange Free State. At this locality three Wilton levels are successively underlain by a Pre-Wilton stratum, 1.5 m of beige sand containing for the most part a sparse and even older "Early LSA" aggregate and 3.0 m of "final MSA" ascribed to the Magosian. Nature, 5/5/72, p 50

[< Magosi water hole in Karamoja, Kenya, where artifacts of this culture were discovered + English -an]

magotla or **makgotla** /mə'gotlə or mə'xotlə/, n pl vigilante law-and-order groups of urban blacks in South Africa, supposedly patterned on traditional tribal courts.

The most notorious has been Soweto's "Magotla" group whose leaders, operating with the silent and not-so-silent blessing of the police and politicians, wield the sjambok (heavy leather whip) on young men accused of assaults and even young girls accused of truancy or immorality. The "legal process" is brisk and arbitrary and the punishment

of a public flogging inflicted
on the spot. Manchester Guardian,
9/24/78, p 8
[< seSutu ma- plural noun pfx +
KGOTLA]

magou /mə'gu: or ma'xu:/, n Also,
mahe(w)u. a drink made of fermented mealiemeal porridge (in
southern Africa).
Police evidence asserted: (a)
That Mr. Biko was given meals
of soup, magou (a vitamin con-
centrate), bread, margarine,
jam, coffee and water; (b) that
he refused the soup and magou
and the bread heaped up in the
cell. The Times, 12/10/77, p 10
[< Zulu (a)mahewu porridge-based
drink]

maharagwe /mahə'ragwei/, n an East
African dish of brown beans, often in a spicy sauce.
[< Swahili ma- plural noun pfx
+ haragwe this bean < Persian]

mahiya or mahia /mə'hi:yə/, n
a traditional toga-like cloth
garment of Swaziland.
The King of the Swazis, once
one of Africa's great warrior
tribes, is equally at home in
formal Western clothes or
"Mahia," the colorful national
costume. New York Times, 9/6/68,
p 8
Several thousand tribal warriors - the emabutfo - wearing
toga-like mahiya cloths around
their waists and feathers in
their hair, paid homage to the
leader they call Ngwenyama, the
Lion, waving wooden knobkerries
and chanting ancient war cries.
The Times, 9/11/72, p V
[< siSwati (e)ma- plural noun
pfx + -hi(y)a (root for) this
garment] See EMAHIYA.

mai /mai/, n title of the King of
Bornu and of the Kanuri (in
western and central Africa).

mailo /'mailou/, n land assigned

in freehold to certain chiefs
and ministers of the Buganda
Kingdom under terms of the Uganda
Agreement of 1900.
The mailo estates have been a
source of envy to men in other
parts of Uganda whose social
and political status would have
entitled them to mailo in Buganda, but the Protectorate
authorities soon came to think
that security for the peasant
was more important than secure
tenure for the chief, and they
resisted demands for the extension of the system. L. Mair,
African Societies, 1974, p 190
The economic strategy must aim
at streamlining land tenure
systems by the creation of legal rather than customary security of tenure. This is particularly urgent in the north
and east of Uganda. Unfortunate-
ly the demagogues and oppor-
tunists have neglected this
problem by a preoccupation with
the Mailo system in Buganda.
Yet it is in Buganda more than
anywhere else that security of
tenure is strongest. Weekly
Review (Nairobi), 4/20/79,
p not recorded
[< Luganda < English mile, because each segment of land was
eight square miles]

Maji-Maji /,madʒi:'madʒi:/, n an
uprising in Tanganyika (now Tanzania) against German rule in
the nineteenth and early twenti-
eth centuries.
In 1905-1906 the widespread
Maji-Maji rebellion of German
East Africa was crushed at
the cost of the lives of more
than 30,000 African men, women and children. Canadian
Saturday Night, 8/25/63, p 2
[< Swahili maji water, which
was sprinkled on warriors during
an oath-taking ceremony as a
sign of unity to convey invul-
nerability]

majimbi /ma'dʒimbi:/, n the root
or roots of a type of taro plant
(<u>Colocasia antiquorum</u>) in eastern
Africa.
> Vegetables are even more numer-
ous, ranging from the familiar
butter beans, corn, spinach,
marrow, and eggplant, to the
exotic cassava, breadfruit,
<u>majimbi</u> root, guarri, lady's-
fingers, and luffa. <u>New Yorker</u>,
10/31/53, p 85

[< Swahili <u>ma</u>- plural noun pfx
+ -<u>jimbi</u> (root for) this root]

Majimbo /ma'dʒimbou/, n regional-
ism or a policy of governing re-
gionally (in Kenya).
> Both he and Mr. Mboya reserved
most of their fire for the African People's Party and the
Kenya African Democratic Union
and their advocacy of <u>Majimbo</u>.
"If they knew what they were
saying when they cry 'uhuru
na majimbo' they would weep,"
Mr. Kenyatta said. <u>The Times</u>,
5/6/63, p 10
> KADU's <u>majimbo</u> (regionalism)
plan is thus aimed at protect-
ing minority rights of the
smaller, often nomadic tribes
against political and territorial domination by the big
tribes. <u>Time</u>, 2/23/62, p 38
> Lubembe was elected chairman
of Kanu's electors group and
nominated by the late President Jomo Kenyatta as leader
of government business in the
then upper house during the
<u>Majimbo</u> constitution. <u>Weekly
Review (Nairobi)</u>, 4/13/79, p 2

[< Swahili, literally, districts,
provinces < <u>ma</u>- plural noun pfx
+ <u>jimbo</u> state, district]

majumboro /ma'dʒəmbərou/, n a
colorful, fringed shirt from
Botswana, worn by "Bushmen."
> Skins, reed, and gameskin mats,
Bushmen's beaded "Majumboro"
shirts, curios, and carved
objects can be found in public
markets and in shops in Gabe-

rone. R. Kane, <u>Africa A to Z</u>,
1961, p 79

[< a southern African language,
? < seTswana]

Makonde /mə'kondei/, n a people
of Tanzania and Mozambique;
their Bantu language.

[< Makonde <u>ma</u>- plural noun pfx
+ <u>konde</u> (root for) these people]

makore /mə'korei/, n a large tree
(<u>Tieghemella heckelii</u>) of West
Africa; its dark, reddish-brown
wood.
> The Ivorian sculptor uses woods
of which few have ever heard -
<u>ikoro</u>, <u>sewe</u>, <u>avodire</u>, <u>makore</u>,
<u>blablengole</u>. <u>Saturday Review</u>,
10/31/70, p 65

[? < a southern African language]

makulu /mə'ku:lu/, adj great; big.
Also as a (plural) noun, <u>Makhulu</u>
or <u>Makulu</u>, a term of respect (in
South Africa).
> "Stay, Makulu," begged the
elderly black man depicted in
the advertisement spread across
the South African edition of
<u>Reader's Digest</u>. "For nowhere
in the world will they need
someone like you as much as
we do."...Zimbabwe Rhodesia's
"Makhulu" - who have been
turning their backs on the
country at a rate of 1,000 a
month - will keep on leaving.
<u>Maclean's</u>, 8/6/79, p 15

[< Zulu <u>ma</u>- noun pfx + -<u>kulu</u>
~Swahili -<u>kuu</u> big, great]

makuta /ma'ku:tə/, n pl of LIKUTA.
> In fact I will go further and
offer a small wager of 10
<u>zaire</u>, 55 <u>makuta</u>, 19 <u>sengi</u> to
152 Ugandan shillings that the
newly-named Lakes Amin and Mo-
butu will have newer names
still before the run of <u>The
Mousetrap</u> ends. <u>The Times</u>,
10/5/72, p 16

[< a Zairean Bantu language <
<u>ma</u>- plural noun pfx + -<u>kuta</u> ~
MACUTA]

malam /'malam/, n = MAALAM.
The conspirators consulted a
malam or Muslim soothsayer,
the prosecutor claimed. The
malam "read the sand", and con-
ducted a salaka, or ritual
slaughter of a goat. He then
made a prediction: "Heart will
spoil, and some people will be
disgraced." The plot went ahead,
nevertheless, but there were
delays, muddle and finally be-
trayal. The Times, 5/31/76, p 5

malanga /ma'langa/, n a type of
taro or yantia.
Malanga, boniato, yuca and
calabaza...are being grown in
Florida by Cuban exiles. New
York Times, 4/26/67, p 3
[< Spanish, ? < Kikongo ma-
plural noun pfx + -langa (root
for) water lily, cf. elanga (singular) water lily]

Malawi /ma'lawi:/, n a country of
southern Africa bordering on
Zambia, Tanzania and Mozambique,
formerly called NYASALAND.
[said to be < the name of an
earlier African empire of this
region < aMaravi the ancestors
of the Nyanja and Chewa, said to
mean people of flames, a reference to Lake Nyasa's glowing sur-
face]

mali /'mali:/, n wealth, money;
property (in eastern, western
and central Africa); the game
BAO, representing wealth or
property.
Yoma and Ebu stayed with me
almost constantly: I taught
them a little French, they
taught me Kimbuti; in between
we played mali, the same game
I had known as lela among the
Bakuba. J. Hallet, Congo Kitabu, 1964, p 280
[< Swahili, property, wealth
< Arabic]

Mali, n an ancient kingdom of
the Mandingo on the upper and

middle Niger, lasting almost
nine hundred years; hence, a
country in West Africa bordering
on Algeria, Mauritania, Senegal,
Guinea, Ivory Coast, Upper Volta
and Niger.
[said to be < Mandingo, literally, where the king, ma, re-
sides]

malikan /mali'kan/, n = MERIKANI.
The African Textile Mill makes
samples of cloths which include malikan, bed-sheets,
rexia for furniture and many
other items. Voice of Uganda,
3/10/73, p 1

Malinke /ma'linkei/, n a people
of Ivory Coast, Guinea, Guinea-
Bissau, Gambia and Mali; their
Niger-Congo (Mande) language,
sometimes considered a dialect
of MANDINGO.

maloti /ma'louti:/, n a unit of
currency in Lesotho, equal to
100 LISENTE; formerly, a gold
coin of that country.
Lesotho. Monetary unit: maloti,
at par with the South African
rand, with (Sept. 18, 1978) an
official rate of .87 malotis
to U.S.$1 (free rate of 1.70
malotis = ₤1 sterling). Britannica Book of the Year, 1979,
p 486
[< seSutu ma- plural noun pfx
+ loti] See LOTI, MALUTI.
--Despite its etymological plural
meaning, this term has attained
a singular meaning, as evidenced
by the addition of the English
plural suffix -s in the above
quotation.

maluti /ma'lu:ti:/, n variant of
MALOTI.
[< seSutu, perhaps named for
the Maluti Mountains, a range
in eastern Lesotho]

mama /'mama/, n mother; a term
of respect for a woman (in
eastern and southern Africa).

I went to a field full of women, colorful as birds in their
long sarongs and making sounds,
as a greeting, exactly like
birds. That field was a mama
shamba. The village women had
cleared the trees and under-
growth from virgin soil and
planted cotton. Atlantic,
9/63, p 43
[< Swahili mama, Zulu (u)mama]

mamba /'mambə or 'maɛmbə/, n a
deadly, venomous green or black
snake (Dendroapsis) of tropical
Africa.
    She earned the respect of her
    farm hands by killing a 9-1/2-
    foot poisonous black mamba
    snake with a shovel on her
    porch - and their devotion by
    founding a school for their
    children. Newsweek, 1/16/56,
    p 45
    "I once had a twenty-foot mam-
    ba that I named Hans. This
    snake was so attached to me
    that I couldn't go anywhere
    without him. He would even
    follow me to church on Sunday,
    and because he didn't care
    much for some of the sermons,
    he would wait for me outside
    under a tree. Not that Hans
    was irreligious. But he had a
    sensitive nature." Flying
    Springbok, 10/79, p 85
    [< Zulu (i)mamba, Swahili mamba]

mambo[1] /mambou/, n 1 the popular
Cuban and Latin American dance
and music of African origin.
    For the next three hours the
    Grand Ballroom and three ad-
    joining rooms rocked to mambos,
    waltzes, and sambas. Time,
    1/3/55, p 18
2 Also, mambu. a priestess of
the voodoo cult (in Haiti).
    Often the peasants turn to
    voodooism to alleviate their
    misery. They seek out the voo-
    doo priest or priestess, the
    hungan or the mambo, for cures.
    Science News Letter, 5/11/63,

p 299
    Mathilda Beauvoir, the "mambo,"
    or voodoo priestess, greets
    the spectators, inviting - or
    rather obliging - them to come
    out onto the floor, too. Man-
    chester Guardian, 1/23/77, p 12
    [< American Spanish < Yoruba,
    literally, to talk]

mambo[2], n, a king of the Rozwi,
who ruled in ZIMBABWE before the
Ngoni takeover.
    Much of what remains today [in
    Zimbabwe], however, belongs to
    the Rozwi period. The Rozwi
    Kingdom of Batua existed to
    the south of Monomotapa's king-
    dom, and just before 1700 the
    Rozwi king, or mambo, succeeded
    the Monomotapa as ruler of an
    area roughly equivalent to the
    present Matabeleland and Masho-
    naland. S. Blumenthal, Bright
    Continent, 1974, p 498
    [< Shona, literally, king < a
    Malawian language]

Mande /'mandei/, n the Mandingo
people; a group of Niger-Congo
languages including Malinke, Bambara, Dyula, Kpelle and others.

mandela /mæn'delə/, n a sub-
atomic particle with a mass about
forty times that of a proton; an
intermediate vector boson.
    The Leeds team...have provi-
    sionally dubbed their proposed
    particle the "mandela". Dr.
    Kellermann speculates that he
    and his colleagues may have
    finally netted the quark at
    their Haverah Park Cosmic Ray
    station. New Scientist, 5/31/73,
    p 532
    [named by its discoverers, sci-
    entists W. Kellerman, G. Brooke,
    and J. Baruch, for Nelson Rolih-
    lahla and Winifred Mandela,
    South African black nationalists]

Mandingo /mæn'diŋgou/, n Also,
Mandinka, MANDE. a people of
Ivory Coast, Guinea, Guinea-

Bissau, Mali, Gambia, and Senegal, including the MALINKE, BAM-
BARA and DYULA; their Niger-Congo
(Mande) language, widely used as
a lingua franca.
[< Mandingo mande the Mande +
-ka people of]

mandrill /'mæn,dril/, n a large
baboon (Mandrillus mormon) of
West Africa, with blue ridges
on the side of the nose.
[< man + DRILL]

Mangbettu or Mangbetu /maŋ'bei-
tu:/, n a people of Zaire; their
Nilo-Saharan (Central-Sudanic)
language.

mangu /'mæŋgu:/, n witchcraft
(among the Azande).
    The Azande ascribe more events
    to witchcraft than any other
    people on record; where any-
    thing at all goes wrong, small
    or great, they see the work of
    a witch. Mangu 'is less an in-
    tellectual symbol than a re-
    sponse to situations of fai-
    lure'. L. Mair, African So-
    cieties, 1976, p 222
[< Azande]

mangwe /'mæŋgwei/, n a tree (Po-
docarpus elongatus) of southern
Africa; its hard, yellowish wood.
[< a southern African language]

mani or Mani /'mani:/, n the title
of a chief or governor of the
Kongo kingdom of the 1400's.
[< Kikongo]

Mansa /'mansə/, n the title of a
hereditary king of the Mandingo
who first ruled the empire of
Mali nearly nine hundred years
ago.
    The earliest English coins of
    that century have been dis-
    covered by assay to be of Af-
    rican gold, and Mansa Musa
    (1312-1337), the pious Mandin-
    go who made a famous pilgrim-
    age to Mecca in 1324, was

known by name in Europe in the
fourteenth century. The Times,
6/29/72, p 16
    On Wednesday morning, everyone
    assembled out at Brikama, 22
    miles from Bathurst, for a
    "mansa Bengo," or gathering of
    chiefs. Harper's, 10/66, p 77
[< Mandingo mansa]

manyatta /man'yatə/, n a kraal,
enclosure, or encampment in
eastern Africa, especially of
the Maasai.
    It is not an uncommon sight to
    see some 3,000 head of cattle
    set out to graze in the morning
    from a single Masai manyatta
    settlement. New Scientist,
    8/24/61, p 450
    Now thousands of Somalis have
    been shunted into manyatta (pro-
    tected villages), a safe dis-
    tance from the Somalia border.
    Time, 9/8/67, p 30
    Each manyatta was enclosed by
    a thick fence of thornbushes
    to protect the cattle from
    lions, hyenas, leopards, and
    other wild animals. Saturday
    Review, 9/9/67, p 41
    The barefoot doctor's main
    function is in prevention, by
    inoculation, health education,
    and hygiene. A similar pro-
    gramme is being tried in Kaji-
    ado district, Kenya, where
    literate girls who are returned
    to the Manyattas when they get
    married are given health train-
    ing so as to become "health ex-
    tension officers." Weekly Re-
    view (Nairobi), 6/1/79, p 64
[? < Maasai]

maridadi /,mari'dadi:/, n osten-
tation; loud decoration; frivol-
ity (in eastern Africa).
    On occasion a noisemaker is
    some flattened bottle caps
    nailed loosely to a stick. A
    woman with loops of colored
    beads in her ears wears a pair
    of smoked welder's spectacles.
    A bit of "maridadi," or non-

sense, they make her friends
laugh, so she is happy. New
York Times, 5/24/63, p 2
The flowered fancy silk and
cotton dresses and the dis-
graceful short-shorts and skin-
tight toreador pants and even
tighter buttocks-squeezing
blue jeans were for their
daughters and granddaughters.
The pipestem cavalry pants
and the maridadi sports shirts
and loud sweaters and horse-
blanket hacking jackets were
for their sons and grandsons.
R. Ruark, Uhuru, 1962, p 89
[< an eastern African language;
? < Swahili]

marimba /mə'rimbə/, n a xylophone-
like musical instrument.
Eventually Boulez and company
departed for the last time,
the orchestras began gathering
their oboes, marimba-phones
etc. together, the applause
reluctantly died down. Listener, 4/18/68, p 502
Another thing possibly brought
by the Indonesians were xylo-
phones, instruments since developed by African musicians
into many types, among them
amadinda, marimba and zeze.
B. Davidson, History of East
and Central Africa, 1969, p 27
[< an African, probably Bantu,
language ~ Kimbundu marimba,
Tshiluba madimba, Swahili marimba, ? ultimately < ma- plural
noun pfx + rimba ~ Swahili -imba
sing]

marissa /mə'risə/, n a beer made
from millet among the Nubians.
Any number of the sheiks present had entertained Brewster
over bowls of marissa, a tribal
beer that has the color of
oatmeal, the consistency of
milk, and the impact of gasoline. New Yorker, 3/5/66, p 112
[< a western or central African
language]

marula /mə'ru:lə/, n a tree (Sce-
lerocarya) of southern Africa
bearing an oval, yellow fruit
used for making beer.
How does an elephant get drunk?
It's fairly simple according
to "Naturwissenschaftliche
Rundschau," a South African
learned journal. The elephants
approach a marula tree and eat
its fruit (Sclerocarya birrea)
- fruit also used by Africans
for brewing near-beer. Manchester Guardian, 3/7/69, p 6
Nearly 300,000 of those people
are in Ovamboland and in adjacent Okavango in the far north,
a land of high grass dotted
with marula, mopani and other
thorn trees, where people live
and rule themselves in tribal
fashion as they have since
time immemorial. Wall Street
Journal, 11/1/63, p 12
[< Afrikaans < seTswana or
seSutu morula]

Masarwa /mə'sarwə/, n = SARWA.
[< a southern African Bantu
language ma- plural noun pfx +
SARWA]

mashairi /maʃa'iri:/, n verses;
poetry; a poem.
All poems composed for public
performance are called mashairi, but there are several
kinds of these: nyimbo, which
are songs of one sort or another, hadithi, which are
tales, and best known, perhaps,
utendi, the heroic poems about
the deeds and lives of famous
men and great events. All these
styles are very old. B. Davidson, History of East and Central Africa, 1969, p 136
[< Swahili ma- plural noun pfx
+ shairi song, line of poetry
< Arabic]

Mashona /mə'ʃounə/, n = SHONA.
[< Shona ma- plural noun pfx
+ SHONA]

112

Maskal /'maskəl/, n a festival in Ethiopia celebrating the Reception of the Cross, a holiday held in late September.

Each year at the Festival of Maskal and on other special occasions, soldiers from all over the country, following their chieftains, pass in review before their emperor. National Geographic, 6/35, p 791
Child deacons await the start of the great Maskal ceremony. The Times, 7/22/72, p IV
[? < Amharic]

Matabele /,matə'belei/, n = NDEBELE.
[< seSutu, said to mean disappearing ones, < ma- plural noun pfx + -tebele < -teba sink down, because of their warfare practice of crouching down behind their spears]

matabiche or matabich /,matə'bi:tʃ or -'bi:ʃ/, n bribe; tip.

Congolese, from children to Cabinet ministers, play the game of je souffre, their long faces proclaiming their suffering even while their hands reach out for matabich – the bribe. Time, 3/13/64, p 31
Some prospective investors decide, after a few days of exploring, that setting up shop in Zaire is more trouble than it is worth. What turns them off, most of all, is a well-established system of graft known as matabiche. Time, 7/10/72, p 34
[< a West African (Zairean) language, ? < French or ? < Portuguese mata kill + biche beast]

matatu /mə'tatu:/, n any vehicle (a car, small truck, etc.) used as auxiliary transport in place of a bus, taxi, etc., often with at least three rows of seats (in eastern Africa).

The musical buses [in London] are scheduled to leave at 10-minute intervals....What music will they play? "Middle of the road music," says London Transport. Perhaps our matatus should feature taped music. "The Bump" would be particularly appropriate! Standard (Nairobi), 2/23/79, p 14
[< Swahili, ? < ma- plural noun pfx + -tatu three, perhaps because originally such auxiliary vehicles were the three-wheeled vehicles common in Somalia]

matoke /mə'toukei/, n a Ugandan dish of baked or mashed and steamed green bananas; the bananas.

On the flourishing black market, an egg costs $1.25. A handful of matoke – green plantains, Uganda's diet staple, costs more than $20.00, up 100 percent since the fall of President Amin 13 months ago. New York Times (Sec. 4), 6/1/80, p 2E
"An infant here is weaned abruptly. One day – generally when the mother realizes that she is again pregnant – he just joins the rest of the family at the matoke bowl. Well, matoke is all carbohydrate and the child falls ill with a disease called kwashiorkor." National Geographic, 11/71, p 715
The Government raised the minimum wage in September from 280 to 400 shillings a month. In the last year, the cost of enough bananas to feed a family of four for a month in the form of a national dish called matoke has risen from 275 shillings to 2,250 shillings. People must steal in order to eat. New York Times (Mag. Sec.), 11/16/80, p 82
[? < Luganda ma- plural noun pfx + -toke (root for) this banana]

Maulana /mau'lanə/, n a teacher, or leader, especially of the Afro-American organization US.

113

The time was not right for revolution, argued Maulana (meaning teacher) Ron, urging that "differences between bloods" be forgotten. Time, 4/19/68, p 17
[< Swahili, literally, lord, sir < Arabic mawlānā learned Muslim scholar]

Mau Mau /'mau,mau/, n the name given to the black nationalist uprising in Kenya against British rule in the 1950's; supposedly a Kikuyu secret terrorist organization that was active in this uprising.
The avowed purpose of the Mau Mau was to drive the British from Kenya's fertile "White Highlands." Its methods ranged from burning the exclusive Nyeri Polo Club...to hamstringing, disemboweling, but not killing herds of cattle. Newsweek, 11/3/52, p 44

--v, maumau. to threaten or terrorize.
In Mr. Wolfe's account of it, "going downtown to mau-mau the bureaucrats got to be the routine practice in San Francisco. The poverty program encouraged you to go in for mau-mauing." Harper's, 2/71, p 107
[said to be < Kikuyu uma uma literally "out out"]

--mau-mauer, n: After a threat is made for the fifth, twelfth or fortieth time, the excitement wears off; boredom becomes contempt when we find out that each hollow boast brings more government money tinkling into the Indian organizations' pockets. American writer Tom Wolfe calls the technique 'mau-mauing'; it's no accident that the most successful mau-mauer, Harold Cardinal, runs one of the strongest Indian organizations in Canada. Maclean's, 12/74, p 108

Mawu /'mawu:/, n the chief deity of the Fon of Benin, the female aspect of the androgynous god of creation, associated with the moon. See LISA.
[< Fon]

mbira /əm'birə/, n a thumb piano.
He was making music with a mbira, a kind of African hand-piano. His brother, who is three years his junior, was accompanying him on a kalimba, he said, which is a modern version of the mbira. New Yorker, 6/4/66, p 27
Among those played are the mbira, timbila, kalimba, guitar-lute, Lozi drums, tampura drone, bamboo pipe, Japanese koto zither, and double respiratory linguaphone. Time, 3/18/66, p 69
[< Swahili or KiMbundu ~ marimba]

mboloko /əmbou'loukou/, n a small forest antelope (Cephalophus sylvicultur) with a dark-brown coat and white spots (in western Africa).
When I reached it, the men were lifting out two mboloko, small antelope, beautiful, gentle-looking creatures (page 422). While two men held each animal by the legs, a third cut its throat, then set it on the earth to die. As the men gathered up the nets to reset them, I heard fragments of the hunting song that they had sung the night before. National Geographic, 3/73, p 420
I opened the gate to the young lions' cage. One of them leaped out and stood uncertainly, swinging his head from side to side. A moment later, a mboloko made the fatal mistake of returning to his home, trotting in daintily through the open front gate. The lion sprang and seized the antelope, cracking his neck; the second cat joined his brother and the pair started to work on the corpse. J. Hallet, Congo Kitabu, 1964, p 434

[< Lingala mboloko small ante-
lope]

mbongi /ə m'bangi:/, n = IMBONGI.
The scope of the mbongi's
poetry has expanded from inter-
tribal to national issues, and
he has become spokesman for a
nation. Celtic and South African bards alike celebrate
national victories and individual achievements, chant the
national laws and customs, re-
cite royal genealogies, and,
on the other side, criticize
the chiefs if they disregard
the laws and customs, abuse
their power, and neglect the
people. R. Dorson, African
Folklore, 1972, p 24

mboziite /ə m'bouzi,ait/, n an
amphibole mineral first discovered in Tanzania. Formula:
$Na_2CaFe_3Al_2Si_6O_{22}(OH)_2$
Mboziite, a new amphibole occurring in a pegmatitic nephe-
line-syenite dike intruded
into earlier syenites north-
east of Mohlileh Hill. 1965
McGraw-Hill Yearbook, 1966,
p 256
[< Mbozi area in southern Tanzania where the mineral was
found + -ite chemical suffix]

mbuga /ə m'bu:gə/, n a steppe or
seasonal swamp in central Tanzania.
[< Swahili]

Mbundu[1] /ə m'bundu:/, n a people
of Angola, also called OVIMBUNDU;
their Bantu language, UMBUNDU.
[< Umbundu]

Mbundu[2], n a people of Angola,
also called Ndongo; their Bantu
language, KIMBUNDU.
[< Kimbundu]

mbuni /ə m'bu:ni:/, n coffee plant;
coffee beans from this plant
(in eastern Africa).
At this time societies and

unions should be collecting
mbuni and dispatching it to
the Kenya Planters Co-opera-
tive Union for milling....As
these arrangements are taking
place, societies and unions
are completing parchment dis-
patches to the KPCU stores and
preparing to pay the members
for their mbuni. Cultivating,
manuring and mulching continues
right through April. Weekly
Review (Nairobi), 2/16/79, p 37
[< Swahili, literally, coffee
plant m- singular noun pfx +
buni < Arabic or Amharic BUNA]

Mbuti /ə m'bu:ti:/, n Also BaMbuti.
a "pygmy" people of Zaire; their
Bantu language.

mchanyato /ə mtʃan'yatou/, n a
Tanzanian dish of yam, cassava,
pumpkin, or bananas mixed with
onions, tomatoes and spices.
[< Swahili m- singular noun pfx
+ -chanyato ∿ chanyata slice up
(cassava, foods, etc.)]

Mende /'mendei/, n a people of
Sierra Leone and Liberia; their
Niger-Congo (Mande) language,
akin to MANDE and MANDINGO.

merikani /,meri'kani:/, n a type
of unbleached, white cotton,
used for sheeting or clothes,
originally made in America.
From the coast all the way inland to Lake Victoria, un-
printed cloth of any descrip-
tion has been called "Merikani"
ever since [the clipper ships
used to put into Zanzibar with
their cargoes of calico]. New
York Times, 1/27/67, p 62
It was impossible nowadays to
obtain cloth or even needles
and thread, there was nothing
for sale in the markets but
the cheapest sort of merikani,
faded bolts the missionaries
must have brought. J. Updike,
The Coup, 1978, p 71
How many Kikuyu bibis have

you seen wearing goatskins in
the last two years, the last
five years, the last ten years?
Not a one of them but hasn't
got a shuka made out of merikani or zanzibari. And shoes
of a sort. And head kerchiefs.
And houses with tin tops. R.
Ruark, Uhuru, 1962, p 189
[< Swahili < English (A)merican]
See AMERICANI.

mesenna or musenna /mə'senə/, n
a tree (Albizzia anthelmintica)
of Ethiopia; its bark, used for
a medicine to expel tapeworms.
[< Amharic məsanna]

mesob /mə'sab/, n a wickerwork
table in Ethiopia.
The restaurant is circular,
as are the local tukul dwellings; the walls are hung with
sabers and beads; the couches
are covered with rich cloths;
and the tables are the traditional reed mesobs. S. Blumenthal, Bright Continent,
1974, p 368
[< Amharic məsob]

Mfecane /əmfə'kanei/, n = DIFAQANE.
By 1833, when the worst of the
wars of wandering were over,
the overall picture had been
drastically changed. Shake
ruled a large empire east of
the Drakensberg Mountains.
North of him were the Swazi,
another Ngoni people....Else-
where the tides of the Mfecane
swept the Ngoni far across Africa. B. Davidson, History of
East and Central Africa, 1969,
p 287
[< Zulu]

mfuu /əm'fu:/, n a tree (Vitex
cuneata) of eastern Africa bearing small edible black berries.
I see a hardwood forest planted
with mzambarau trees for furniture, mvinje trees for construction, eucalyptus for telephone poles. Whoosh! A two-

foot monkey with a baby on
her back lands overhead in a
mfuu tree. She's after its
cherry-size fruit. National
Geographic, 4/75, p 503
[< Swahili m- singular noun
pfx + fuu (root for) this tree]

mganga /əm'gaŋgə/, n a doctor or
witch doctor in eastern Africa.
Even some whites turn to the
resident M'ganga now and then.
...Symon Thuita is an M'ganga
and he is one of Kenya's best.
Time, 1/1/65, p 22
John Agunga awoke...to find a
snake coiled around his neck.
"It did not bite me and I was
not afraid," he recalls. "Then
I knew I would be a mganga
like my grandfather." New York
Times (Mag. Sec.), 10/19/80,
p 68.
[< Swahili m- singular noun pfx
+ -ganga ～ ganga mend (what is
injured)]

mgwisho /əm'gwiʃou/, n the tail
or hairs of a tail from an animal tied to a stick, used as a
fly whisk (in eastern Africa).
Jomo Kenyatta leads his fledg-
ling nation along the path
toward self-help, hard work,
and racial good will. Here,
over a Voice of Kenya microphone, he calls on Kenyans of
all tribes to forget grudges
and unite for future great-
ness. From his wrist dangles
a silver-handled horsehair
fly whisk, or mgwisho - a
Kenyatta trademark. National
Geographic, 2/69, p 151
[< Swahili m- singular noun
pfx + gwisho (root for) this
whisk]

milo /'mi:lou/, n a hardy, wild
grass; grain sorghum (Sorghum
vulgare).
Another 108-acre plot planted
to millet, milo and kaffir
corn supplied more than 20,000
geese with good eating for

some time in the fall. <u>Science
News Letter</u>, 4/12/58, p 240
Budding corn and milo crops
were wiped out, but there is
still time for replanting, officials said. <u>Wall Street Jour-
nal</u>, 1/18/62, p 24
[< seSutu <u>maili</u>]

miombo /mi'ambou/, <u>n</u> a sparse, dry,
open woodland area; the tree or
trees (<u>Brachystegia</u>) of these
areas.
The plateau supports tracts of
relatively open <u>miombo</u> forests
of mainly leguminous trees,
deep-rooting and productive
of protein-rich beans. <u>Scien-
tific American</u>, 11/60, p 125
Vast stretches of <u>miombo</u> ex-
tend from the eastern edge of
the plateau to beyond the boun-
daries with Zambia and Mozambique.
Trees such as the African Black-
wood and other hardwoods grow
on the ridges and along the
edge of streams. In the valleys
strips known as dambos, are
waterlogged in the rainy season, and tall grasses and poor
acacias grow. R. and E. Steel,
<u>Africa</u>, 1974, p 162
[said to be < Swahili]

miyembe /mi'yembei/, <u>n</u> a mango
tree (in eastern Africa).
During our three years of marriage in Canada, Sarah had
often ignited my imagination
with her tales of her native
Uganda. She...conjured images
of her mother's home island in
Lake Victoria - a fairyland of
<u>miyembe</u> trees pregnant with
drooping mangoes. <u>National Geo-
graphic</u>, 7/80, p 74
[< Swahili <u>miembe</u>, strictly,
mango trees, < <u>mi-</u> plural noun
pfx + <u>embe</u> mango; the Swahili
singular form for mango tree is
more properly <u>mwembe</u>]

mkeka /əm'keikə/, <u>n</u> an oblong
straw mat, used as a symbol of
tradition in celebrating KWANZA

(an Afro-American festival). See
the quotation under KWANZAA.
[< Swahili <u>m-</u> singular noun pfx
+ -<u>keka</u> (root for) this mat]

mlala /əm'lalə/, <u>n</u> the hyphaene
or dwarf palm of eastern and
southern Africa.
We made camp under a thunderous
mahogany tree that slammed
shade onto the ground. The virgin camp where a Mlala palm
sussurated dryly in a soft
breeze and rattled its nuts together with the sound of a distant rain. <u>Rand Daily Mail Supplement (Johannesburg)</u>, 1/25/80,
p 1
[< Swahili <u>m-</u> singular noun pfx
+ -<u>lala</u> (root for) this tree]

mlanji or mlanje /əm'landʒi: or
əm'landʒei/, <u>n</u> Also, <u>milanji</u>. a
tall tree (<u>Widdringtonia whytei</u>]
of eastern and southern Africa,
similar in appearance to a cedar.
With a large and rapidly increasing population and less
than one fifth of its land surface under forest, much of it
of low intrinsic worth, Nyasaland likewise has good reason
to be interested in afforesta-
tion. So far the species that
have given the best results
under plantation conditions are
the native Mlanje cedar and
some of the exotic pines and
eucalyptus. G. Kimble, <u>Tropical
Africa I</u>, 1960, p 195
[< Mt. <u>Milanji</u> or <u>Mlanje</u> in
Malawi]

Mmo or muwo /əm'mou or əm'mwou/,
<u>n</u> a masquerade cult of Ibo origin
that uses a variety of carved
masks, such as horned masks for
male figures and white-faced,
gentler masks for females.
He no longer understands the
transpositions and abstractions
of, say, an Ibo Mmo mask. He
prides himself on his ability
to produce a likeness and believes his pictures to be

quite realistic. The Times,
12/1/77, p not recorded
[< Ibo, literally, ghosts, spir-
its]

mmoza /ə m'mouzɔ/, n = BAZIMO.
[< a Bantu language]

mngwa /əm'ŋgwə/, n an animal supposedly found in Tanzania, resembling a giant cat with stripes
and bands like a tabby.
     The Mngwa. A man-eating carni-
     vore found only along the coast
     of Tanganyika. Rather like a
     leopard, but as big as a don-
     key and striped with grey like
     a tabby-cat. Not to be con-
     fused with the Ndalawo of Ugan-
     da, also unknown to science,
     and certainly not with the
     Nandi bear, which Dr. Heuvel-
     mans thinks may turn out to
     be a non-extinct Chalicotherium.
     Punch, 12/31/58, p 859
[< a Bantu language, ? < m-
singular noun pfx + ngwa ~ Luyia,
Zulu, Xhosa, siSwati ingwe
leopard]

mninga /əm'niŋgɔ/, n a tree (Pterocarpus) of eastern and southern
Africa; its hard, valuable wood.
     Furniture materials include
     glass-reinforced plastic, satin
     chrome, M'ninga wood, mylon
     fur and bent plywood veneered
     in black bean. Punch, 5/31/61,
     p 832
[< Swahili m- singular noun pfx
+ -ninga (root for) this tree]

moamba /mou'ambə/, n a Zairean dish
of chicken cooked in palm oil and
served with a hot, spicy sauce
and rice.
     One type of oil (palm oil) which,
     when freshly extracted, is
     bright orange-yellow or reddish
     in color. It is used extensive-
     ly as cooking oil by the Congo-
     lese. One of the excellent na-
     tive dishes I ate in the Congo
     was moamba, chicken cooked in
     the oil. National Geographic,

3/52, p 361
     He is a gentle man, popular but
     often broke, and lives in a
     small house at the end of a
     puddle-filled dirt road. We
     often visited his kin. At a
     cousin's house we lunched on
     moamba. National Geographic,
     3/73, p 423
[? < Lingala]

mohonono /mouhou'nounou/, n a
tree (Terminalia sericea) of
Botswana and southern Africa.
[< Lozi]

moinmoin /'moin,moin/, n a Nigerian dish of mashed, highly
seasoned black-eyed peas, mixed
with vegetables and steamed.
     Because Nigeria has every-
     thing - fruits, vegetables,
     grains, tubers - her repertory
     of national dishes is one of
     the most varied in black Afri-
     ca. Pepper chicken, egusi soup
     (made from ground melon seeds),
     moinmoin...are specialties. S.
     Blumenthal, Bright Continent,
     1974, p 176
[< Yoruba]

mojo /'moudʒou/, n magic; magical
power; practice or ability of
casting spells.
     He was the one that no jail
     could hold overnight and no
     bloodhounds could track beyond
     a certain point. Because he
     worked a mojo on them that no-
     body ever heard of before or
     since. Harper's, 2/69, p 61
     Muddy Waters sang about trou-
     bled love and about his "mojo,"
     a voodoo conjuration which
     would work on anyone but the
     one he wanted. London Sunday
     Times, 7/10/60, p 6
[< Gullah moco witchcraft < a
West African language ~ Fulani
moco'o medicine man]

molimo /mou'li:mou/, n a month-
long festival of the Mbuti celebrated after moving from a camp

where a fellow tribesman died.
The real meaning of the song,
its importance and power, is
in the sound. In the crisis
festival of the molimo, the
closest approximation to a
ritual in the unformalized
life of the Bambuti, the men
of the band will sing, night
after night, through the night
until dawn. The function of the
sound now is to "awaken the
forest" so that it will learn
the plight of its children or
hear of their joy in its boun-
ty. Scientific American, 1/63,
p 31
[< Mbuti]

mondele /moun'delei/, n a term of
address for a white man; a white
man (in central Africa).
"Mondele Van Derveer and mondele Fallet were not here last
night, they had both gone to
Lisala."...Then, at his employer's departure, he might
inherit lots of old junk, like
a couple of pots and pans; may-
be some kitchen utensils; may-
be a folding cot or his mondele's cast-off tropical clothes.
L. Kenney, Mboka, 1972, p 40
[< a central or western Bantu
language ~ Ngombe mondélé; cf.
Jamaican English mundella (weza),
literally, white man (is coming)]

mongongo /moŋ'goŋgou/, n an African tree whose fruit, kernels
and flesh are staple foods of
the !Kung.
It is the rich nuts of the
mongongo they rhythmically
pound in those mortars, often
mixed with roots or meat, all
roasted in fire coals and sand.
Scientific American, 6/80, p 36
Asked why he hadn't taken to
agriculture a Bushman replied,
"Why should we plant, when
there are so many mongongo nuts
in the world?" New Scientist,
9/2/71, p 528
[? < !Kung or a related Khoisan

language, ? ultimately < a
southwestern Bantu language]

Monomotapa /,mounəmə'tapə/, n a
kingdom or dynasty of the Shona
from about 1400 to 1600 centered
in the Zambezi area; a king of
this dynasty.
[< Portuguese < Shona, said to
mean "lord (or master) of the
ravaged lands (or of the mines),"
a praise name of Mutota, the
dynasty's founder; ? alteration
of mwenemutapa < mwene lord, master (~ Swahili MWINYI, mwenye,
or dialectal mwene one who possesses, a complimentary title)
+ mutapa, ? ~ Swahili mtapa
iron ore]

moochi or muchi /'mu:tʃi:/, n
Also, mucha, moocha, mutsha/-i.
a loincloth worn by Zulu men,
made of animal skins or tails.
"O my uncle. I am Ignosi, right-
ful king of the Kukuanas!"
Then, with a single movement,
he slipped off the "moocha,"
or girdle round his middle,
and stood naked before us.
"Look," he said; "what is this?"
and he pointed to the mark of
a great snake tattooed in blue
round his middle. H. Haggard,
King Solomon's Mines, 1885,
p 114
[< Zulu umutsha loincloth]

mopani /mou'pani:/, n Also, mopane. a tree (Copaifera mopane)
of tropical Africa, used for
its hard, durable wood and as
a source of copal.
From "reefs" or lodes, gold
is extensively mined in the
Bulawayo district, an undulating country much overgrown
with mimosa and mopani bush.
National Geographic, 6/35,
p 765
He gets out his carving tools,
finds a piece of wood and
works on miniature figures.
His work is based on the people he meets while on Military

duties, and varies from District
Assistants to Selous Scouts.
Most of the work is done with
Mopani wood and Mr. Chadwick
has been nicknamed "Chief Mopani" by members of Internal
Affairs. (Rhodesia) Herald,
1/8/79, p 7
[< seTswana mopane]

moran /mo'ran/, n a Maasai age-set
of young, unmarried males who
form the warrior group; a member,
warrior, etc. of this group.
  Ah, the Masai moran, or warrior!
Tall, proud, ready to kill a
lion with his spear, drinker
of a stern concoction of cow's
milk and cow's blood. National
Geographic, 2/69, p 194
  A great Masai ceremony near
Narok when the Morans or young
warriors are shaved and set
free to marry and found families. London Sunday Times,
10/17/71, p 39
  Andrew Dick thought he would
impose "law and order" in the
community; so he descended the
Rift Valley and, using his
gun, succeeded in capturing
several Maasai cattle. He was
pursued and killed by the
Maasai moran. S. Sankan, The
Maasai, 1971, p xxii
[< Maasai (ol)muran warrior or
warrior group]

More /mə'rei/, n Also, Mole. =
MOSSI.
[< Mossi mole the self-designation of these people and their
language]

Moro Naba /'morou 'nabə/, n the
title of the king or a chief
among the Mossi.
[< Mossi moro a Mossi + naba
king; said also to mean big lord]

Mossi /'masi:/, n a people of Upper
Volta; their Niger-Congo (Gur)
language.

mpani /əm'pani:/, n = MOPANI.

Mr. Bottomley, with Lord Gar-
diner, talked with Mr. Nkomo
in the shade of a spreading
mpani tree on the banks of the
Lundi river. The Times, 2/25/65,
p 12

mpembe /əm'pembei/, n = PEMBE.
  It was depressing to picture
myself all alone in my bunga-
low whose whitewashed walls
were still reeking of the
mpembe....I smiled at two women squatting beside me and
they grinned back, showing
their triangularly filed teeth.
One of them, instead of red,
was coated with mpembe that
had dried in uneven streaks on
her thin, shriveled body. L.
Kenney, Mboka, 1972, p 27

msasa /əm'sasə/, n an African
tree (Brachystegia) with compound leaves and small, white
flowers, common in Zimbabwe savannahs.
  The Makabusi woodlands consist
of about 30 species of indigenous trees, of which msasa, mu-
hacha, mukarati and hamobohobo
predominate. (Rhodesia) Herald,
1/8/79, p 3
  I often set a tea table on the
wide green lawn...and invited
ladies to morning or afternoon
tea. The scene always reminded
me of a certain picture in Kate
Greenaway's "Marigold Garden,"
...Unlike the Greenaway tea
table, mine was in the shade
of a spreading msasa tree.
New Yorker, 2/19/66, p 39
[< Shona, ? ~ Swahili msasa
plant or shrub with coarse leaves]

mseto /əm'seitou/, n a Tanzanian
dish of rice mixed with lentils.
[< Swahili m- singular noun pfx
+ seto ~ -seta mash (soft things)]

msitu /əm'si:tu/, n an area of
dense bush (in Zambia).
[< Swahili m- singular noun pfx
+ -situ (root for) this type

of land]

mtemi /əm'temi:/, n = NTEMI.
By 1500 most of the peoples of
western Tanzania were ruled by
chiefs. These chieftainships
each consisted of a small group
of villages ruled by a single
chief whom the villagers ap-
pointed. Such chiefs were known
as ntemi or mtemi. B. Davidson,
A History of East and Central
Africa, 1969, p 52
[< Swahili m- singular noun pfx
+ -temi ∿ tema cut, < a Bantu
language ? Nyamwezi, adaptation
of NTEMI]

mtepe /əm'teipei/, n a sailing
vessel of eastern Africa with a
long prow and square matting
sail.
[< Swahili]

mtoto /əm'toutou/, n = TOTO.
"Kidogo said you could see
from a longer distance out on
that side - bush thinner and
patchier. In any case it looks
steep enough for us not to
shoot into each other. I'd
hate to widow Peggy Bruce, her
as big as a house with that new
mtoto she's building in her
tummy." R. Ruark, Uhuru, 1962,
p 54
[< Swahili m- singular noun pfx
+ -toto]

mugongo /mu'gaŋgou/, n an African euphorbia tree (Ricinodendron
rautanenii and africum); its very
light wood.
[< a Bantu language < mu- singular noun pfx + -gongo ∿ Swahili
gongo dense wood, thicket]

mugumo /mu'gu:mou/, n a type of
wild fig tree held sacred by
the Kikuyu.
And Ngai took me to a mugumo
tree which was bigger and
higher than all the other[s]
in the forest, a tree that
was like a father of all trees.

I. Henderson, Man Hunt in
Kenya, 1958, p 144
Brian and Don stopped at the
entrance to the thick forest
to rest in the shade of a big
mugumo, where the almost physical presence of Ngai was often
felt. R. Ruark, Uhuru, 1962,
p 43
[< Kikuyu]

muhimbi /mu'himbi:/, n a tree
(Cynometra) of eastern Africa;
its wood, called Uganda ironwood.
[< Lunyoro]

muhogo /mu'hougou/, n cassava,
or manioc, in eastern Africa.
Mbarara has a reputable standard of cleanliness. But with
the incoming indigenous citizens the Town Council has expressed fears the standards
may go down. Whereas the Asians
had a special type of food
which would not bring in rub-
bish, the citizens have moved
in with matoke, muhogo and
what have you. Voice of Uganda,
3/21/73, p 2
[< Swahili]

--muhogo tamu, n a beef and
cassava stew.

mujiba /mu'dʒi:bə/, n a young
scout of the black nationalists
in Zimbabwe.
More than 17,000 Patriotic
Front soldiers had turned
themselves in at Commonwealth-
supervised assembly points.
However, Rhodesian military
officials contended, thousands
were "mujibas" - youngsters
as young as 8 years old who
function as scouts - leaving
other thousands of guerrillas
still at large. New York Times
(Sec. 4), 1/6/80, p 2E
[? < Shona]

mukama /mu'kamə/, n a king or
ruler among the Nyoro and Toro
of Uganda.
[< Lunyoro]

Mulungu /mu'luŋgu:/, n the supreme
deity of the Zulu, Chewa, and
other Bantu people of southern
Africa.
[< various Bantu languages < mu-
singular noun pfx + -lungu ~ Swahili (M)UNGU]

mumbo-jumbo, n an idol, deity,
or object supposedly worshipped
in Africa; gibberish.
[said to be < Mumbo Jumbo the
idol worshipped, or < the name
of a Mandingo secret society (or
a diviner of that society who
speaks in a secret language); ?
< Mandingo mama ancestor +
dyumbo pompom-wearer]

Mungu /'muŋgu:/, n the supreme
deity of the Swahili and other
peoples of eastern Africa.
    In Kenya, the Communist-leaning
    Minister for Home Affairs prayed
    before 5,000 people to Mungu
    (God) to give Kennedy a good
    place in heaven. Time, 12/6/63,
    p 36
[< Swahili mu- singular noun pfx
+ -ungu ~ -unga join fasten to-
gether]

munt or muntu /'munt(u):/, n an
offensive, derogatory term for
a black person (in southern Africa).
    A young Rhodesian was arguing
    with the black barman over the
    price of a drink he was buying
    for a colored friend. "You damn
    munt," he said to the barman,
    who smiled nervously. A colored
    drinker explained quietly that
    the term "munt" is worse than
    "kaffir." "'Kaffir' is, I sup-
    pose, like 'nigger;' 'munt'
    means the thing that moves."
    New York Times, 4/1/76, p 4
    History has gone too fast for
    most of these people. They re-
    main totally paternalistic in
    their relations with Africans.
    They run little dispensaries
    and give land for schools, but
    some still refer to Africans

as "munts," and to the African
families farming on parts of
their land which they have sold
to settlement as "my Africans".
Integration has not happened
as it has in Nairobi. Manchester
Guardian, 7/30/78, p 9
[< a Bantu language < (u)mu-
singular noun pfx + -ntu (root
for) person, creature ~Swahili
m-tu Luyia (o)mundu person; ~
BANTU]

muran /mu'ran/, n = MORAN.
    "Shall we talk to the chief?"
    "He went to the manyata to see
    the muran." That really in-
    trigued me. I knew that the
    muran (or moran, as they are
    sometimes called) were the
    warriors, and I had some hazy
    notions about the manyata. Ac-
    cording to all I had heard, it
    was a special warrior village,
    resembling to some extent the
    gladiator schools of the ancient
    Roman empire. J. Hallet, Congo
    Kitabu, 1964, p 133

murram or murrum /'mərəm/, n a
lateritic, reddish material in
soils, used for unpaved but lev-
eled roads in parts of Africa.
    The better drained ones are
    red 'Murram' soils, with iron
    as the prominent cation, and
    leached of most soluble mater-
    ials. W. Pearsall, New Biology,
    Vol. 17, 1954, p 12
    There are also plans to improve
    the existing murrum roads and
    bitumanise them. Bucunku road
    - one of the seven feeder roads
    has already been marked for bi-
    tumanisation. Voice of Uganda,
    3/21/73, p 2
[< an African language]

muti /'mu:ti:/, n medicine; spells,
incantations; herb or herbs used
in healing; witchcraft; any treatment for a real or imagined illness, disease, etc., (in southern
Africa).
    "Muti" for money - the money

was "presumably Kruger sovereigns" was the motive for murder....Witness Johannes Shongwe said a ritual was performed to obtain "muti for the digging of underground money." Times of Swaziland, 6/22/73, p 1
Just read the instructions on the packet or bottle of the muti and you are likely to find the contents [of a pesticide spray] are dangerous to children and animals, must not be sprayed on vegetables and fruit within so many days of eating. (Rhodesia) Herald, 1/6/79, p 6
[< Zulu umithi tree, shrub (as used in preparing medicines) < umu- singular noun pfx + -thi ~ Swahili (m)ti tree]

muzungu /mu'zuŋgu:/, n = MZUNGU.
When Mohinder Singh came to work the next morning and described News From Britain to Sam Fong ("dancing with a Muzungu girl and goodness knows what"), Sam Fong wept. Atlantic, 7/68, p 75

mvinje /əm'vindʒei/, n a tree (Casuarina equisetifolia) of eastern Africa; its hard, durable wood used for masts of dhows.
Heading southeast, I visit a state farm: Rice farmers tend individual plots, and the state does the plowing for a share of the yield. I see a hardwood forest planted with mzambarau trees for furniture, mvinje trees for construction, eucalyptus for telephone poles. National Geographic, 4/75, p 503
[< Swahili m- singular noun pfx + vinje (root for) this tree]

mvule or mvuli /əm'vu:lei/, n an African tree (Chlorophora excelsa) also called IROKO; its hard, durable wood.
Tall mvule trees soared dark and green around the compound, and the air grew loud with the furious cheeps of gold-and-black weaverbirds in the palm trees. National Geographic, 11/71, p 714
The Kenyan market has relied on importations from Uganda, but when this source was closed the timber dealers went for the few remaining trees along the lake basin and in Busia District, in particular, and induced farmers in whose plots these trees stand to sell them at very low prices. The Mvule in this area has traditionally been protected from exploitation because the people revered the tree and used it only for dug-out canoes. Weekly Review (Nairobi), 4/20/79, p 29
Kilaguni Lodge in Kenya's big-game country even had a special 7-ft. bed of mahogany-like m'vuli wood. Time, 2/2/70, p 28
[< Swahili m- singular noun pfx + -vule ~ Luganda muvule this tree]

mwalimu /mwa'li:mu:/, n the title of Julius K. Nyerere, president of Tanzania; literally, teacher.
Then (as now) Mr. Nyerere declared that Mr. Kenyatta was the inevitable hero-leader of the united state. However, Tanganyika was independent first and Mr. Nyerere - the Mwalimu or Teacher - enjoyed a prestige ensuring him the second place, which meant that Mr. Obote could only be third. The Times, 8/16/65, p 9
"Countries like South Africa would like to confuse the issue," said the 53-year-old President, who was addressed as mwalimu. New York Times, 4/27/76, p 2
The recent Summit of five front line Heads of State in Dar es Salaam, was a series of initiatives started by Mwalimu Nyerere in his search for the liberation of Africa. Sunday News (Dar es Salaam), 9/19/76, p not recorded

[< Swahili, teacher (because Nyerere was once a schoolteacher) < mw- singular noun pfx + -alimu (~ elimu study, subject matter) < Arabic]

Mwami or Mwame /ə' mwami: or ə'mwamei/, n the title of the Tutsi king; a ruler.

The Watutsi exercised their supremacy not so much through the ownership of land, which all belonged to the Mwami or king, as through grants of cattle. Manchester Guardian, 2/13/64, p 2

Mwame (King) Ntare the Fifth, who had reigned only three months and just turned 19 on Friday had gone off on a visit to the Congo without his drum - a sign and source of his mystical powers. New York Times, 12/4/66, p E5

"We in the Soviet Union need uranium. The United States needs uranium. To maintain a facade of neutrality, Mwami Kibangu, President of Boende [a fictional country of Africa], in reality an American puppet, set a quota on what he would sell us, while at the same time he sold the United States three times as much." I. Wallace, The Second Lady, 1980, p 66

[< Kirundi mw- singular noun pfx + -ami ~ Luyia (o)mwami ruler]

mwana /ə' mwanə/, n a child; one's son or daughter (among numerous Bantu peoples).

"Have I not given birth to one mwana? Why can I not have another child?" Mokolo said nothing. L. Kenney, Mboka, 1972, p 120

[< a Bantu language ~ Swahili mwana, Luyia omwaana, Luvale mwana, Lingala mwana < mw- singular noun pfx + -ana (root for) a child]

mwene /ə m'weinei/, n a king or chief of certain Bantu peoples

(of West and southern Africa).

[< Kikongo, Kimbundu, Shona, etc. ~ Swahili MWINYI, mwenye]

mwinyi /ə m'winyi:/, n Also, Mwenye. a chief (in eastern Africa); sir. The [boat] owner may control the marketing and may own the means of transport. He may also be instrumental in the acquisition of dynamite and its subsequent distribution. He may have social status as a mwinyi or a sheikh, or he may be a corrupt individual with some capital and a "get-rich-quick" mentality. New Scientist, 10/12/78, p 115

[< Swahili ~ mwenye one who possesses, < mw- singular noun pfx + -enye having]

mwiru /ə m'wi:ru:/, n sg of ABIRU.

[< Kinyarwanda mw- singular noun pfx + -iru (root for) such an expert]

mzambarau /ə mzam'barou/, n a tree (Syzgygium jambolanum) of eastern Africa; the Java plum tree. See the quotation under MVINJE.

[< Swahili, ? < Portuguese jambalao]

Mzee /ə m'zei/, n the title of the late Jomo Kenyatta, president of Kenya from independence until 1978; literally, (respected) old man, elder.

Kenyatta used such tensions to rally support for the government and cement national unity. His successors will have to do that and more if Kenya's stability, Kenyatta's chief legacy, is to survive the leader his countrymen called Mzee. Maclean's, 9/4/78, p 48

The late Robert Shaw for many years among the best of the all-rounders on the screen is the defector Marenkov; Lee Marvin, silver haired and (I think) getting to be a bit mzee for

the romantic bit, is still good
value helping to hold up the
C.I.A. end of the operation.
(Nairobi) Standard, 11/30/79,
p 21
[< Swahili m- singular noun pfx
+ -zee aged, old ∿ -zaa to be
born]

mzungu /ə m'zungu:/, n a derogatory
term for a white person (in
eastern Africa).
   The other slogan in Kenya is
   "Africanization," which is to
   say that a black man should
drive around in the Mercedes-
Benz, instead of an Asian or
mzungu. Harper's, 8/76, p 66
They all fell silent as we entered. One stopped washing himself under a stand-pipe. Then
a few voices called out that
the "mzungu" (white man) had
visitors. I turned a corner to
see Astles, a small, grey pale
man, walking towards us. The
Times, 11/18/79, p 5
[< Swahili m- singular noun
pfx + -zungu (root for) Euro-
pean]

N

₦ or N, abbreviation of NAIRA.
Nigeria's rapidly increasing
wealth is shown by the rise in
the level of federal revenues
and spending....For the 1979-80
year the projected figures were
₦8,805 million and ₦2,534 million. Americana Annual, 1980,
p 373
The West African Automobile
and Engineering Company Limited
will make a giant stride in its
commercial venture [sic] when
it opens its N400,000 showroom
and other centres in Benin
City this month. Nigerian Observer, 10/1/74, p 93

Nabagereka /ˌnabəgəˈreikə/, n the
title of the wife of the KABAKA
(in Uganda).
News of their ruler's exile hit
the Baganda like a tropical
rainstorm. The Kabaka's 300-1b.
sister, Princess Zalwanga, col-
lapsed and died; his pretty
young Nabagereka (Queen) retired
with her ladies in waiting and
sent out a message that she was
"bewildered and grief-stricken."
Time, 12/14/53, p 34
[< Luganda]

naboom /nəˈbuːm/, n a southern African tree (Euphorbia ingens)
with candelabra-like branches and
a highly toxic latex.
[< Afrikaans < Khoikhoin ngha

this tree (～gnap powerful) +
Afrikaans -boom tree]

Nachikufan or Nachikufu /ˌna-
tʃəˈkuːfən or ˌnatʃiˈkuːfuː/,
adj of or relating to a late
Stone Age culture of south-east-
ern Africa.
[< Nachikufu, said to be an area
in Malawi where artifacts of this
culture were discovered (+ English
-an)]

nagana /ˈnagənə/, n a disease of
cattle and domestic animals in
southern Africa, with fever,
lethargy and bodily swelling,
transmitted by the TSETSE fly.
It was found that the dreaded
cattle disease, nagana, was
present in the bloodstream of
wild game. It had no effect on
the animals themselves, but
the tsetse fly transferred the
disease from the wild hosts to
domestic cattle, in which it
was fatal. National Geographic,
9/60, p 381
[< Zulu (u)nakane]

naira /ˈnairə/, n a unit of currency in Nigeria, equal to 100
KOBO.
On Jan. 1, 1973, Nigeria will
scrap her system of Nigerian
pounds, shillings and pence,
borrowed from her colonial ruler, Britain, and begin a

decimal currency system with
units of money called the naira
and the kobo. New York Times,
8/9/72, p 14
Nigerian gangster chief "Mighty
Joe" and his lieutenant died
here yesterday before a six-man
military firing squad after being convicted of violently rob-
bing a man of ten Naira (15
U.S. dollars). Ghanaian Times,
6/8/73, p 2
[an alteration of Nigeria]

nakong /nə'kaŋ/, n an antelope related and similar to the SITA-
TUNGA.
[? < seTswana]

nakuruitis /nə,kuru'aitis/, n a
disease affecting sheep or cattle,
caused by a deficiency of cobalt.
When nakuruitis threatened to
sweep away settlers' cattle
and sheep in Kenya, the malady
was found to be related to a
trace element deficiency. With
a dressing of cobalt, the land
now carries excellent live-
stock. Bulletin of Atomic Scientists, 3/54, p 102
[< Nakuru town in Kenya where
the disease was discovered +
English -itis inflammation]

Nama /'namə/, n a people of western
South Africa; their Khoisan language, sometimes considered a
dialect of KHOIKHOIN.

Namaqua /'namə,kwa/, n 1 = NAMA.
2 Also, Namaqua dove, an African
dove (Oena capensis) with a strikingly long tail.
[< Nama nama the name of these
people + -qua man, people ～
Khoikhoin khoi man; def. 2 <
Namaqualand region in western
South Africa]

Namibia /nami'bi:ə/, n a country
of southern Africa bordering on
Angola, Zambia, Botswana and
South Africa, formerly known as
South West Africa.

[< Khoikhoin namib desert region in that country]

Namoratunga /na,morə'tuŋgə/, n
the name of an archaeoastronomi-
cal site in northwestern Kenya
where 19 basalt pillars dating
to 300 B.C. are believed to have
been used in aligning the rising
points of a seven-star formation
that is of present-day significance
in Cushitic calendars.
The most interesting of many
short reports on post-Pleisto-
cene archaeological activities
in Africa was that of an align-
ment of basalt pillars at Namoratunga in Kenya. The stones
were oriented to certain stars
and constellations and suggested the existence of a calendar at about 300 BC. 1979 Compton's Yearbook, 1979, p 20
[said to mean stone people in
the local Cushitic language]

nancy-story or nancy, n a folk
tale of the Caribbean of West
African origin, the hero of which
is usually the trickster Anansi,
the spider. Also, ANANSI-TORI.
[by folk etymology < Nancy a
girl's name < Akan ananse spider,
the trickster + English story;
the tales in Akan are called
anansesem]

Nandi bear /'nandi:/, n a large,
bear-like animal supposedly found
in eastern and southern Africa.
He is more concerned with such
creatures as the abominable
snowman, the Australian bunyips,
the Nandi bear, the African
dragon St. George did not kill,
...the little hairy men, moas,
giant sloths, the orang pendek
of Sumatra, and so on. Observer,
12/7/58, p 16
[< Nandi a Nilotic people of
Kenya]

nandine /'nædi:n/, n a West African civet (Nandinia binotata
and gerrardi) with spotted sides.

127

[< a West African language]

nanger or **nanguer** /'nᴂŋgər/, n
an ADDRA from Senegal.
[< French < a West African language, ? ~ Wolof]

naras /'narəs/, n a shrub (Acantho-
sicyos horrida) found in desert
areas of southern Africa, with a
melon-like fruit and oily, edible
seeds.
[< Khoikhoin (Nama) bnarab]

ndagaa /əndə'gaə/, n = DAGAA.
In East Africa the large lakes
Tanganyika and Malawi harbour
rich populations of small clu-
peid fishes canned ndagaa. New
Scientist, 1/28/71, p 180
[< a Bantu language < n- noun
pfx + DAGAA]

ndagala /əndə'galə/, n = DAGAA
(in central or western Africa).
Once I watched an old Hutu
magician burn about three
pounds of agahuza - little
herring-like fish that came
all the way from Lake Tanganyika where the Congolese called
them ndagala. J. Hallet, Congo
Kitabu, 1964, p 116
[< a central African Bantu language < n- noun pfx + dagala alteration of Swahili dagaa (because
in many cases Swahili drops an
l between two vowels)]

ndalawo /əndə'lawou/, n a carni-
vorous animal supposedly found
in Uganda.
The Mngwa. A man-eating carni-
vore found only along the coast
of Tanganyika. Rather like a
leopard, but as big as a donkey
and striped with grey like a
tabby cat. Not to be confused
with the Ndalawo of Uganda,
also unknown to science, and
certainly not with the Nandi
bear. Punch, 12/31/58, p 859
[< an East African language]

N'dama /ən'damə/, n a West-African

breed of small, fawn or red cattle with lyre-shaped horns, noted
for its resistance to trypanoso-
miasis (sleeping sickness).
Cattle resistant to tsetse-fly
attack in West Africa, and in-
habiting the hot, wet-forest
belt, very small and slow growing, little use for beef or
draught, and giving almost no
surplus milk, Ndamas present
many fascinating scientific
problems, which seem to call
for much bolder investigations
than anyone has yet started.
Science News 34, 1954, p 105
[? < Swahili ndama the young of
cattle; a calf (because of its
small stature)]

Ndebele /ˌəndə'beilei/, n 1 a
people of Zimbabwe, also known
as MATABELE; their Bantu language,
also known as SINDEBELE. 2 a
people of South Africa; their
Bantu language.
[def. 2 < seSutu]

ndege /ən'deigei/, n an airplane
(in eastern Africa).
In a recent letter to a New
York friend, Mrs. Hemingway
described Hemingway's all-out
conversion to the air age:
"Poppa is so keen on scouting
in the Ndege at 600 or something shillings a half day
[about $84], which includes
bumps and rolls and swooping
down on the deck and wing-
brushing the chulu hills, that
we will shortly have no money
left except for gin and cab-
bage." Time, 2/1/54, p 31
[< Swahili, literally, bird]

ndizi na nyama /ən'di:zi: na
'nyamə/, n a Tanzanian stew of
plantains and beef or other meat.
Tanzanian specialties such as
nyama ya mbuzi (goat meat),
and ugali na nyama (fufu with
meat), and ndizi na nyama (bananas with meat) are served
at the Forodhani Hotel. S.

Blumenthal, Bright Continent,
1974, p 427
[< Swahili, literally, bananas
and meat]

Ndlovukazi /ənd,louvu'kazi:/, n
the title of the queen in Swaziland.
At the head of this [democracy
in Swaziland] is the King and
the Ndlovukazi at which [sic]
council everyone is free to
speak his mind. Times of Swaziland, 7/6/73, p 8
Cyprian's happy subjects saluted
her with the honorary title of
Ndhlovukazi. Time, 4/27/59, p 33
[< siSwati, literally, female
elephant < ndlovu ～ Swahili ndo-
vu elephant + kazi ～ Luyia -xasi
woman]

ndoro /ən'dorou/, n a small,
round shell with a spiralling
groove and a hole in the middle,
worn as a badge, used by witchdoctors, and once used as money
in southern Africa.
There is extant a photograph
of him wearing a military tunic with four stripes, a headdress of ostrich feathers (a
sign of his eminence in African eyes), and on his breast
the "ndoro" or badge of chief-
tainship. Manchester Guardian,
10/2/58, p 13
[? < Shona]

ndugu /ən'du:gu:/, n a term of
address used in Tanzania meaning
"comrade."
Sweden supports the Patriotic
Front alliance of Ndugu Joshua
Nkomo and Ndugu Robert Mugabe,
the Swedish Minister for International Development and Co-
operation Mr. Ola Ullsten, has
said. Daily News (Dar es Salaam),
2/21/77, p 1
[< Swahili, literally, brother,
sister, fellow tribesman, citizen, etc.]

negbie /neg'bei/, n Also, negwe.

an oval, ornamental cover for
the buttocks, worn by Mangbettu
women.
"Congo women wearing ornamental
fenders, called negbie." B.
Rudofsky, The Unfashionable
Human Body, 1974, p 60, illus-
tration legend
The negwe is made from sycamore
bark that has been beaten and
dyed with earth, and the combination of colours and of
geometrical patterns that adorn
it is evidence of a vivid
aesthetic imagination. J.
Paudrat in M. Huet, Dance, Art
and Ritual of Africa, 1978,
p 194
[< Mangbettu]

negus /nei'gəs/, n a title of the
former emperor of Ethiopia,
Haile Selassie.
HIM is short for His Imperial
Majesty - Haile Selassie I,
Emperor of Ethiopia. His titles
also include Negus Negusti
(King of Kings) and Conquering
Lion of Judah. New York Times,
2/14/67, p 2
[< Amharic negus]

Ngai /əŋ'gai/, n the supreme
deity among the Kikuyu, Maasai,
and others of eastern Africa;
belief in such a deity.
Brian and Don stopped at the
entrance to the thick forest
to rest in the shade of a big
sacred fig tree the Kikuyu
called mugumo, where the almost physical presence of
Ngai was often felt, and where
some of the more devout gang
leaders...came often to pray
and replenish the spirit. R.
Ruark, Uhuru, 1962, p 43
Surprisingly, Kihoro says he
believes in religion, but of
a certain kind. He is a tra-
ditionalist Ngai. Not a bad
Marxist, come to think of it.
Weekly Review (Nairobi), 5/25/
79, p 11
[< Kikuyu, Maasai, and other

eastern African languages]

Ngala /əŋ'galə/, n a people of Zaire and Congo; their Bantu language, on which LINGALA is based.

ngalawa /ɔŋgə'lawə/, n an outrigger canoe or boat of eastern Africa, propelled by poles and sails.

But Dar es Salaam was my favorite city, in a six-week tour. At sunrise, when the dhow-rigged outrigger ngalawas came in, a crowd of fish peddlers on bicycles collected for the auction held on the beach. Harper's, 8/76, p 68 He worked hard, going out beyond the reef each day in his little outrigger canoe, the type of boat which is called a ngalawa. Manchester Guardian, 7/17/69, p 14
[< Swahili]

nganga /əŋ'gaŋgə/, n = MGANGA.
In the Congo, boys at the age of fifteen are declared dead, taken into the forest and there subjected to purification, flaggelation, and intoxication with palm wine, resulting in anesthesia. The priest-magician (nganga) who is in charge teaches them a special language and gives them special food. Harper's, 6/65, p 18
[< a Bantu language n- singular noun pfx + ganga ∼ Swahili mganga doctor]

ngege /əŋ'geigei/, n a fish (Tilapia esculenta) found in Lake Victoria and used for food.
[< a Bantu language]

ngoi /əŋ'goi/, n = KIKOI.
She didn't have anyone to help her take care of me whilst she was working on the field. She therefore strapped me to her back in the ngoi whilst working. This was very tiring

as she had to bend down all the time using a long knife for cultivation or a hoe 'jembe'. Sometimes I would be crying on her back or sleeping. But so long as I was fed and dry my mother would continue working. R. Gatheru, Child of Two Worlds, 1965, p 12
[< Kikuyu n- noun pfx + goi ∼ Swahili kikoi]

ngola[1] /əŋ'goulə/, n title of the former king of the Mbundu of Angola.
Early in the 1620s the reigning ngola's sister, Queen Zhinga, went to Loanda to make peace with Joao Correia de Sousa, a governor who had just arrived. He refused her a chair, whereon she called up one of her servants and, seating herself on his back, began to negotiate. B. Davidson, In the Eye of the Storm: Angola's People, 1972, p 81
[< Kimbundu; the name Angola was derived from ngola]

ngola[2], n = NGULA.
Baloki's young body was freshly coated with ngola. Nearly all the local village women used it. That coat of finely powdered red bark blended with oil probably protects more efficiently against sun and insects than clothes, and it looks attractive, too. The ngola covering Baloki's mother, however, was blotted out and smeared in several spots and its color had faded. L. Kenney, Mboka, 1972, p 58

ngoma /əŋ'goumə/, n 1 a dance, party, or festival in eastern and southern Africa.
My baby, the last one, little Jock, is more or less a Kikuyu. You were away, Brian, you weren't at the christening, but there was a hell of a big do. All the clans from both

sides of the ridge came and pitched up on the farm. I killed some sheep and cattle and we had a whacking great ngoma. It carried on for days. R. Ruark, Uhuru, 1962, p 102 About the only hint of racial discontent on the island concerns this club...because the Africans resent the fact that by law their ngomas, or dances, must stop at eleven in the evening while every Saturday the roof of the English Club is raised until four or five in the morning. New Yorker, 10/31/53, p 84

2 a drum or drums.
The royal drums, the ngomas, were symbols of his mystical power, and the drum beaters belonged of necessity to the aristocracy. J. Paudrat in M. Huet, Dance, Art and Ritual of Africa, 1978, p 194
[< Swahili and other Bantu languages, literally, drum]

Ngombe /əŋ'gambei/, n a people of Zaire; their Bantu language.
[? < Bantu ng'ombe cow]

Ngoni /ən'gouni:/, n a people of Tanzania, Mozambique, Malawi, Zambia and Zimbabwe; their Bantu language.
[said to be < a Zulu praise name]

ngubu /əŋ'gu:bu/, n a blanket; clothing for a black African (in southern Africa).
[< Nguni ingubu blanket ~ Swahili nguo clothes]

ngula /əŋ'gu:lə/, n a red or orange-red powder made from the pounded bark of a tree (Pterocarpus tinctorius), applied to the body or the face as a cosmetic. Also, NGOLA[2].
The color of the ngula is highly significant: red is the nearly universal symbol of love and happiness among primitive peoples everywhere (black, obtained from charcoal powder, enjoys a similar status with some Bantu tribes and the Pygmies). Unlike ourselves, almost all Africans agree that white, derived from a clay called pembe, is associated with death and sorrow. J. Hallet, Congo Kitabu, 1964, p 46
[< a Bantu language ~ Kuba ngula]

Nguni /əŋ'gu:ni:/, n a group of southern and southeastern African peoples comprising the Zulu, Xhosa, Swazi, Ndebele (def. 2), Shangaan, and Ngoni; their group of Bantu languages.
[< Zulu, literally, one of ancient stock]

nguo /əŋ'gu:ou/, n a piece of cloth, especially used as clothing.
At the teeming marketplace of a Kenya village deep in the bush country, a bronze teen-ager, wearing only a brilliant red and white nguo (sash) around his middle, sold us a large bunch of bananas for half a shilling. Saturday Review, 9/9/67, p 41
They scrambled up and, dropping their hoes, ran to me. They lifted up the little nguo with which they had covered me and to their horror found I was bright red all over, like a pepper! They were very frightened. R. Gatheru, Child of Two Worlds, 1965, p 12
[< Swahili]

Nguzo Saba /əŋ'gu:zou 'sabə/, n the seven principles of blackness proposed by MAULANA Ron Karenga, founder of US: unity, self-determination, collective works and responsibility, cooperative economics, purpose, creativity, and faith.

[< Swahili nguzo fundamental
principles + saba seven]

Ngwazi /ən'gwazi:/, n the title of
Dr. Hastings Banda, president of
Malawi.
> They built him up as the Lion
> of Malawi, Ngwazi (Supreme
> Chief), and called him Messiah.
> Time, 10/2/64, p 25B
> Now an invitation from the
> Ngwazi (Chief of Chiefs) is a
> mark of social and political
> acceptance. Scotsman, 5/26/64,
> p 9

[< Chichewa, literally, chief,
provider]

ngwee /ən'gwei/, n a unit of currency in Zambia, equal to 1/100th
of a KWACHA.
> Zambia, for instance, announced
> last week that, when it goes
> over to decimals next January
> 100 Ngwee will equal one Kwacha.
> Manchester Guardian, 4/20/67,
> p 6

[< Chinyanja, literally, bright;
? ~ Lele nghei a measure of salt
used as a unit of trading raffia
cloths]

Ngwenyama /ən'gwen,yamə/, n the
title of the king of Swaziland;
paramount chief.
> In Swaziland, elections under
> a new constitution are to be
> held in June. The Swazi Nation-
> al Council, which with the
> Ngwenyama (King) has been
> strongly opposing the consti-
> tution, has now agreed to co-
> operate and, presumably, to
> take part in the elections.
> The Times, 2/14/64, p 8

[< siSwati, literally, lion, ?
< ngwe ~ Luyia ingwe leopard +
nyama ~ Swahili nyama meat, ani-
mal]

niaye /ni'ayei/, n a marshy depression between dunes and parallel with the coast (of northern
Senegal).

[? < Wolof, said to mean

clump(s) of oil palms]

Niyabingi /,niya'bingi:/, n a
secret society among the RASTA-
FARIANS advocating racial war
against white domination; originally a warrior group in Ethiopia supposedly organized by
Haile Selassie for similar purposes.
> Extremists of the Ras Tafarian
> movement are the Niyabingi,
> the Men of Dreadlocks, who do
> not shave or cut their hair.
> ...Niyabingi means "death to
> the white man," which the de-
> vout anticipate in the ruthless
> manner of Revelations. Punch,
> 11/13/63, p 711

[? < Amharic]

--**Niya man**, n: In Jamaica, "Niyabingi" came to be defined as
"death to all black and white
oppressors." Some men locally
known as "Ras Tafaris" came to
be called "Niya men"; their idea
of violence as a tool of freedom
spread like wildfire. T. Nicholas, Rastafari, A Way of Life,
1979, p 24

Njoroan /ən'dʒorouən or 'nyorən/,
adj of or relating to the remains, artifacts or culture of
a late Stone Age people in East
Africa who used polished stone
axes. See the quotation under
GUMBAN.

[< Njoro variant of Nyoro a
Bantu people of Uganda + English
-an]

Nkosi Sikelel'i/-'e Afrika
/ən'kousi: sike'leili: 'afrika/,
n a hymn sung in South Africa
and regarded by black nationalists as the country's national
anthem.
> From inside the van came the
> sound of the African anthem
> Nkosi Sikelele Afrika (God
> Bless Africa). The Times,
> 2/17/70, p 5

[< Xhosa, literally, God Bless

Africa; the first verse was written by Enoch Sontonga in 1897]

Nok /nak/, n̲ a civilization of West
Africa (ca. 500 B.C.-200 A.D.)
noted for its terra-cotta sculpture and iron works, located in
present-day Nigeria.
[N̲o̲k̲ name of a village in Nigeria where evidence of this culture was discovered]

Nommo /'nomou/, n̲ a spirit among
the Dogon of Mali, representing
order, structure and reason in
the universe.
    The Dogon universe is governed,
on the one hand, by a deity,
Nommo. His power is balanced
to some degree by his brother,
who has the form of a white
fox. The Fox is depicted as
the obverse of order – not a
sinister obverse but a richly
creative one. L̲i̲s̲t̲e̲n̲e̲r̲, 9/12/68,
p 328
    Carrying on the craft of his
ancestors, a weaver works his
crude loom in Yenndouma. Tribal myth says weaving originated
with N̲o̲m̲m̲o̲, or spirit, who spat
out sacred thread and wove it
on a loom made from his jaws,
teeth, and lips. As he worked,
he spoke words of revelation,
which his forked tongue wove
into this first fabric. N̲a̲t̲i̲o̲n̲-
a̲l̲ G̲e̲o̲g̲r̲a̲p̲h̲i̲c̲, 3/69, p 438
[< Dogon]

nomoli /nou'mouli:/, n̲ p̲l̲ small
soapstone (steatite) figures
from Sierra Leone, believed to
have been carved by the ancient
Mende and used as talismans in
farms.
    These soapstone n̲o̲m̲o̲l̲i̲ were
being made during the sixteenth
century by the ancestors of
the present Sherbro and possibly Temne tribes, who in those
days occupied large areas of
the country from which the
Mande-Fu-speaking Mende later
drove them. The identity of

style (and some striking details of subject matter) between the nomoli and the major-
ity of the Afro-Portuguese
ivory saltcellars, spoons and
hunting horns which appeared
in European collections at
that time is supported by the
praise given by contemporary
Portuguese travellers to the
ivory-workers of Sherbro. W.
Fagg & M. Plass, A̲f̲r̲i̲c̲a̲n̲ S̲c̲u̲l̲p̲-
t̲u̲r̲e̲, 1964, p 22
[< Mande]

nsenene /ənse'neinei/, n̲ p̲l̲ locusts; a Ugandan dish of steamed,
dismembered, and fried locusts.
    A French-Canadian volunteer
in Chad who feasted on fried
flying termintes assured me
they were delectable ("taste
like crackers"), and I assume
the n̲s̲e̲n̲e̲n̲e̲ taste similar. S.
Blumenthal, B̲r̲i̲g̲h̲t̲ C̲o̲n̲t̲i̲n̲e̲n̲t̲,
1974, p 456
[< Luganda, ? ~ Swahili n̲z̲i̲g̲e̲
locust]

nshima /ən'ʃi:mə/, n̲ a Zambian
dish of cornmeal and water mush.
    A typical Zambian meal: [is]
a stew of beef accompanied by
a porridgelike cereal called
nshima. N̲e̲w̲ Y̲o̲r̲k̲ T̲i̲m̲e̲s̲, 11/6/
67, p 14
[< Bemba]

nsolo /ən'soulou/, n̲ = BAO.
    Men have planted soya beans
and other crops and have been
kept busy road building and
constructing more huts. I saw
one man making an Nsolo board,
used for an African version of
draughts. T̲h̲e̲ T̲i̲m̲e̲s̲, 4/13/65,
p 9
[? < Swahili n̲- noun pfx + s̲o̲l̲o̲
seed(s) of a thorny shrub (C̲a̲e̲s̲a̲l̲-
p̲i̲n̲i̲a̲ c̲r̲i̲s̲t̲a̲t̲a̲) used as counters
in games]

ntemi /ən'temi:/, n a ruler,
chief, or king in eastern and
central Africa.

The <u>ntemi</u> was not different from the king or chief of the West Lake region. He had to possess certain sacred symbols; he had to lead in certain rituals and, above all, his own well-being was identified with that of his chiefdom. In some cases his position was more ritualistic, and in others the <u>ntemi</u> was politically more active. I. Kimambo & A. Temu, <u>History of Tanzania</u>, 1969, p 22
[< various Bantu languages < <u>n</u>-singular noun pfx + -<u>temi</u> ~ Bantu -<u>tem</u>- cut ("decide")] See ABATEM-BUZI.

Nuba /'nu:bə/, <u>n</u> a people of the Nuba hills of the Kordofan region of Sudan; their Nilo-Saharan (Chari-Nile, Eastern Sudanic) language.

Nubia /'nu:bi:ə/, <u>n</u> an ancient kingdom between Egypt and Ethiopia, now an area in present-day Sudan.
[< Nuba (Mahass) <u>nob</u> slave + -<u>ia</u>]

Nuer /'nu:ər/, <u>n</u> a people of the Sudan and Ethiopia; their Nilo-Saharan (Chari-Nile, Eastern Sudanic) language.

nug /nəg/, <u>n</u> a plant (<u>Guizotia abyssinica Cass</u>) of Ethiopia related to the sunflower and cultivated for its seeds which yield oil.
Nor let us forget the Ethiopians, who clutter our docks with antelope pelts, rugs, spears, dried green peas, castor seeds, lentils, haricot beans, nug seeds, and portraits of Haile Selassie. <u>New Yorker</u>, 5/23/59, p 32
[< Amharic]

num-num /'nəm,nəm/, <u>n</u> an evergreen shrub of southern Africa; its edible purple or red fruit.
[< Afrikaans, ? < Khoikhoin

(Nama) //^{n}um//^{n}um]

nyala /'nyalə/, <u>n</u> a bluish-gray antelope (<u>Strepsiceros</u>) with white stripes, found in eastern and southern Africa.
Several exotic African animals were brought to the National Zoological Park in Washington, D.C., this year. One of these, the gerenuk from Kenya, is a rare mammal that requires no drinking water. Other unusual species imported by the park include the nyala, dibatag, cape buffalo, gazelle, and beisa oryx. <u>Collier's Encyclopedia Yearbook</u>, 1968, p 626
[< a southern or eastern Bantu language, ~ Tsonga, Venda <u>in</u>-<u>yala</u> ~ Luyia <u>inzala</u> antelope (diminutive: <u>axa-yala</u>)]

nyama /'nyamə/, <u>n</u> 1 meat; flesh (of an animal) (in eastern and central Africa).
Tanzanian specialties such as <u>nyama ya mbuzi</u> (goat meat), <u>ugali na nyama</u> (fufu with meat), and <u>ndizi na nyama</u> (bananas with meat) are served at the Forodhani Hotel. S. Blumenthal, <u>Bright Continent</u>, 1974, p 427
Many poachers believe that they have a God-given right to kill the game. There is a Swahili phrase, <u>nyama ya Mungu</u>, which literally means "meat of God." That sums up their attitude toward the animals. <u>National Geographic</u>, 2/72, p 160
At Lulonga, where your great-grandfather was a great chief, there was plenty of <u>nyama</u> to eat, but I would not be given the tiniest morsel. That is the law of your tribe. L. Kenney, <u>Mboka</u>, 1972, p 25
2 an animal or animals (in eastern and central Africa).
The villagers are forced to accept the situation with relative passivity, and indeed find ways of rationalizing it. They do this either by referring

to the Mbuti as <u>nyama</u> (animals),
thus excluding them from the
realm of normal moral behavior,
or else they openly admit the
Mbuti's right to raid their
plantations. <u>New Scientist</u>,
8/11/63, p 332
[< Swahili and other Bantu languages; e.g. ∿ Chiluba, animal,
Zulu -<u>nyama</u> meat; cf. Jamaican
English <u>nyam</u> to eat; <u>ninyam</u> food
∿ Wolof <u>nam</u>, <u>namnam</u> to eat, ∿
Hausa <u>na:ma</u> flesh, meat, Akan
<u>nam</u> flesh, meat]

Nyanja /'nyandʒə/, <u>n</u> a people of
Malawi; their Bantu language,
also known as CHINYANJA.

nyanza / n'yanzə/, <u>n</u> a lake or
large inland body of water (in
central and eastern Africa);
formerly in place names, hence:
<u>Albert Nyanza</u> = Lake Albert;
<u>Albert Edward Nyanza</u> = Lake Ed-
ward; <u>Victoria Nyanza</u> = Lake
Victoria.
[< a central or eastern Bantu
language; ∿ Luganda, Luyia,
Haya (i)<u>nyanza</u> lake ∿ Chichewa
<u>nyasa</u> lake; cf. NYASALAND]

Nyasaland /'nyasə,lænd/, <u>n</u> the
former name of MALAWI.
[< Lake <u>Nyasa</u>, large lake in
Malawi < Chichewa <u>nyasa</u> lake]

nyayo /'nyaiyou/, <u>n</u> a slogan and
rallying cry in Kenya, calling
on the citizens to follow in
the footsteps of the late President Mzee Jomo Kenyatta.
  President Daniel arap Moi made
  the word <u>Nyayo</u> - the catch-
  phrase of his administration
  - a specified word under the
  National Flag, Emblems and
  Names Act, as from March 15,
  1979...It is not general practice to put names on flags.
  At least that has not happened
  so far even with the word
  <u>harambee</u> which expresses the
  nation's motto [and] appears
  on the coats [sic] of arms...

Moi coined the word <u>Nyayo</u> to
express his administration's
philosophy late last year.
<u>Weekly Review (Nairobi)</u>, 3/30/
79, p 17
  Mr. Boit who was also the Returning Officer for Nairobi,
told the M.P.s to honour their
pre-election pledges of fos-
tering the "Nyayo" philosophy
of love, peace and unity for
rapid progress. <u>Standard (Nai-</u>
<u>robi)</u>, 11/23/79, p 3
[< Swahili, literally, foot-
prints, tracks <u>n(y)</u>- plural
noun pfx + -<u>ayo</u> (root for) foot-
print]

nyika /'nyi:kə/, <u>n</u> wilderness
area; open forest or dry bush,
often with acacias, euphorbias,
etc. in eastern Africa.
  Within a distance of little
more than 300 miles it is possible to observe coral reefs,
coastal forest, thick nyika
bush, open savannah, lava
desert, montane forest and
alpine grassland. <u>The Times</u>,
12/16/68, p VII
  Many other African explorers
were treated with the same
arrogance "that over the next
hundred years would inflame
the scientists' dealings with
any number of committed field
workers in the <u>nyika</u>, and to
which the 8,000 square mile
Tsavo wasteland now stands as
a monument." Quoting P. Beard's
<u>The End of the Game</u> in <u>New</u>
<u>Scientist</u>, 3/8/79, p 782
[< Swahili; cf. TANGANYIKA]

nyimbo /'nyimbou/, <u>n</u> <u>pl</u> songs,
especially songs of the Swahili.
There are numerous <u>nyimbo</u> in
this form, most of them dealing with the subject of love
in a light manner. J. Knappert
in E. Skinner, <u>Peoples and</u>
<u>Cultures of Africa</u>, 1973, p
550
[< Swahili <u>n(y)</u>- plural noun
pfx + -<u>imbo</u> ∿ <u>imba</u> sing]

135

Nyimi /'nyi:mi:/, n (the title
of) the king among the Bakuba of
Zaire.
   The Nyimi was forbidden to
touch the ground, to come into
contact with blood or to be
seen by a woman in the act of
eating. He sat on a living human throne...and he was not allowed to die a natural death.
Instead, when he was believed
to be mortally ill, he was rit-
ually smothered by his eldest
son. J. Hallet, Congo Kitabu,
1964, p 55
   The Nyimi, kings of the Bakuba,
were then recruited into the
Bushoong clan and became the
custodians of this fragment of
divine power on earth. J. Paudrat
in M. Huet, Dance, Art and Ritual of Africa, 1978, p 193
[< Kuba]

nyumba /'nyumb /, n a Kikuyu
hut or dwelling for women and
young children. See the quotation under THINGIRA.
[< Kikuyu ~ Swahili nyumba house]

Nzinga / n'zing /, n a "corn-
row" hair style (short braids
or pigtails flat against the
scalp in rows) of Nigerian origin, popular among Africans and
Afro-Americans. See the quotation under ASHIA.
[< Nzinga a 15th century Nigerian leader]

O

oba /'oubə/, n 1 a chief or (divine) king among the Yoruba and other peoples of West Africa.

In Western Nigeria the Obas combine grassroots machine politics with honorific tribal positions. The Times, 7/27/63, p 9

Benin was one of Africa's oldest and most powerful kingdoms. It is best known for its "Benin bronzes," highly sophisticated sculptures depicting the obas, or kings, who ruled during its zenith in the 16th century. New York Times, 7/16/63, p 11

2 a title of a leader in the candomblé, a religion of African origin in Brazil.

Mr. Amado is enmeshed in the cultural heritage of the slaves. He holds the title of "oba," which is bestowed in Bahia on the top 12 lay leaders in candomblé. New York Times, 10/1/77, p 7

[< Yoruba]

obeah /ou'beiə/, n a ritual or system of magic and sorcery in the Caribbean; a sorcerer or medicine man, obeahman, who practices such magic.

In Trinidad and Tobago the sorcerors and obeahmen serve identical functions - they are multi-purpose and they can as easily be male or female, Indian and Negro, educated or illiterate, Christian or pagan. Sunday Guardian, 5/6/73, p 4

For decades, a Jamaican in trouble has turned automatically to his local "obeah man" - a cross between witch doctor, medical practitioner, herbalist, faith healer, marriage counsellor, careers adviser and fortune teller. The Times, 4/17/77, p 12

[< a West African language ~ Efik ubio charm-like thing ~ Akan ɔbayi(fó) witch; wizard; sorcery ~ Edo obi poison]

obeche /ou'beitʃei/, n a West African tree (Triplochiton scleroxylon); its wood, used for plywood and veneers.

The seat is despatched complete with handsome, adjustable brass fittings and fixings. There are two types, one of obeche wood which has a lustrous, rosewood type of finish. The Times, 3/25/78, p 6

[< a Nigerian langauge]

obi[1] /'oubi:/, n the hut of a head of a household (among the Ibo).

Okonkwo's prosperity was visible in his household. He had a large compound enclosed by a thick wall of red earth. His

own hut, or <u>obi</u>, stood immediately behind the only gate
in the red walls. Each of his
three wives had her own hut,
which together formed a half
moon behind the <u>obi</u>. C. Achebe,
<u>Things Fall Apart</u>, 1958, p 13
[< Ibo]

obi[2], <u>n</u> = OBA.

After an audience with another
obi, author Noel Grove rose
before the obi did. "You must
sit down, Noel," a Nigerian
friend quietly advised. "In
the old days he could have had
your head for that." <u>National
Geographic</u>, 3/79, p 426

obitenge /oubi'tengei/, <u>n</u> = KI-
TENGE (in Angola).

He hurled provocative questions
at me: "Why did you, a progressive, join a reactionary
organization like Unita?"...
and he spoke with a frightening
certainty. I was sure that he
believed everything he said
even if it were not true. I
liked him, he was black, he
wore an obitenge shirt, and
he was intelligent. <u>Manchester
Guardian</u>, 3/14/76, p 16
[? < Kimbundu ⌐KITENGE, cf.
plural, <u>vitenge</u>]

obosom or obosum /ou'bousəm/,
<u>n</u> a deity among the Akan, similar
to the Dahomean VODUN.

Among various sources of help
by far the most important were
certain rural shrines where
the spirit of the <u>obosom</u> or
local deity would enter into
the body of the priest of the
shrine and, through his agency,
would bestow magical protection
on the supplicants who came
before him. <u>Listener</u>, 3/2/61,
p 387
[< Akan ɔbosom deity]

odum /'oudəm/, <u>n</u> a type of forest
tree and its wood from Ghana.

Mahogany has been joined by

such woods as walnut, sapele,
and <u>odum</u> - all of which are
suitable for interior work,
decorative veneers and furniture. <u>The Times</u>, 3/11/77, p 26
[Akan odúm tree]

ofay /'oufei/, <u>n</u> a derogatory
term for a white man (in the U.
S.).

[? < a West African language
< o- a common Niger-Congo nomi-
nal pfx + <u>fay</u> ~ Bamum fɛ, Gola
<u>fua</u> white; thought also to be
< Pig Latin <u>foe</u> -> o-f-ay]

ogbanje /og'bandʒei/, <u>n</u> a child
believed by the Ibo to die and
re-enter its mother's womb to
be born again.

Ezinma bubbled with energy like
fresh palm-wine. At such times
she seemed beyond danger. But
all of a sudden she would go
down again. Everybody knew she
was an <u>ogbanje</u>. These sudden
bouts of sickness and health
were typical of her kind. But
she had lived so long that perhaps she had decided to stay.
C. Achebe, <u>Things Fall Apart</u>,
1958, p 72
She is an <u>ogbanje</u>, a free spirit.
<u>The Times</u>, 8/25/66, p 14
[< Ibo] See IBEJI.

ogi /'ougi:/, <u>n</u> a Nigerian dish
of porridge wrapped in a leaf
and served as breakfast.

Ogi could be prepared in a
much more advantageous way,
without altering its consistency, by copying the techniques
used in Latin America to produce "tortillas." Ogi accounts
for up to one-third of the total energy content in the Nigerian diet and many children
who are fed on it suffer from
malnutrition. <u>New Scientist</u>,
5/4/67, p 271
[? < Yoruba]

Ogun /'ougən/, <u>n</u> a Yoruban deity,
god of war and iron, retained in

certain cults of African origin in Latin America.

Today, many Nigerians of the region practice the deadly juju; some still swear only on hunks of iron in fealty to their blacksmith god, Ogun. Time, 8/6/65, p 40

In this long poem the Nigerian poet and dramatist associated Ogun, the Yoruba God of Iron and War, and Sango, the God of Lightning, with the pylons and tension wires of electrical power. Listener, 6/20/68, p IV Bewsher hit upon his celebrated idea of turning the thunder god Ogun into the god or more strictly the Saint of Electricity and Vital Energy. According to Mrs. Dobson he produced it immediately after supper and it was then quite new - an inspiration. J. Cary, An American Visitor, 1963, p 139
[< Yoruba]

ogusi /ou'gusi:/, n = EGUSI.
Stephen Spielman, a Brooklyn College student who has just returned from a year at the University of Nigeria, shared the student diet, which consisted of such things as ogusi soup, pawpaw, and fufu. New Yorker, 9/28/63, p 33

okapi /ou'kapi:/, n the well-known animal with a giraffe-like neck and leg stripes like a zebra.
[< a West African language]

Oklo phenomenon /'ouklou/, n a nuclear chain reaction that took place naturally during the accretion of a rich uranium deposit more than one billion years ago.
It appears that our planet earth may have produced its own nuclear reactor long before the human race existed - as much as 1,800,000,000 years ago. The evidence for this apparent event in the earth's history is known to scientists as the Oklo phenomenon. Grolier Science Supplement, 1976, p 140
[< Oklo the uranium mine in southeastern Gabon where this took place]

okoumé or okume /ou'ku:m/, n a large forest tree (Aucoumea klaineana) of West Africa; its semi-hard, pink-red wood, used in plywood.
The winds of change which sweep over all Africa are not stopped by any wall of mahogany and okoume trees. Schweitzer is still the great witch doctor to the old, but the young evolués dislike the hospital. Atlantic, 11/61, p 55
[< French okoumé < a West African language, ? ~ Akan o-kúm tree similar to oak]

okra /'oukrə/, n the well-known green vegetable.
[< a West African language ~ Akan ŋkrúmã okra]

Oldowan or Olduwan /'ouldə,wan/, adj of or relating to a stone-tool technology and culture of hominids living almost two million years ago in eastern Africa.
Composed roughly of primitive choppers, scrapers, and flakes, this technology has been called "Oldowan." The Oldowan design continued to be the basic tool kit of the Olduvai hominids for a million years, a staggering continuity! The stone-tool culture didn't remain static for the whole of that time, however. It gradually became more complex, so that by 1.5 million years ago there were more than ten identifiable implements in the tool kit compared with the six in the basic Oldowan. Mary Leakey named the "new" technology "Developed Oldowan." R. Leakey & R. Lewin, People of the Lake,

1978, p 89
The most outstanding find in
the first category is the discovery by Dr. Louis S. B. Leakey of an extremely primitive
skull and a tibia at Olduwai,
Tanganyika, at the level of
the Olduwan culture. This culture of the lower Pleistocene
is well known from various
parts of Africa and is particularly characterized by hammer
stones and choppers. Collier's
Encyclopedia Yearbook, 1960,
p 46
[⋖ Olduvai Gorge, a gorge in the
Rift Valley area of Tanzania
where artifacts of this culture
were first discovered ◄ Maasai
OLDUVAI]

olduvai /'ouldǝ,vai/, n a succulent plant, the bayonet aloe
(Sansevieria) of eastern Africa,
notable for its healing medicinal properties.
　　Twisting the thick ridged
　　leaves produces a clear liquid
　　which has remarkable powers
　　for healing open wounds, act-
　　ing both as an antiseptic and
　　as a natural bandage in binding
　　the wound together. Nomadic
　　peoples in the Rift use Oldu-
　　vai, as have two generations
　　of Leakeys following accidents
　　during field excursions. It is
　　certainly preferable to any-
　　thing that twentieth-century
　　pharmaceuticals can offer....
　　One wonders whether our an-
　　cestral hominids had discovered
　　the properties of the plant,
　　for it undoubtedly was growing
　　in those distant times past.
　　R. Leakey & R. Lewin, People
　　of the Lake, 1978, p 55
[< Maasai ol- singular noun pfx
+ duvai (root for) this plant]

olowo /o'louwou/, n a type of
hair style popular in West Africa.
　　The older style, called Olowo
　　in Yoruba, requires parting
　　the hair into sections and

meticulously combing and
braiding each section into
various designs. These styles
can be seen on wood carvings
and statues that date back to
the mid-19th century. New York
Times, 1/6/77, p 22
[< Yoruba olowu title of a chief
of Owu]

ol-umigumi /,oulumi'gu:mi:/, n
a plant eaten by Maasai warriors
to give them courage.
　　Leite...showed me a small plant,
　　ol-umigumi, taken as a stimu-
　　lant with meat before a lion
　　hunt. New Yorker, 9/16/72, p 67
[< Maasai　ol- noun pfx + umi-
gumi, ?< a Bantu language umi-
noun pfx + -gumi (root for) this
plant]

Omanhene /,oman'he:ne/, n the
paramount chief of the Fanti.
　　The Omanhene...jiggled by in
　　a palanquin carried by his
　　people. This powerfully big
　　man looked familiar. Where had
　　I seen him before? Then I re-
　　membered. The night before,
　　at a dance in the open court-
　　yard of a hotel at Sunyani, a
　　big man in a tuxedo had been
　　the master of ceremonies....
　　He had danced the "High Life,"
　　a sort of cakewalk, none too
　　sedate. "I go for this jazz,"
　　he had told me. It was the
　　Omanhene. National Geographic,
　　9/60, p 317
[< Akan oman state + -hene king,
chief]

Omukama /oumu'kamǝ/, n the title
of the chief or king of the
Nyoro and Toro peoples of Uganda.
　　The new agreement has been ac-
　　cepted by the Omukama and Ru-
　　kurato (council) of Bunyoro
　　and her Majesty's Government.
　　The Governor, in full uniform,
　　was greeted on his arrival by
　　the Omukama, resplendent in
　　his gold-braided and turquoise
　　blue robes and gold-tasselled

scarlet tarboosh. The Times,
9/5/55, p 6
[< Lunyoro omu- singular noun
pfx + -kama] See MUKAMA.

omuramba /oumə'rambə/, n a dry
bed or valley near a periodical
river in the Kalahari (and other
parts of Namibia).
[< Herero < omu- singular noun
pfx + -ramba (root for) this
area, ? ∿ dambo]

Oni /'ouni:/, n the title of the
king of Ife.
The Queen had approved the appointment of Chief Joseph Ode-
leye Fadahunsi as Governor of
the region in succession to
Sir Adesoji Aderomi, the Oni of
Ife. The Times, 1/1/63, p 9
Bronze head believed to be a
portrait of an Oni (ruler) of
Ife from about the twelfth
century. Atlantic, 4/59, p 55
[? < Yoruba or Edo]

o'nyong-nyong /ou'nyoŋnyoŋ/, n
a virus-caused disease similar
to DENGUE.
One of the most dramatic of
the new infections has been the
"huge epidemic" of o'nyong-nyong
which has swept through Uganda.
The symptoms of infection by
the o'nyong-nyong virus [are]
feverish paroxysms, pains in
the bones and muscles and swol-
len joints. New Scientist,
12/14/61, p 670
[< an East African language ∿
Swahili (ki)nyong'onyo (anything
causing) tiredness, weakness,
fatigue]

opah /'oupə/, n a large, brilliant-
ly-colored elliptical fish found
in the warmer parts of the Atlantic Ocean in West Africa.
[< Ibo uba]

opepe /ou'peipei/, n an African
tree (Sarcocephalus); its hard,
yellow-brown wood.
[< Yoruba opepe]

oribi /'oribi:/, n a rufous antelope of Africa with small,
straight horns.
[< Afrikaans < Nama orab]

orisha /'oriʃə/, n a Yoruba spirit
or deity worshipped in certain
Caribbean cults.
An orisha is personal, universal, and transcendental, and
each individual may have his
own orisha whom he worships.
Communication with the orishas
is possible through possession,
a trancelike state in which
the individual symbolically
takes on the characteristics
of the specific orisha he worships. E. James in P. Carril,
Shango de Ima (A Yoruba Mystery
Play), 1970, p 42
[< Yoruba]

Oromo /o'roumou/, n = GALLA.

Osagyefo /ousə'gyeifou/, n a
title assumed by Kwame Nkrumah,
former leader of Ghana.
His High Dedication is the lat-
ist title given Kwame Nkrumah
by his admirers, who once were
content with Osagyefo, or Re-
deemer. Time, 10/20/61, p 32
When he [Nkrumah] was installed
as President under a new re-
publican constitution last
July, the word went out that
he was to be referred to as the
Osagyefo, which is variously
translated as "mighty warrior"
and "deliverer from war and
maker of peace." Wall Street
Journal, 2/27/61, p 1
[< Akan]

Oshun /'ouʃən/, n a river goddess
of Yoruba origin, worshipped also
in Cuba and Trinidad.
The four hundred and one orisha
were worshiped there....Shango,
...Oshun,...and all the rest
were given their due sacrifices
and they were speaking to the
people through the kola nuts.
"When Life is Good for Us We

Become Bad" in C. Brooks (ed.), African Rhythms, 1974, p 52
[< Yoruba]

otavite /'outɔ,vait/, n a white crystalline mineral, a carbonate of cadmium.
[< Otavi town in Namibia where it was discovered]

ouabagenin /,wabɔ'dʒenin/, n a substance obtained by hydrolysis of OUABAIN.
[< OUABA(IN) + -genin]

ouabain /wa'baiɛn/, n a poisonous substance obtained from seeds of certain dogbane plants (Strophantus gratus) or from the wood of OUABAIO, used as an arrow poison (in northeastern Africa) and medicinally as a substitute for digitalis.
    Drugs which stimulate the sodium pump enzyme activity... appear to modulate memory formation during the lifetime of labile memory and can overcome cyclohexamide and ouabain induced amnesias. New Scientist, 1/25/79, p 263
    These [fetal mice] hearts responded normally to a number of cardioactive drugs, such as acetylcholine and ouabain. McGraw-Hill Yearbook of Science and Technology, 1971, p 53
[< French < Somali wabayo the plant from which the substance is obtained + -in chemical substance]

ouabaio /wa'baiyou/, n one of the two trees (Acocanthera) from which OUABAIN is obtained.
[See OUABAIN]

ouanga /'wɑɛŋgɔ/, n = WANGA. November 22 is a significant date in voodoo numerology, and Duvalier had cast a ouanga a mort ("death curse") on the President in May of 1963. Atlantic, 11/67, p 84
[< Haitian Creole, cf. WANGA]

Ovambo /ou'vambou/, n = AMBO.

Ovimbundu /,ouvim'bundu:/, n = MBUNDU.
[< Umbundu, said to mean people of the fog]

owala /ɔ'walɵ/, n an African tree (Pentaclethra africana) yielding a lubricant and cooking oil.
[< Mpongwe owala, ovala, obala owala tree]

oware /ou'wari:/, n = WARI. The most interesting buy is a game board for playing Oware, a pursuit game requiring skill and concentration. The Oware board is a rectangular piece of wood with 12 or 14 cups scooped into it; some boards are beautifully carved and decorated. (Commercial versions of Oware are available in the States: Kalah, by Products of The Behavioral Sciences, Oh-Wah-Ree, by the 3M Company. S. Boone, West African Travels, 1974, p 366

P

P, p, abbreviation of PULA, PESEWA. Finance. Monetary unit, pula, P1 = US$1.255. Collier's Encyclopedia Yearbook, 1979, p 187 Stake with Confidence. Your National Football Pools. Certified Dividends for 22nd March, 1980...22 1/2 Points...¢5596.80 for 1p...699.60 for 1/8p. Ghanaian Times, 4/22/80, p 5

Pahouin /'pawæ̃n/, n = FANG. [< French]

panga /'pæŋgə/, n a large, machete-like knife used for heavy work (in eastern and southern Africa). "Are they, so to speak, carrying any - how shall I say? - persuasive instruments?" I asked, suddenly conscious that my mucous membrane was coated with flannel. "Yes siree," declared the young man. "Pangas, and sharp ones." New Yorker, 8/14/54, p 23
Mr. John Gilbert, 20...and Miss Hilda Moses, 26, were walking to his home at 5 am on Saturday when a group of about 20 men threatened them with sticks, pangas and a firearm. The couple ran away. Argus (Cape Town), 1/21/80, p 9

--v to cut with a panga. Our cabin steward hearing that we were going to Kenya told me that as soon as Kenya got Uhuru we would all be pangaed! Punch, 3/30/66, p 465
[< Swahili, ? < Malay parang large, heavy knife]

pangola grass /pæŋ'goulə/, n a perennial grass (Digitaria decumbens) from southern Africa, used as pasture grass in the U.S. Other drought-resistant varieties are Pangola grass with roots six feet deep in three months, and Bermuda and Dallis grass with roots four feet deep in that time. Science News Letter, 12/12/53, p 377
[? < a West African (Bantu) language, ? < pa- locative noun pfx + NGOLA]

papa /'papə/, n an East African dish of shark meat, cooked with chili, coconut milk and salt. [< Swahili, literally, shark]

patha-patha /'patə'patə/, n a type of dance or dance music from black South Africa, popularized by Miriam Makeba in a song of the same title. Instead, Soweto families prefer to visit a beer garden for "Bantu beer" (made of slightly fermented maize), or a shebeen (speakeasy) for stronger drink and the sensuous local music

called patha patha. Time, 6/28/
76, p 34
[< Nguni, reduplication of patha
touch ∼ Swahili pata get, seize]

Pedi /'pedi:/, n a people of South
Africa akin to the SOTHO; their
Bantu language.

pembe /'pembei/, n a white clay
for coating the body in dances
and rituals associated with death
or sorrow (in central and western
Africa); MPEMBE.
In former times this dance was
part of an obedience ritual....
[The dancers] wore feather headdresses or raffia caps and
their bodies were coated with
white clay, or pembe. They
leapt around all over the place,
brandishing their weapons and
striking aggressive attitudes.
J. Paudrat in M. Huet, Dance,
Art and Ritual of Africa, 1978,
p 193
[? < Lingala or Bateke (a Bantu
language of Zaire]

pesewa /pe'seiwa/, n a unit of cur-
rency in Ghana, 1/100th of a
CEDI.
The pesewa means a penny in the
Ghanaian Fante language. The
Times, 7/14/65, p 11
A 30-year-old trader who sold
a spool of thread 30 pesewas
above the control price was on
Tuesday sentenced to a year's
imprisonment with hard labour.
Ghanaian Times, 11/8/79, p 8
[< Akan pésɛwa(bo) dark blue
seed of a plant, used as the
smallest gold weight]

Peul /pu:l/, n = FULANI.
[< French < Fulani pulo, sg. of
fulbe, the Fulani people; cf.
FULANI]

pili-pili /,pili:'pi:li:/, n Also,
periperi. = PIRIPIRI.
Those in search of Africa can
wave off the Texas beef in
preference to the filet of

zebu fried in palm oil and simmered in peanut sauce, or the
chicken Grand Bassam spiced
with pili pili until it whistles.
Saturday Review, 10/24/70, p 38
[< Swahili and numerous African
language, ? < Persian or Arabic]

pinder or **pindar** /'pindər/, n
the peanut (in southern U.S.).
[< Portuguese pinda < Kikongo
mpinda peanut]

piripiri /,piri'pi:ri:/, n spicy,
hot red pepper; a dish made with
such peppers.
Usually the traveler is presented with food that is no
more than a pale, vapid reflec-
tion of international cuisine.
But there is one notable excep-
tion: the so-called piripiri,
or hot-pepper dishes, utilizing
the tiny, ferocious peppers of
Mozambique. Piripiri is Mozambique's national favorite, and
its major contribution to the
art of cooking in Portuguese
Africa. L. van der Post et al.,
African Cooking, 1970, p 120
Calamari piri piri...is ready
when it turns a light brown
in color. To prepare the piri
piri sauce, mix all the ingredients except the tomato puree
in a pan and stir-fry. Weekend
Argus (Cape Town), 2/17/79, p 9
[< numerous African languages,
? < Persian or Arabic]

pishi /'pi:ʃi:/, n a cook (in
eastern, central and southern
Africa).
Although we had a big fire burning they marched right through
the camp and all the boys except Paulo the pishi were so
terrified they spent the whole
night up a tree and would not
come down even for their posho.
Paulo thought it all a huge
joke and could scarcely cook
dinner for laughing. Punch,
8/8/62, p 200
[< Swahili (m)pishi cook < -pika

(to) cook]

pitso /'pi:tsou/, n a tribal con-
ference or gathering of council-
lors among the Sotho (in Lesotho).
Eventually the Imperial Government grudgingly yielded to the
importunities of the Cape Cabinet, a pitso confirmed that the
Basuto wanted to be British
subjects, and Basutoland became
a Crown Colony in 1884. M. Benson in C. Legum (ed.), Africa,
A Handbook to the Continent,
1966, p 315
[< seSutu] See KGOTLA, LIBANDLA.

pombe /'pambei/, n beer, especially locally made from maize.
Nyerere set off at Christmas
on a tour of the country's
[Tanzania's] regions, deriding
farmers who left the work to
their wives while they dozed
in the sun sodden with "pombe."
Atlantic, 6/67, p 37
"Then kill me. Kill me in the
square by the Mosque of the
Day of Disaster and show the
people my head. Water the land
with my blood. I have no fear.
My ancestors bubble in the
earth like pombe brewing. The
thought of death is sweeter to
me than honey dipped from the
tree." J. Updike, The Coup,
1978, p 30
At night there was improvised
music – and pombe: no thin in-
dustrial fluid, but a thick,
yellow-brown millet brew, sour,
strong, satisfying as soup, the
delight of men who, like the
local road menders or the guides
we took on mountain walks,
would rather do a hard day's
work for a pot of beer, or of
waragi, the distilled spirit,
than for cash. The Times,
7/23/66, p 11
[< Swahili]

pombeiro /pam'beirou/, n a black
African or Portuguese slave trader hired by the Portuguese to

act as an interpreter or to
establish new trade routes.
Lastly there were the pombeiros, the "barefoot blacks" who
"are the agents of the aviados
for the retail trade; at this
they are skillful and always
give good account of their
loads."...This governor "for-
bade under pain of heavy penal-
ties the entry into the interior
of all whites, mulattoes, and
shod blacks, allowing permis-
sion only to the pombeiros."
B. Davidson, In the Eye of the
Storm: Angola's People, 1972,
p 92
[< Portuguese, said to be < an
Angolan language (? Mbundu) pombe
wilderness or pombo market, fair
+ Portuguese -eiro agent suffix]

pombo /'pambou/, n an East African
dish of okra boiled with chili
peppers and simmered with shrimp
or crayfish.
[< Swahili, literally, any
cooked, viscous vegetable obtained from a plant or tree]

pongo /'pangou/, n the genus of
apes that includes the orangutans.
[< Kikongo mpongo, mpongi, im-
pungu]

poor joe, n a blue heron, common
in the southern United States.
[< Gullah < Vai pojo heron]

Poqo /'poko/, n an outlawed black
nationalist guerrilla organization in South Africa, originally
an arm of the Pan Africanist
Congress.
This period coincided with two
holiday weekends when people
became disturbed by...rumours
that the Poqo terrorist organization was planning an upheaval
of some sort. The Times, 4/18/63,
p 8
The murders, which occurred
early last February, were the
work of the secret Poqo organization. New York Times, 7/31/63,

p 2
[< a South African Bantu language, said to mean "ourselves
alone" and "pure, completely"]

Poro /ˈporou/, n a men's secret
society among the Mende, Kru,
Kpelle, and Temne in Liberia and
Sierra Leone, exerting consider-
able political and social influ-
ence.
> The Poro secretly penetrates
> all life; birth, initiation,
> marriage, conflict and death
> are dominated by it more than
> the cathedral ever dominated
> the life of Chartres. Scienti-
> fic American, 5/67, p 161
[< Mende, Kru, Kpelle and Temne]
See SANDE.

posho /ˈpoʃou/, n a ration, especially of porridge made from
ground corn (in Swahili-speaking
areas).
> Albert, the fat-tailed sheep,
> thrust his comic rump up into
> the light, his sleek black
> head down into a bowl of posho,
> or cornmeal porridge. Harper's,
> 9/60, p 60
> East Africans will still pre-
> fer their posho to Chlorella
> and Western steak-guzzlers their
> prime Angus to cuts of hippo
> and kangaroo tail. New Scien-
> tist, 9/5/68, p 476
[< Swahili < -posha give rations
to]

poto-poto /ˌpoutouˈpoutou/, n an
adobe-like clay (in western and
central Africa).
> Once more in Nigeria, we are
> journeying southward toward
> the heavy forests. After the
> fatigue of dry, corrugated mo-
> tor roads and then the frustra-
> tion of sticking fast in the
> poto-poto, or slippery clay,
> it is a real delight to travel
> by pirogue, the gently gliding
> boats of the Niger Delta. Na-
> tional Geographic, 8/59, p 243

> The coveted house would more
> than likely have raised my eye-
> brows in other circumstances.
> There had been enough locally
> made bricks for the floors
> only; the walls were built of
> piles driven vertically into
> the ground, with the empty
> spaces filled with potopoto,
> Congolese style. L. Kenney,
> Mboka, 1972, p 13
[< numerous West African languages ~ Akan pɔtɔpɔtɔ slimy
sediment, cf. Poto-Poto name of
an area in Braazaville]

potto /ˈpatou/, n a lemur-like
mammal of Western Africa; the
sloth.
> Pottos are between lemurs and
> monkeys on what zoologists call
> the primate tree. New Yorker,
> 6/13/59, p 23
[< a West African language ~
Akan aposo ~ Wolof pata]

prama do /ˈpraməˌdou/, n communal gathering area of the Fanti.
> We are told of the communal
> life of our fore-fathers where
> people living in the same
> house gathered at one big hall,
> "prama do" (as the Fantis would
> call it) and had their meals
> in common. Ghanaian Times, 4/30/
> 73, p 6
[< Akan prama space or lane between houses]

pula /ˈpuːlə/, n a unit of currency in Botswana, equal to 100
THEBE.
> The introduction of Botswana's
> own currency, the pula, last
> month in place of the South
> African rand is an indication
> of the Government's growing
> economic self-confidence. The
> Times, 9/21/76, p II
> Estimated cost of the Works.
> Pula 335,000 equivalent to ap-
> proximately 320,000 European
> units of account. Weekly Re-
> view (Nairobi), 5/18/79, p 31

[< seTswana, literally, rain,
hope, blessing (and a term used
as a greeting) ∿ Swahili (m)vua
rain]

puku /'puːkuː/, n a reddish antelope (Adenota vardonii) similar
to the KOB and related to the
waterbuck.
 Territorial systems of breed-
 ing have been described in the
 waterbuck, in the Grant's and
 Thomson's gazelles and the com-
 parable southern springbok, in
 the hartebeest and topi and
 puku. The Times, 10/17/70, p 17
[< Zulu (m)puku]

putu /'puːtuː/, n a South African
dish of mealie-meal made into a
stiff paste.
 The Zulus could tell Dr. Botha

nothing about the child's origin, save her name....Mavis,
however, loved her soft mattress
and liked salads better than
the Zulu putu (porridge). Time,
9/28/53, p 28
[< Nguni (u)phutu porridge,
crumbly earth]

puza /'puːzə/, n an alcoholic
drink (in southern Africa).
 The slogans shouted at the
 meeting described what is on
 the minds of ZAPU officials
 and all nationalist politicians
 these days. First the speaker
 shouts, "Z," and the thunderous
 reply is "Zimbabwe," the nationalist name for Rhodesia. Next,
 he cries out, "ZAPU," and the
 refrain is Puza. Manchester
 Guardian, 7/30/78, p 17
[< Zulu (uku)phuza to drink]

Q

---

quagga /'kwagə/, n a wild ass
(Equus quagga) of southern Africa related to the zebra, now
extinct.
> A poster in one corner said
> "Extinct Is Forever" and pre-
> sented line drawings of van-
> ished creatures, each with the
> approximate year of its demise
> - quagga (1883), Cape Lion
> (1860), northern kit fox (1938).
> New Yorker, 2/19/79, p 75

[< Afrikaans < Nguni (i)qwara
something striped < Khoikhoin
qua-ha quagga (< onomatopeic
of its braying)]

quashee /'kwaʃi:/, n 1 (formerly)
a term for any black person,
especially of the West Indies;
2 variant of QUASSIA.
> Neighbors dosed each other
> with rhubarb and senna, castor
> oil, Daffy's Elixir, tea made
> of quashee root or nettles;
> they made plasters of honey and
> flour, onion, garlic, and deer
> fat. Atlantic, 11/66, p 102

[< an Akan proper name Kwasi
male child born on Sunday]

quassia /'kwaʃi:ə/, n a genus
of shrub or tr-e (Simaruba) of
the West Indies and South America; the drugs obtained from its
wood, used as a tonic, beer
additive, etc.

> Why not, then, fall back on
> the old alum solution spray or
> quassia tisane? Because in the
> first shower or misty day it
> becomes so diluted as to be im-
> potent. Sunday Telegraph, 3/8/
> 64, p 19

[< Graman (Grandman) Quassi or
Quacy, the name of a black Surinam slave who discovered its
medicinal properties < Akan
Kwasi (see QUASHEE)]

quelea /'kwi:li:ə/, n a type of
red-billed weaverbird of Africa.
> Sorghum has attracted consid-
> erable interest this year as
> an alternative crop to maize,
> especially in drought areas.
> Many farmers have grown the
> crop, but are now suffering
> damage caused by swarms of
> queleas. Rhodesia Herald,
> 2/23/73, p 20

[< New Latin quelea, ? < an East
African Bantu language ∾Swahili
kwelea climb to or on (a reference to the way these birds
climb onto their upside-down
hanging nests)]

Qwaqwa /'kwa,kwa/, n a homeland
(region in South Africa set a-
side by the government for
blacks) for the Sotho, located
in the Orange Free State.

R

Rada /'radə/, n a pantheon of
deities in the VOODOO cult of
Haiti; a cult surrounding this
pantheon.
   In this second definition,
Saraka resembles the Yoruba
cult of Shango in Trinidad
despite the fact that Rada, as
described by Andrew Carr, originated in Dahomey and came
here with Papa Antoine and his
ancestors. Sunday Guardian,
4/22/73, p 8
[< Allada town in southern Benin
and former capital of the Daho-
meyan kingdom]

ras /ras/, n 1 title of a prince
or overlord in Ethiopia.
   Haile Selassie I, then a noble-
man known as Ras Tafari, was
chosen regent in 1916, but
formal power was held by Em-
press Zauditu until 1938, when
Haile Selassie was crowned
Emperor. S. Blumenthal, Bright
Continent, 1974, p 361
2 a title or term of respect for
a RASTAFARIAN.
   The price to be paid for wrong
living is a heavy one. Ras
Hu-I explains: "The Paris peace
talks, SALT, all these things
cannot bridge the gap between
destruction and life. Not one
shall stand." T. Nicholas,
Rastafari, A Way of Life, 1979,
p 31

[< Amharic, literally, head,
prince < Arabic ra's head]

Rasta /'raestə/, n short for
RASTAFARIAN.
   When the plane landed and he
saw all those thousands of
weirdo, half-naked half-
stoned Rastas waiting to
greet him, Selassie was terrified. Maclean's, 12/13/76,
p 52

Rastafarian /raestə'fari: n/ or
Rastafari /raestə'fari:/, n
(adj) a member of a religion
popular especially in the Caribbean that deifies the former
ruler of Ethiopia, Haile Selassie.
   The first [trip] was to the
West Indies, where he [Haile
Selassie] was particularly
warmly received in Jamaica by
the Rastafari sect. Annual
Register, 1967, p 349
   Jamaica's ugly "Back-to-Afri-
ca" Rastafarian sect is back
in the news this month, though
only in an indirect fashion.
...The Rastafarians, or Rastas
as they are known colloquially,
haven't been in the news much
lately. San Francisco Chronicle,
12/26/63, p 42
[< Amharic Ras Tafari title
and surname of Haile Selassie
< ras RAS (head, prince) +
tafari < təfəri to be feared]

reg /reg/, n a flat, plain area
(in Ethiopia).
    After 20 miles of patches of
fesh-fesh, we run on the reg
that extends some 130 miles
to the first rest stop at
Tindouf. Reg is hard, flat
gravel. To the astonishment
of the skippers, it abounds
in acacia trees here. _National Geographic_, 11/67, p 710
[said to be < Amharic ~ ERG]

riga /ri:gə/, n a long, richly
embroidered robe worn by Hausa
men.
    Once a heavy smoker, Abubakar
swore off after his 1957 pil-
grimage to Mecca, now combats
the tensions of his job by
chewing the bitter kola nuts
that he keeps in the pocket of
his long white riga. _Time_,
12/5/60, p 25
[< Hausa]

ruga-ruga /,ru:gə'ru:gə/, n pl
mercenary warriors (in eastern
Africa).
    Another set of pressures were
a bitter fruit of the Ngoni
invasions and the rise of the
ruga ruga companies, tough
military units put together
from men who had lost homes
and families, from runaway
captives, and from all manner
of adventurers. These operated
in southern Tanzania and northern Malawi. Backed by ruga ruga
fighters, who served for pay
or for plunder, inland merchants or other ambitious men
went into the slave trade without mercy for anyone whom they
found in their path. B. Davidson, _History of East and Central Africa_, 1969, p 196
[< Swahili rugaruga messenger;
police in plain clothes, ? <
Arabic]

Rukurato /ruku'ratou/, n a council of the Nyoro people of Uganda.
    Mr. Kenyon Gowers - to whom a
number of sincere tributes
were paid at the ceremony -
drew up the new agreement
which has been accepted by the
Omukama and Rukurato (council)
of Bunyoro and by her Majesty's
Government. _The Times_, 9/5/55,
p 6
[< Lunyoro]

rungu /'ruŋgu:/, n a cane or
stick with a knobbed end, used
as a weapon (in eastern Africa).
    The dancers...in the main body
begin to leap straight up and
down, spears glinting in the
sun; they shoot the chin out
as they rise and stamp with the
right foot as they touch the
ground, and on each rise the
upright spears and clubs, or
rungus, are twirled all the way
around. P. Matthiessen, _Tree
Where Man Was Born_, 1972, p 64
We have some candidates who try
all sorts of tricks in their
bid to get votes. The worst of
these acts is the way wananchi
have been harassed and threatened by the so-called youthwing-
ers of a particular candidate
who, armed with rungus and
stones vow they will beat up
anyone who will not vote for
this particular candidate.
Innocent travellers are no ex-
ception to these. _Weekly Review
(Nairobi)_, 5/11/79, p 2
[< Swahili]

Rusanga /ru'sæŋgə/, n the
royal bull of the king of
Rwanda.
    The Royal Drum of Ruanda was
considered even more sacred.
A perpetual flame burned in
its honor and the people saluted it, just as they greeted
the King, with three hand claps.
The drum ranked equally with
Rusanga, the Royal Bull, and
both were equal to the King.
J. Hallet, _Congo Kitabu_, 1964
p 119
[< Kinyarwanda ru- singular

noun pfx + SANGA]

Rwanda /rə'wandə/, n Also, Ru-
anda. a country of eastern Africa bordering on Burundi, Zaire,
Uganda and Tanzania.
[< a Bantu language ? Kinyarwanda < rw- singular noun pfx +
-anda (root for) the Rwanda
people]

S

S, Sh or /, abbreviation or symbol for SHILINGI.

Saba Saba /ˌsabə 'sabə/, n 1 a
holiday in Tanzania commemorating
the 1954 founding of TANU (Tanganyika African National Union)
celebrated on July 7.
> A group of Africans celebrat-
> ing Saba Saba at the pombe bar
> milled out to greet the Land
> Rover as it rumbled down out
> of the hills. P. Matthiessen,
> Tree Where Man Was Born, 1972,
> p 213

2 saba-saba, n the Tanzanian
artillery barrages fired in the
1979 war with Uganda.
> Careening around the front
> car, we lurched between piles
> of rubble left by the terrible
> days of the saba-saba. Nation-
> al Geographic, 7/80, p 74
[< Swahili, literally, seven
seven, because July 7th is the
seventh day of the seventh month]

sabon gari /ˌsaboun 'gariː/, n pl
a district or settlement inhabited by non-Moslems, especially
Ibo workers, in Hausa areas of
Nigeria.
> The civil service posts...went
> largely to the Ibos, who lived
> in the Strangers' Quarters, or
> sabon garis, as segregated
> units. New York Times, 9/9/68,
> p 42

Crying "Heathen!" and "Allah!",
the mobs and troops invaded
the sabon gari, ransacking,
looting and burning Ibo homes
and stores and murdering their
owners. Time, 10/14/66, p 27
[< Hausa sabon strangers +
GARI²]

sadza /'sadzə/, n a Zimbabwean
dish of mealie-meal or cornmeal
paste.
> Infantry soldiers in black
> kit and camouflage are simply
> dropped off on a main road to
> walk into the jungle. There
> they may remain for two or
> three weeks without relief
> or resupply, living off the
> land or out of their rations
> (including rice and a thick
> African corn-meal paste called
> sadza). Time, 2/27/78, p 38
> The main complaint was about
> their confinement and the
> monotonous diet of sadza (a
> maize dish), porridge, coffee
> and meat. Some who have been
> in captivity for many years
> will need time to readjust to
> freedom. The Times, 4/14/78,
> p 9
> The abolition of discrimination
> has been felt more in the so-
> cial sector. Blacks have re-
> cently complained that hotels
> have not moved with the times
> in providing sadza (mealy

porridge) on their menus in
spite of it being their staple
diet. The hotels replied that
if there were sufficient demand
it would be provided. Manchester
Guardian, 3/11/79, p 7
[? < Shona or Nguni]

safari /sə'fari:/, n an expedition
for hunting or viewing wildlife;
any journey; trip.
I was on safari when I met the
Masai for myself. East Africa
overworks the word "safari."
It can mean anything from an
hour's drive to six months in
the bush with a white hunter,
15 African "boys," and a fleet
of cross-country safari cars.
My safari lay somewhere in
between. National Geographic,
9/60, p 336
The House Select Committee on
Assassinations...is attacking
the FBI, the CIA in particular
and law enforcement in general
with its idiotic safaris into
a criminal world it knows not
of. Time, 9/18/78, p 64

--v to go on a safari, trip,
journey, etc.
In Kampala, Uganda, where the
dollar used to bring 10 shillings on the black market,
safariing Americans were lucky
to get five. Time, 8/30/71,
p 15

--adj (in numerous attributive
uses:)
The place is amusing enough,
put popcorn on the car hood
and a baboon will check your
oil and water, then leave a
deposit on the windshield.
Johnny Weissmuller extras herd
the cars along, Land Rovered,
safari jacketed. National Review, 10/13/72, p 1140
Elsewhere, it is known by such
names as the safari suit and
leisure suit, but in Jamaica
the Kareeba - a stylized con-
traction of Caribbean attire
- is something special. Wearing

it is not only a question of
comfort and fashion. It is
politics as well. New York
Times, 3/24/76, p 51
There were sneers about commercial zoos (which actually make
money) and about safari-parks
(which have been making it paw
over fist) but all zoos have
to get the stuff from somewhere.
New Scientist, 5/11/72, p 335
[< Swahili, literally, journey
~ safiri travel < Arabic safariy]

Safohene /,safou'heinei/, n =
ASAFOHENE.
Tomorrow morning, Mr. Aggrey-
Fynn will be outdoored as the
new Safohene followed by the
funeral rites for his prede-
cessor in the afternoon. Ghanaian Times, 3/2/73, p 10

sakabula /sakə'bu:lə/, n a long-
tailed southern African bird
(Diatropura progne); the widow
bird of the weaver family.
With a Sakabula feather in
his hair and a leopard skin
around his waist, he [King
Sobhuza] danced with his warriors and watched his air
force...fly past. Maclean's,
9/14/81, p 50
[< Zulu (i)sakabuli]

salongo /sa'loŋgou/, n a rallying
cry or slogan in Zaire, calling
for a major development effort,
to make something work, etc.
The show currently in question
is next week's heavy-weight
title fight between champion
George Forman and Muhammad
Ali, and it's taking a heap
of salongo for the underde-
veloped African nation of 23
million to pull it off. Newsweek, 9/23/74, p 72
[< Lingala (ko)sala (to) work]

samango monkey /sə'mæŋgou/, n
a dark-headed, forest-dwelling
monkey (Ceropithecus labiatus)
of southern Africa, somewhat

like a vervet.
[? ◄ a southern Bantu language]

samba[1], n the well-known Brazilian
dance of African origin.
[Portuguese an African lan-
guage]

samba[2] /'sambə/, n = OBECHE.
[< a Nigerian language]

Sambo /'sambou/, n a derogatory
term for a black person, especially a black man or child.
I'm not going to reject that
man because some misinformed
person, some prejudiced person,
sees him as the embodiment of
Uncle Tom, or Sambo. Harper's,
3/67, p 83
[< the American story of Little
Black Sambo < West African personal names: Hausa Sambo, Mandingo Sambu, Wolof Samb, thought
to be ~ Kikongo nzambu monkey]

samosa /sə'mousə/, n a small meat
or vegetable pie, usually triangular in shape, popular in eastern Africa.
The three-cornered curry cook-
ies called samosas are still
the most popular sidewalk
snack, but now there is a ham-
burger stand on the circle in
the center of town. New York
Times, 1/27/67, p 64
[< Swahili, ? < Hindi]

sampan /'sampən/, n = TAMPAN.
[< Khoikhoin samban]

sancho /'saŋkou/, n a type of
simple guitar of West African
origin, with fiber strings and
a body consisting of a wood box
covered with animal skin.
[< a West African language ~
Akan (ɔ)sãnkú, Ewe sàngkú]

sanda /'sandə/, n a festival or
celebration among the Nuba.
With the harvest came festival
time, the days and nights of
the sandas - wild jamborees

of dancing, singing, and wres-
tling. The barren valleys
stirred with life, and between
December 15 and January 25 the
village chiefs arranged a score
of greater and lesser sandas.
They were staged in rotation
outside the seven Masakin villages. National Geographic,
11/66, p 692
[< Nubian]

Sande /'sandei/, n a women's
secret society among the Mende,
Kru, Kpelle, Temne and others in
Liberia and Sierra Leone, exerting considerable political and
social influence.
The bush society, which may
well have had a surreptitious
hand in those proceedings, is
probably the feature of Liberian life that has most impressed
- or appalled - foreigners who
have visited the hinterland.
There are two branches of the
society - one for the men,
called the Poro, and one for
the women, called the Sande.
Every member of the tribe must
belong, and the prestige of
the society is so great that,
outside the control exercised
by government officials, it is
the de-facto ruler of the country. The Poro and the Sande
hold alternate sessions, each
of which lasts three years.
New Yorker, 1/11/58, p 94
[< Mende sane ~ Kru, Kpelle and
Temne] See PORO.

Sanga or Sangu /'saŋgə or 'sa-
ŋgu/, n either of two breeds of
cattle: a long-horned cattle of
eastern and southern Africa called the Abyssinian ox; a cross-
breed of Zebu and other cattle of
western Africa.
These two breeds, Zebu and Sanga, have been of central importance to the growth and wel-
fare of the populations of East
and Central Africa. B. Davidson,
History of East and Central Af-

rica, 1969, p 22
[? < a Bantu language ~Kinya-
rwanda -sanga < RUSANGA;?< Amharic]

Sango[1] /'sæŋgou/, n = SHANGO, the
Yoruba god of thunder and lightning.
> If the patient hears voices
and cannot sleep, he must pla-
cate Ogun, the god of iron...
If he sees and talks to spirits
it is Sango, the god of thunder, who must be appeased. Harper's, 12/65, p 59
[< Yoruba]

Sango[2], n a Niger-Congo (Adamawa-
Eastern) language used as a lin-
gua franca in the Central African
Republic.

Sangoan /'sæŋgouən/, adj of or relating to an Achuelean culture of
Africa characterized by the use
of hand axes as picks and working
tools.
> At some time around 50,000 B.C.
bands of Achuelean hunters entered the Congo basin (later
than the Kalambo Falls settlement). They quickly discarded
their axes for wood-working
tools, evolving a culture called Sangoan. Science News,12/4/-
65, p 361

sangoma /saŋ'goumə/, n a witchdoctor or diviner among the Zulu,
usually a woman, capable of detect-
ing witches.
> The three witches are trans-
formed into sangomas (witchdoctors) who upset all Western
notions of the sinister by con-
ducting jolly dances round the
cauldron shaking with seemingly innocent laughter. The
Times, 4/4/72, p 6
[< Nguni isangoma]

sansa /'sænsə or 'sænzə/,n = SANZA.

sanyan /'sænyæn/, n a type of
fawn-colored clothmade in Nigeria.
See the quotation under ETA.
[?< Yoruba]

sanza /'sænzə or 'sænsə/, n
= ZANZA (a thumb piano).
> The woman, it is rumored,paints.
The children, the neighbors
attest, take violin, piano, and
sanza lessons. The small black
man can be seen sitting at
round white tables along the
Quai. J. Updike, The Coup, 1978
1978, p 316
[< ZANZA]

sapara /'sapərə/, n a West African gown for men, made of light-
weight fabric with sleeves that
fold back over the shoulders.
> One evening after the day's
shooting, for example, American Negro Actor Raymond St.
Jacques wandered into the
Plage bar dressed in a gaudy,
pajama-like African garment
called a sapara, accented by
a gold earring in his left
ear. Time, 2/3/67, p 33
[?< Yoruba]

sapele /sə'peli:/, n a West African tree (Etandrophragma cylindri-
cum); its mahogany-like wood.
> Desk tops, in six sizes come
in oak, sapele, teak, rosewood
and laminate, and are lacquered
to give a non-glare scratch-
resistant finish. The Times,
9/5/73, p 14
[< a West African language
sapele or sapeli]

saphie or saffi /'sæfi:/, n a
talisman, amulet, or charm from
West Africa.
[< Mandingo safaye, ? < Arabic]

Sara /'sarə/, n a people of Chad
and Central African Republic;
their Nilo-Saharan (Chari-Nile,
Central Sudanic), spoken widely
in southern Chad. See UBANGI.

Sardauna /sar'daunə/, n a spiritual leader of the (Muslim) Hausa
of northern Nigeria.
> Major Chukwuma Nzeogwu, 29...
once even led his troops
through a mock invasion of

the sprawling white palace of
Sir Ahmadu Bello, the Sardauna
(Emir) of Sokoto, religious
leader of 12.5 million Nigerian Moslems, boss of the nation's
ruling political party, and
the real power behind the Ba-
lewa government. Time, 1/28/66,
p 19
At the heart of our real life
political drama was the theatri-
cal figure of the Sardauna: as
rich, cruel, and power hungry
as any who might step from the
pages of "The Duchess of Malfi."
Manchester Guardian, 2/17/66,
p 7
[< Hausa]

Sarki /sar'ki:/, n a Hausa ruler
of a small agricultural area;
later, a ruler of a city.
If one sought a Hausa word to
render "Prince," "Sarki" would
seem to be the best one. Manchester Guardian, 2/24/66, p 15
[< Hausa; sarkin is the form
used in connective constructions]

Sarwa /'sarwə/, n a name for the
San ("Bushman") people or their
language (in Botswana).
[< a Bantu language < MASARWA]

sasabonsam /ˌsasə'bounsam/, n a
mythical, evil forest-dwelling
monster of the Ashanti, a tall
creature with long legs and feet
which point both ways.
The Government men opposite
him in Parliament apologized in
private that the party system
would force them to vote for
something they knew to be wrong.
In his final speech on that
occasion he spoke about a monster of Ghanaian folklore
called Sasabonsam, who lives
in the forest and eats children; when he runs out of other
people's children he is driven
to eat his own. Later, when
some of Nkrumah's men joined
him in prison, having fallen
foul of the dictator, he was

able to say, "I told you so."
The Times, 8/10/77, p 14
[< Akan sasabonsam, ? < sāsā to
haunt + ɔbonsám devil]

sassaby /'s s bi:/, n a hartebeest (Damaliscus lunatus) of
southern Africa, dark purple
with a black back and face.
Herds of eland, kudu, tsessebe
(or sassaby), impala, and diminutive duikers detoured skit-
tishly within a stone's throw
of our car as we circled the
roadless veld. National Geographic, 6/35, / 774
[< seTswana tshêsêbê]

sassywood, n a West African tree
(Erythrophloeum guineense) that
yields a poisonous bark used in
ordeal trials; a medicine man
who determines wrongdoers by
ordeal trials.
These accounts often contain
gruesome anatomical details,
and are sometimes accompanied
by an editorial demand for
the reinstitution of trial by
sassywood, a judicial process
in which the suspect drinks a
deadly poison...and supposedly
recovers from it if he is innocent. New Yorker, 1/11/58,
p 89
"The cash register was robbed,"
said Reggie. "The manager
called the police. They could
not find the thief. So the
manager called the sassywood,
the medicine man. He set palm
oil to boiling in an iron kettle and dropped in a pin. 'Take
the pin out,' said the old
sassywood to the suspects. The
innocent ones felt only a cool,
damp sensation as they reached
in their arms. The guilty one
did not dare try. He would
have been badly burned." National Geographic, 9/60, p 310
[< a West African language ∼
Akan sésé Ewe séséwú]

saza /'sazə/, n a county in the

Buganda kingdom.
Mr. Kintu is a saza chief, and
his wife is the daughter of Sir
Aplo Kagwa, who was Katikiro
from 1889 to 1926. The new Katikiro was chairman of the Lukiko drafting committee which
went to draw up new Buganda
agreements in London. The Times,
8/25/55/, p 6
[< Luganda]

seafari /'si:,fari:/, n a pleasure
trip by sea.
[< sea + safari]

Sechuana /,se't∫wanə/, n = SETSWANA.

sekere /'sekərei/, n a percussion
instrument, similar to a maraca,
made from a calabash (in West
Africa).
Unlike Jamaican reggae, it is
difficult to understand without
a grounding in fundamentals.
There is a heavy, driving sound
from an unusual array of instruments: Western drums, trumpets
and trombones mixed in with
Konga drums, lip sticks and the
sekere. New York Times (Mag.
Sec.), 7/24/77, p 11
[< Yoruba shɛkɛre gourd; cf.
Jamaican English shaka] See
SHAKAREY.

Sekiapu /seki:apu:/, n = EKINE.
The funerary screens of deceased
heads of trading houses in the
Kalabari towns of Degema, Bu-
guma and Abonnema...were made
for them in their capacity as
chiefs in the Ekine cult, otherwise known as the Sekiapu
('Dancing People') society, and
they were represented on them
in the headdresses which they
were entitled to wear in the
Ekine plays in honour of the
Water Spirits. W. Fagg & M.
Plass, African Sculpture, 1964,
p 87
[< Ijo]

Senegal /'senə,gal/, n a country

of West Africa bordering on
Guinea, Guinea-Bissau, Gambia,
Mauritania and Mali.
[< French, said to be < Zenaga
a name for the Berbers of Mauri-
tania]

sengi /'sengi:/, n a unit of cur-
rency in Zaire, 1/100th of a
LIKUTA.
[? < Kikongo]

senti /'senti:/, n a unit of currency in Tanzania, equal to
1/100th of a SHILLINGI.
[< Swahili < English cent]

Senufo /sə'nu:fou/, n Also, Senou-
fo. a people of Ivory Coast, Mali
and Upper Volta; their Niger-
Congo (Gur) language.

Serer /sə'rer/, n a people of
Senegal; their Niger-Congo (West
Atlantic) language, also known
as Serer-Sin.

seSutu or SeSutu /se'su:tu:/, n
Also, seSotho or Sesotho. the
Bantu language of the SOTHO.
[< seSutu se- singular noun
(language) pfx + sutu Sotho]

seTswana or Setswana /se'tswanə/,
n the Bantu language of the Tswana,
the national language of Botswana.
[< seTswana se- singular noun
(language) pfx + TSWANA]

shakaray /'shakərei/, n a stringed
musical instrument of West Africa, made from a calabash.
A Ghanaian band played on a
drum, a guitar and a stringed
gourd called a shakarey, as
models swirled by in caftans
and bubus made of batiks and
the fascinating embroideries
of the African tribes. New
York Times, 5/21/76, p B2
[< Yoruba shɛkɛre gourd; see
SEKERE]

shamba /'∫æmbə or ∫ambə/, n a
farm, garden, or agricultural

plot (in eastern Africa).
> So we went up only as far as
> the Land-Rover could go, through
> the verdant coffee plantations
> that march up the mountainside.
> Africans own most of these
> thriving shambas, selling their
> crops through a cooperative.
> National Geographic, 9/60, p 341
> The court was told that the land
> belonged to a Mr. Kiprotich arap
> Chuma who had rented his land
> to the accused in 1977. Mr.
> Chuma learned that Matheri had
> obtained the loan by taking his
> shamba as security. (Nairobi)
> Standard, 2/23/79, p 7
[< Swahili, thought to be ultimately < French champ field because the Zanzibaris learned
about clove plantations from
nearby, French-speaking Mauritius]

sham(m)a or shemma /'ʃamə or
'ʃemə/, n a white shawl or wraparound, toga-like garment with
patterned trim, worn by men and
women in Ethiopia.
> The Ethiopian independent
> fighting man - Shifta, they're
> called - is a long, rangy in-
> dividual dressed in a white
> polo-necked shirt called a
> shama tucked into riding breeches,
> with long leather boots, a belt,
> full of brass cartridges. Lis-
> tener, 8/29/68, p 269
> Unlike other East Africans,
> who like bright colors and pat-
> terns, Ethiopians prefer white.
> The traditional costume is
> shama, which consists of a
> dress (kemise) and head cover-
> ing. This dress, in handwoven
> white cotton gauze with silk
> borders, was designed to order
> by Alem Zewd Imru. New York
> Times (Mag. Sec.), 4/11/76,
> p 99
> Children in bright blue, yellow
> and scarlet clothes clapped
> enthusiastically when the Em-
> peror approached. Behind them
> stood groups of elders dressed
> in shemma. The Times, 5/19/72,

p 8
[< Amharic šemma]

Shangaan or Shangane /ʃaŋ'ga-
n(ə)/, n a people of Zimbabwe,
Mozambique and South Africa;
their Bantu language.
[< Zulu shangane wanderer]

Shango /'ʃæŋgou/, n the Yoruba
god of thunder and fertility;
a cult in Africa, Trinidad and
Brazil worshipping this god.
> The rich legacy of myth and
> legend of Spanish, Amerindian,
> and African art remains....The
> talking drums of shango and
> gayal did not die with older
> generations. They provide the
> deep reservoir from which the
> entertainment of today's
> younger artistes flows. Sunday
> Guardian, 4/8/72, p 17
> I would guess that Shango in
> his latest avatar may be on the
> way to becoming the god or
> let's at least say the emblem
> of a second Cuban revolution.
> And why not? Massive + [sic]
> agile, masculinely sexual but
> recognizing his good female
> strengths + red colorations in
> likeness of Saint Barbara, he's
> got what it takes, not least
> of all his hot tropical light-
> nings + the sweet angry African
> face that's so true to Cuba's
> life + revolutionary potential.
> J. Rothenberg in P. Carril,
> Shango de Ima (Yoruba Mystery
> Play), 1970, p 25
[< Yoruba]

Shankalla /,ʃæŋ'kalə/ or Shangalla /ʃaŋ'galə/, n a derogatory term in Ethiopia for a non-
Arab or non-Ethiopic black tribesman, especially one from the
western lowlands.
[< Amharic šank'illa a black
person; Negro; ? < GALLA]

sharo /'ʃarou/, n a male initiation rite of the Fulani, in which
each young man must withstand

blows from a stick without be-
traying emotion.
    Probably the Fulani themselves
have the best explanation: The
sharo is simply a test of endurance and courage which tough-
ens young men to bear suffering
without complaint and to prove
themselves before taking a
bride. Youths who wince during
the performance are disgraced
in the eyes of the young women.
National Geographic, 8/59, p 239
[< Fulani]

shauri /'ʃauri:/, n business; affair; concern; intention (in
eastern Africa).
    The rest of my friends simply
had no time for her [Margaret
Thatcher]. "The only saving
grace is that Britain is now
a toothless bulldog in international affairs. If they prefer to be ruled by two women,
the Queen and the Thatcher woman, it is their shauri," one
of my friends observed. Weekly
Review (Nairobi), 5/25/79, p 48
Anyhow, the wretched thing disappeared without a trace, and
of course I lost my head and
started a big shauri about
everybody being searched. New
Yorker, 12/26/70, p 22
[< Swahili < Arabic]

--shauri ya Mungu, the concern
or affair of God; fate.

shea tree /ʃei or ʃi:/, n a West
African tree (Butyrospermum
parkii) with rough bark and a
nut that yields an oil to make
shea butter.
    Certain trees may be left
standing; trees such as the
baobab which are too big; and
those which supply people and
animals with food e.g. oil
palm and shea trees. Ghanaian
Times, 3/12/73, p 4
[shea < Bambara si this tree]

Shebuja /ʃei'bu:dʒə/, n the title
of a Tutsi overlord (in Burundi).

[< Kirundi]

shenzi /'ʃenzi:/, n a derogatory
term for a black African considered "uncivilized," "uneducated," or "heathen"; stupid
(person) (in eastern and central
Africa).
    "Same old me," Brian grinned
...and gestured mockingly at
himself. "Same old shenzi shanty
Irish. No change in me. It's
you who've changed." R. Ruark,
Uhuru, 1962, p 21
[< Swahili, literally, barbarous,
uncivilized, ? < Persian] See
BASHENZI.

sheytani or shetani /ʃei'tani:/,
n the devil (in eastern and central Africa).
    The complex demon world of
Zanzibar encroaches - especially
I felt by night - on the all-
things-are-explicable world
of the hard-working socialist
state. Side by side with the
huge housing blocks and cocktail hour at the modern bar
of the Hotel Ya Bwawani, people
profess to see ghostly Arab
ladies disappear before their
eyes on country roads and tell
you that the sea before vener-
able Africa House is perennially
afflicted by a sheytani or
devil who lives in the caves
where he claims a fresh victim
every year. Geographical Magazine, 6/79, p 649
"The claw of an eagle and the
bone of a Mutwa, rolled up in
a dog's placenta and wrapped
in banana bark. That will protect you from harm!" Andre
rolled his eyes at Kamende and
expressed his own opinion: the
lion was Shetani himself. J.
Hallet, Congo Kitabu, 1964,
p 349
[< Swahili shetani evil spirit,
devil, Satan < Arabic]

shifta /'ʃiftə/, n an outlaw,
bandit, or insurgent (in eastern

Africa).
> About 1,000 shiftas - armed
> nomads of the Western Somali
> Liberation Front - periodically
> mount hit-and-run attacks along
> the Somali frontier. Time,
> 5/23/77, p 46
> East African poaching is carried
> out by Somali shifta (raiders)
> who, according to Talbot, are
> "supported, backed and armed
> by Russians..." ICUN's Adrian
> Phillips likened the ruthless
> shifta to "highly organized
> and militaristic bands of
> pirates." Science News, 11/17/79,
> p 348

[? < Somali, said to mean wanderer; ? < Amharic šift ~səffətə he rebelled]

shillingi or shilingi /ʃi'liŋgi:/,
n a shilling (in eastern Africa).
> Out in the bush I have encoun-
> tered Masai herdsmen whose
> stoic disregard of hardship
> and danger compelled my admira-
> tion. But I have also seen
> Masai beg money from tourists,
> with harsh cries of "shillingi!
> shillingi!' in return for
> posing for a photograph. Nation-
> al Geographic, 2/69, p 194

[< Swahili shilingi < English]

shimiyana /,ʃi:mi'yanə/, n an alcoholic drink of southern Africa,
made from fermented treacle and
water.
> Armed clashes between police-
> men and 1,000 Africans claimed
> at least nine lives in Cato
> Manor, a Negro township outside
> Durban, South Africa. The vio-
> lence started when police went
> to Cato Manor to search for
> shimiyana, a deadly native brew
> made secretly. Wall Street Jour-
> nal, 1/25/60, p 1

[< Zulu (isi-)shimeyana]

Shona /'ʃounə/, n a people of Zimbabwe and South Africa; their
Bantu language.

shrimpi /'ʃrimpi:/, n a bush partridge (Francolinus subtorquatus)
considered a delicacy (in South
Africa).

[< Zulu swempe]

shuka /'ʃu:kə/, n a piece of calico, worn as a toga-like garment
or as a skirt (in eastern Africa).
> Across the border in Tanzania
> the authorities are now getting
> the Masai out of their red
> ochre and blankets and into
> trousers, or at any rate into
> pants worn under their shuka.
> The Times, 10/17/71, p 39

[< Swahili, ? < Arabic]

Shum /ʃum or ʃəm/, n a village
chief (in Ethiopia). See the
quotation under DEJASMATCH.

[< Amharic šum ~šomə rule]

siafu /si'afu:/, n a small, reddish-brown driver ant.

[< Swahili]

sik sik wat /sik sik wot/, n an
Ethiopian dish, a WAT of beef
stewed in red pepper sauce and
served with INJERA.

[< Amharic]

simba /'simbə/, n lion; a rebel
group in Zaire.
> Stuffed simba "roars" at ad-
> mirers through the window of
> Zimmermann's shop in Nairobi.
> The sight of a life-size lion,
> even a stuffed one, awes not
> only tourists but many Afri-
> cans as well. Many native-born
> Kenyans living in well-settled
> areas have never seen a lion,
> buffalo, or elephant in the
> wild. National Geographic,
> 2/69, p 185
> The Simba uprising of 1964
> under the banner of the martyred
> Patrice Lumumba, tore the Con-
> go apart all over again after
> the Katanga secession had been
> put down. The Simba, a jungle
> army of tribal warriors high
> on dope and the exhortations

of witch doctors, held Stanley-
ville in a savage reign of ter-
ror for 110 days. Harper's,
4/76, p 53
[< Swahili]

simbil /'simbil/, n a white-bellied
African stork (Sphenorhynchus ab-
dimi) having a greenish and brownish plumage. Also, simbere.
[? < a southern African language]

simi /'simi:/, n a short, two-edged
sword or long knife (in eastern
Africa).
Mr. Kenyatta presented them to
the cheering crowd as they
handed over their arms to him
- two home-made guns and a
few knives and simis. The Times,
12/17/63, p 6
[< numerous East African languages: Kikuyu, Kamba, Maasai;
~ Swahili sime]

simsim /'simsim/, n sesame (in
eastern Africa).
Maximum Prices of Controlled
Commodities...Goods:...9. Simsim
1/90 per kg.; 10. Pure White
Maize Flour (Posho) 1/20 per
kg. Voice of Uganda, 2/23/73, p 7
[< Swahili < Arabic]

Sindebele /,sinda'beilei/, n the
Bantu language of the NDEBELE.
[< Sindebele si- singular noun
(language) pfx + ndebele]

sirige /'sira,gei/, n a mask of
the Dogon topped by a high blade
which exhibits patterns of parallel lines and opposing triangles,
creating the image of a multi-
storied house.
The dancer of greatest skill
and strength wore the...sirige
mask, 15 feet high. National
Geographic, 3/69, p 447
The sirige mask has a rectangular face divided by a verti-
cal ridge with two hollowed
spaces....Several meanings are
concentrated into this term.
There are the different stages

of creation, the degrees sever-
ing the earth from the sky, the
curve of the arch, the genetic
sequence, and also, in the ver-
tical parallel lines, the front-
age of the ginna or 'family
house', representing by analogy
the vast human family. J. Paudrat
in M. Huet, Dance, Art and Ritual of Africa, 1978, p 101
[< Dogon, literally, storied
house]

siSwati /si'swati:/, n the Bantu
language of the SWAZI.
[< siSwati si- singular noun
(language) pfx + swati Swazi]

sitatunga /sita'tunga/, n an
aquatic, greyish-brown antelope
(Tragelaphus spekei)with a white
mark between the eyes.
[< a Bantu language, ? < Tonga,
? < Swahili sita six + tunga tail
bones, perhaps a reference to the
six white stripes on its back]

siwa /'si:wa/, n a large horn of
ivory, wood or metal, formerly
used as a symbol of chieftaincy
in eastern Africa.
The building was later occupied
by a string of District Com-
missioners. The museum is a
celebration of the Lamu and
Bajuni cultures, containing
exhibits of carved doors and
chests, antique ebony thrones
inlaid with bone and ivory,
rich costumes, embossed and
incised silver, long canoes
and dhows and siwas - great
horns of ivory or brass, jeal-
ously guarded symbols of kingship, usually sounded only on
state occasions. New York Times
(Sec. 10), 10/26/80, p 17
[< Swahili < Arabic]

snofari /'snoufari:/, n a walking
trip or hike in snowy or moun-
tainous regions, usually with
skis.
Tourists are invited to take
a 20-mile guided snofari for

£15, space suits included.
The Times, 12/12/70, p 5
[< snow + safari]

sobosobo /,soubou'soubou/, n a
plant (Solanum nigrum) of southern Africa yielding a berry similar to the blackberry and sometimes made into jam.
[< Nguni umsobosobo < um- singular noun pfx + sobosobo (root for)
this plant]

Sobukwe clause /sou'bu:kwei/, n
a South African law giving police
greater powers of arrest and de-
tention, especially of political
dissidents.
  Obituaries. Robert Sobukwe...
  spent 18 years in prison or
  under severe government restric-
  tions aimed at neutralizing his
  political power; the "Sobukwe
  clause," an open-ended deten-
  tion of political dissidents,
  was...enacted in response to
  his case. Compton's Yearbook,
  1979, p 272
[< Robert Mangaliso Sobukwe
(?1926-1978), black nationalist
political leader and founder of
the Pan African Congress in the
1950's]

sodabi /'soudəbi:/, n a potent
schnapps-like drink of Benin,
made from palm kernels.
[said to be < the proper name
of a European who brought stills
to Dahomey]

sokoto /'soukoutou/, n a men's
garment of tunic and trousers
(in Nigeria).
  One robber dressed up for his
  execution in the stylish traditional garb of lace-trimmed
  buba and sokoto. London Sunday
  Times, 9/26/71, p 9
[< a West African language]

Somali /sə'mali:/, n a people of
Somalia, Ethiopia and Kenya;
their Afroasiatic (Eastern Cushitic) language.

[< Somali; said to be < somaal
< so- go maal to milk, because
of their liking for camel's milk]

Somalia /sə'mali:ə/, n a country
of eastern Africa bordering on
Ethiopia and Kenya.

somalo /sə'malou/, n a unit of
currency in Somalia; a Somali
shilling. Pl.: somali.
  The budget of the trust territory was balanced at 113.2 million somali in 1958 (the somalo equals U.S. $0.14). Ameri-
  cana Yearbook, 1962, p 689
[< Italian < Somali the people
of Somalia]

Somba /'sambə/, n a people of
northwestern Benin; their Niger-
Congo (Gur) language.

Songhai /saŋ'gai/, n Also, Songhoi.
a people of Mali; their Nilo-
Saharan language, a separate
language family.

songololo /songə'loulou/, n a
millipede (Juras terestris) of
southern Africa that coils up
when frightened.
[< Nguni songololo ~ukusonga
to roll up < uku- infinitive pfx
+ -songa ~ Swahili songa(ma) be
rolled together + -olol- itera-
tive suffix]

Soninke /sa'ninkei/, n a people
of Mali and Senegal; their Niger-
Congo (Mande) language.

Sotho /'soutou or 'souθou/, n
BASOTHO; their Bantu language,
SESUTU.

soukala or soukhala /su:'kalə/,
n a round house or dwelling with
a conical, thatched roof and
sometimes two doors (in Togo
and Ivory Coast).
  The road between Mango and
  Dapango is not only picturesque
  - undulating terrain sprinkled
  with soukala - but passes

through a region inhabited by
the Moba people, the traditional clothing of whose women is
(or was, as recently as independence) bunches of leaves
fore and aft hanging from a
belt. S. Blumenthal, Bright
Continent, 1974, p 258
[< French < a West African lan-
guage]

sufuria /sufə'ri:ə/, n a metal
cooking pot (in eastern Africa).
A temporary ban on the following items has been imposed until further notice. The reason
is that most of them are produced locally and some appear
to be of a luxury nature:
Radios and radiograms. Grama-
phones and tape recorders.
Passenger cars. Matches....
Electric and non-electric ket-
tles, cooking utensils, sufurias and karais. Voice of Uganda,
2/23/73, p 1
[< Swahili < Arabic]

sukuma wiki /sə'ku:mə 'wi:ki:/,
n an East African dish of ground
beef, served with rice and IRIO.
[? < Kikuyu or < Swahili sukuma
push, roll out (dough) + wiki of
unknown meaning; (Swahili for
week, < English, but the connec-
tion is obscure)]

suman /su'maŋ or su'man/, n a charm
or amulet with supernatural
powers (among the Akan).
[< Akan sumaŋ, diminutive of
asumãmma charm]

sumuni /sə'mu:ni:/, n a coin of
Ethiopia.
[< Amharic, literally, one-
eighth < Arabic; cf. Swahili
thumni one-eighth < Arabic]

suni /'səni: or 'su:ni:/, n a
tiny, graceful brownish-gray
antelope (Nesotragus moschatus)
of eastern and southern Africa,

with ringed horns.
[? < a Bantu language]

sunsum /'sunsəm/, n the soul,
or spirit (among the Akan); the
soul or spirit of all the Akan
people as contained in the gold-
en stool.
Ashanti tribesmen "stool" their
chiefs, rather than crown them,
and hide the Golden Stool, containing their sunsum (soul),
to prevent its capture. Newsweek, 6/28/54, p 41
[< Akan sunsúm; cf. Jamaican
English sunsum the soul of man]

Susu /'su:su:/, n Also, Sousou.
a people of Guinea and Sierra
Leone; their Niger-Congo (Mande)
language.

Swahili /swa'hi:li:/, n a people
of Kenya and Tanzania; their
Bantu language, a national language of Tanzania and Kenya.
[said to be < Arabic sāḥil
coast; the self-designation for
the language is KISWAHILI]

Swazi /'swazi:/, n a people of
Swaziland; their Bantu language,
also known as SISWATI.
[< Mswazi name of a Swazi king]

Swaziland /'swazi,laend/, n a
country of southern Africa bordering on South Africa and Mozambique.

syli /'si:li:/, n a unit of currency in Guinea.
The latter part of the year was
dominated by the introduction of
of a new currency, the "syli."
The aim was partly to find out
who had been profiteering in
Guinea francs, as all the money
had to be changed within a
week. Annual Register, 1973,
p 254
[< Susu, literally, elephant,
the symbol of the Guinean Democratic Party]

T

t, abbreviation of TAMBALA (symbol used on postage stamps).

Taata /'taəta/, n a term of respect for a man among the Baganda; a father or paternal uncle. We were seated in the mud hut of Sarah's uncle, Taata Musa - Father Moses. Among the Baganda, fathers and paternal uncles are called taata, mothers and maternal aunts maama. National Geographic, 7/80, p 78
[< Luganda; ? ~ Jamaican English taata father (or grandfather) ~ Chiluba tatu, Kimbundu tata, ~ Ngombe, Ewe tata] See BABA.

tabby /'tæbi:/, n a cement-like material of oyster shells, lime, sand and water. Meanwhile, 150-year-old mansions of tabby are slowly going to ruin while old women inside sit by and cling to another age. Saturday Review, 4/22/72, p 12
[(< Gullah tabi) < a West African language ~ Wolof tabax wall of a house made of sand, lime, mud; ~ Hausa ta'bo mud; ~ Kikongo and Chiluba ntaba muddy place where building mud is obtained]

tabernanthine /tæbər'nænθi:n/, n a bitter, crystalline alkaloid usually found in IBOGAINE.
[< New Latin tabernanthe genus name of the ibogaine plant < a central African language + English -ine chemical suffix]

tabki /'tabki:/, n a small pond in the savannah regions of northern Nigeria.
[< Hausa]

tagati /tə'gati:/, n adj bewitched; under the spell of a witchdoctor or witchcraft (in southern Africa). They found a couple of unbroken bottles, and knocking the tops off drank the contents. But they had not allowed for the expansion caused by the fizz in the wine, and feeling themselves swelling, rolled about in the bottom of the boat, calling out that the good liquor was "tagati". I spoke to them from the vessel, and told them that it was the white man's strongest medicine, and that they were as good as dead men. H. Haggard, King Solomon's Mines, 1885, p 29
[< Nguni umthagathi wizard] See ABATAGATHI.

taha /'taha/, n a black and yellow weaverbird (Euplectes taha) of southern Africa.
[< Zulu taka]

talakawa /,talə'kawə/, n a free

164

man among the Hausa; the common folk.

In a region ruled by the emir aristocracy, Abubakar's rise was especially noteworthy, for he was a talakawa, child of a poor commoner. Time, 3/7/60, p 29

[< Hausa]

talla /'talə or 'tələ/, n an Ethiopian beer made from barley and GESHO leaves.

The ensuing night-long palavering around a campfire, while the horn beakers of talla, the local beer, passed from mouth to mouth, robbed me of much-needed sleep. National Geographic, 12/70, p 878

[< Amharic]

tambala /tæm'bælə/, n a unit of currency in Malawi, equal to 1/100th of a KWACHA.

In 1971 a new decimalized currency was introduced, the kwacha (dawn) which is subdivided into 100 tambala. Statesman's Yearbook, 1980, p 814

[?< Chichewa or Chinyanja, said to mean cockerels]

tambookie or tambouki /tæm'bu:-ki:/, n a shrub or tree (Erythrina acanthocarpa) of southern Africa; its light wood.

[< Afrikaans tamboekie a member of the Tembu people (< tamboe Tembu) + -kie diminutive suffix]

--tambookie grass: a grass (Sorghum verticilliflorum) of southern Africa used for thatching.

tambouti /tæm'bu:ti:/, n a southern African tree (Spirostachys africanus); its fragrant, golden-yellow wood.

[< Afrikaans tamboetie < tamboe Tembu, a tribe of southern Africa + -tie diminutive suffix]

tampan /'tæmpæn/, n a southern African tick (Argasidae) with a venomous bite; a chicken or fowl tick.

[< seTswana tampane < Khoikhoin samban]

tango, n the well-known Caribbean dance.

[< American Spanish < a Niger-Congo language ~ Ibibio tamgu to dance]

Tanganyika /ˌtæŋgə'ni:kə/, n name of a former territory in East Africa, now part of TANZANIA.

[< Tanga town in northeast Tanzania, formerly an important trade center + NYIKA]

tann /tan/, n Usually tannes, pl. long, flat land areas in Senegal, especially marshy depressions near the rivers; the soil of these areas.

Other soils or special cases include alluvial soils, cultivated mainly in drier areas (they are avoided in wetter areas because of the dangers to health and flooding problems in valley bottoms);... 'poto-poto' or estuarine clays of the south-west, suitable for cultivation if flushed free of salt or sulphur; and 'tannes', the highly saline alluvium of the Senegalese estuaries. A. Mountjoy & C. Embleton, Africa, New Geographical Survey, 1966, p 615

[? < Wolof]

Tanzania /ˌtænzə'ni:ɔ/, n a country of East Africa bordering on Zambia, Zaire, Burundi, Rwanda, Uganda, Kenya and Malawi comprising Tanganyika and Zanzibar.

[< Tanganyika + Zanzibar + -ia]

tanzanite /'tænzəˌnait/, n a rare, semi-precious stone discovered in Tanzania, a variety of zoisite consisting of calcium-aluminum silicate and ranging from yellowish-green to brown, blue and violet.

Tiffany's, the international jeweller which first promoted Tanzanite, is helping to launch tsavorite, a green grossular garnet first discovered in the Teita hills. The Times, 12/14/76, p V
[< Tanzania + -ite mineral suffix]

tata /'tatə/, n a family compound or village of the Somba consisting of two-storied thatched houses joined by turreted walls.
The Somba live in...tatas, the walls of which are embellished with circular turrets. Animals and equipment occupy the ground floor, while the family members live above. The principal activity of each unit is centered about the enclosed courtyard. R. Kane, Africa A to Z, 1961, p 102
[< Somba]

Tata, n father; a term of respect for a man (in southern Africa).
[< Nguni utata; cf. TAATA]

tchi-wara /tʃi:'warə/, n = CHIWARA.

teff or tef /tef/, n an Ethiopian cereal grass (Eragrostris abyssinica) with grain that yields a nourishing white flour, used in making INJERA.
Grain - particularly teff, which is specially fine stuff made from a prairie grass harvested only in Ethiopia is in very short supply. It is not available in the kebele stores, and the bread lines in front of the commercial stores testify to the demand. The price of teff, which now manages about seventy-five cents per kilogram, has, I was told, gone up four hundred per cent in the past year. New Yorker, 7/31/78, p 49
[< Amharic t'əf, t'ef ~Tigre taf]

tej /tedʒ/, n an Ethiopian beverage made from fermented honey; mead.
The restaurant was in a tukul, the traditional Ethiopian dwelling, actually just a mud hut. We sat on the floor cross-legged on monkey skins, and drank a great amount of tej, the wine of the country, a delicious kind of mead. It's sleep-inducing stuff, and the pauses in our talk grew longer. Punch, 4/17/63, p 567
[< Amharic t'əj]

--tej-bet: a popular, inexpensive wine bar.

tembe /'tembei/, n a low, rectangular hut of eastern Africa with a lean-to roof that is flat or sloping to the rear; a compound of such huts.
The food, some of it brought in from the coast, was excellent - chicken, lamb, sherbet, almonds, and gumdrops - and the tembes were furnished with Persian carpets and magnificent bedding. New Yorker, 5/14/60, p 154
Here the land becomes flat and the space between the square earth houses, the tembes, widens, and tufts of dry grass where footsteps neglect to tread evoke the savanna that once flourished here, before goats and God killed it. J. Updike, The Coup, 1978, p 123
[< Swahili]

tembo /'tembou/, n an alcoholic drink (in eastern Africa).
Kidogo dug into his only adornment, a leather pouch, and handed Brian a flat, dented silver flask which contained tembo - Scotch whisky. The time for tears was over. Now it was time for a couple of drinks to celebrate, and then they could drive back to camp. R. Ruark, Uhuru, 1962, p 20
In the evening some Africans would be found playing cards and draughts. Others would be

drinking some stinking muni-
cipally brewed drink - 'Tembo'
- at Pumwani as an outlet for
their handicapped life. R.
Gatheru, Child of Two Worlds,
1965, p 104
[< Swahili, literally, palm wine]

Temne /'temnei/, n a people of
Sierra Leone and Liberia; their
Niger-Congo (West Atlantic) lan-
guage.

temtem /'temtem/, n a headpiece
or turban (in Ethiopia).
His turbanlike temtem, the
standard headpiece of debteras
and married priests, shadowed
his face; I could not see his
eyes well enough to know whether
he winked. National Geographic,
12/70, p 877
[< Amharic təmtəm]

tere siga /tə'rei 'si:gə/, n an
Ethiopian dish of raw meat, often
beef cubes with a red pepper
sauce.
[< Amharic t'ire siga]

thahu /'θahu:/, n a charm, curse,
or spell (of the Kikuyu).
In his small Kikuyu village,
Mugo is set apart; frail and
unprotected, he has been since
infancy under a...thahu, so he
cannot join in the games or
the training of his peers.
Saturday Review, 2/18/67, p 42
They had the power, too, to
remove the curses known as
'thahu', that wicked people
were supposed to have placed
upon others, or that men brought
upon themselves. R. Gatheru,
Child of Two Worlds, 1965, p 1
[< Kikuyu]

thebe /'θeibei/, n a unit of currency in Botswana, equal to
1/100th of a PULA.
The new unit - the pula, which
will be divided into 100 thebe
- will have the same value,
however, as the rand. New York

Times, 8/15/76, p 6
[< seTswana, literally, shield
(part of Botswana's national
emblem)]

thiebou-dien /'chebu:,dʒin/, n
a Senegalese stew of rice, fish
and vegetables.
[< Wolof]

thingira /θiŋ'gi:rə/, n a Kikuyu
hut that only a man or men may
occupy.
Brian had been a full-fledged
Game Warden with a neat stone
house and uniformed askaris
and flowers in the boma....It
was a nice house, primly painted
and achingly neat, but it was
sternly and antiseptically a
bachelor hut, a thingira, and
it needed a woman's touch to
make it more homelike. R. Ruark,
Uhuru, 1962, p 35
Our homestead, like that of
all other Kikuyu families, included two circular houses
made of logs and with thatched
roofs. One was for my mother
and the young children and was
called a 'nyumba'. One was for
my father and the older boys
and was called a 'thingira'.
In the centre of both the nyumba and the thingira was a
stone fireplace used for cooking. R. Gatheru, Child of Two
Worlds, 1965, p 18
[< Kikuyu]

tiang /'ti:æŋ/, n a topi of West
Africa, especially a small, pur-
plish red Senegalese topi (Damaliscus korrigum tiang).
[< Dinka]

Tigre /tə'grei or 'ti:grei/, n
an Afroasiatic (Semitic) language
spoken in Ethiopia and Eritrea.

Tigrinya or Tigrina /tə'gri:nyə/,
n Also, Tigrigna. an Afroasiaitic
(Semitic) language of Ethiopia
and Eritrea, closely related to
GEEZ.

167

tikolosh(e) /tiːkə'louʃei/, n
= TOKOLOSHE.
    "They're following a little man
    no bigger than a boy - he's got
    hair all over his body and a
    long white beard, and claws in-
    stead of fingers." The mothers'
    hearts froze. For this, they
    knew at once, was Tikoloshe -
    the evil sprite who tempts South
    African black men to murder and
    worse...who has the power to
    lure children away with tales
    of a marvelous playland, which
    leaves their brains addled for
    life...Tikoloshe is invisible,
    of course, to all but children
    or evil men. Time, 7/23/56,
    p 51
[< Xhosa utikoloshe]

timbila /tim'biːlə/, n = MBIRA
(in southern Africa). See the
second quotation under KALIMBA.
[< a Bantu language ti- noun
pfx + mbila variant of MBIRA]

Timkat /tim'kat/, n the Ethiopian
festival of the Theophany.
[? < Amharic]

tin-apa or tinapa /'tinəpa/, n
a Ghanaian dish of smoked fish,
especially canned fish in tomato
sauce.
    Somehow, after independence, we
    failed to understand why our
    money should be used for capital
    projects, such as the Akosombo
    Dam, and not for bringing in
    more milk and tin-apa. Ghanaian
    Times, 11/8/79, p 4
    He likes simple food. For break-
    fast he may have orange juice
    and tinapa. He is fond of cara-
    bao milk with coffee. New York
    Times (Mag. Sec.), 1/9/55, p 47
[< English tin + Akan apa(taa)
fish]

tipoye /tə'poiyei/, n a chair
somewhat like a hammock mounted
on poles and carried by four or
more men (in central Africa).
    The official habitually travelled

by tipoye, the native sedan
chair. New Yorker, 10/22/66,
p 231
    My goal would be achieved
    neither by standing aloofly by,
    the member of a "superior" and
    "civilized" race, nor by en-
    forcing any rigid system of
    regulations and punishments,
    and certainly not by riding in
    a tipoye and playing Bwana Mu-
    kubwa. J. Hallet, Congo Kitabu,
    1964, p 25
    Chief Bulukulu, who had arrived
    unobserved and had listened
    from his tipoye, carried by a
    team of four husky Africans,
    broke the spell. L. Kenney,
    Mboka, 1972, p 96
[? < a Zairean language]

tjwala /'tʃwalə/, n a beer made
from maize in Swaziland.
    The main food item for ema-
    Swati is porridge and the
    mealie-meal or sorghum...Further,
    emaSwati brewed beer - tjwala
    for everyday drinking, cere-
    monies and festivities. Times
    of Swaziland, 7/6/73, p 11
[< siSwati ~ JOALA]

tocusso /tə'kuːsou/, n an Ethiopian
cereal grass (Eleusine tocussa)
with edible seeds used to make a
black bread.
[< Amharic tokusso]

Togo /'tougou/, n a country of
West Africa bordering on Ghana,
Upper Volta and Dahomey.
[said to be < Ewe, literally,
behind the sea, a reference to
a tiny coastal village where the
Germans first established themselves in the 1800's]

toich /'touiːtʃ/, n an inundated
marshland area used in the dry
season for pasturage (in southern
Sudan).
    High water in the river spills
    over the banks and inundates
    large areas of toich land. New
    Scientist, 4/20/78, p 141

Lush pastures are available as the waters recede and the cattle are brought down to feed on toich grass and water meadows. The Times, 1/10/78, p 10
[< Dinka]

tokoloshe /,toukə'louʃei/ or tokoloshi /,toukə'louʃi:/, n Also, tokolossi(e). an evil or mischievous spirit in the form of a small man living in the water who entices children and is believed capable of causing adults to commit evil deeds (in southern Africa).
They accept that Dr. Mangane has chased away the tokoloshe, or evil spirit. The Times, 1/31/66, p 8
And all the time I am praying, "Jesus, Our Saviour, get me out of this long-grass before these damn tokolossies catch me for the Devil." New Yorker, 2/1/64, p 27
We younger children, even my Kaffir playmate, Pete, had too healthy a fear of the tokoloshi to interfere with her. The Times, 7/27/64, p 12
[< Zulu utokoloshe] See TIKOLOSHE.

tolly or tollie /'toli:/, n a male calf (in southern Africa).
Large Slaughter Stock Sale... 500 Prime Sheep 500. Also Afrikaner Tollies And Heifers. Cape Times, 3/7/59, p 17
[< Xhosa intole]

topi /'toupi:/, n a large antelope (Damaliscus korrigum) with a purplish-brown coat.
Some, such as wildebeest, kongoni and topi eat grass and herbs; rhinoceros browse on thorn bush; and the giraffe bite off the leaves and small branches of taller trees. New Scientist, 8/24/61, p 453
[< a West African language ~ Mende ndopa, ndope antelope]

tora /'torə/, n a reddish harte-beest (Alcelaphus tora) of northern and eastern Africa.
[said to be < Amharic tora]

tote /tout/, v to carry. n a haul; a large handbag.
[? < a West African language Kikongo tota pick up, Kimbundu tuta carry, load ~ Swahili tuta pile up, carry]

toto /'toutou/, n a child (in eastern and central Africa); a disrespectful term of address for a black man.
The word toto (child) when referring to African filling station attendants or grocery clerks has been publicly condemned, and the preferred term is now "rafiki" (friend). San Francisco Chronicle, 12/21/63, p 8
LOCAL and IMPORTED FOOTWEAR for LADIES, GENTS and TOTOS at VERY LOW PRICES Maridadi Footwear, Tom Mboya Street. Weekly Review (Nairobi), 5/11/79, p 27
[< Swahili (m)toto child]

toubab /'tu:bab/, n a usually derogatory term for a white person in West and Central Africa; originally, a white doctor.
The last elephant north of the Grionde gave up its life and its ivory in 1959, with a bellow that still reverberates. "The toubabs took the big ears with them," is the popular saying. J. Updike, The Coup, 1978, p 16
Dr. Dedet had served as toubab [sawbones] in just such a North African village. Saturday Review, 2/3/68, p 25
The arrival of toubab - foreigners - was a great event. The whole village crowded round as we talked to the 77-year-old chief, who was dressed in a yellow robe. National Geographic, 11/80, p 602
[? < French < numerous West African languages < Arabic]

touraco /'tu:rəkou/, n a large
bird (Musophagidae) of west and
central Africa with brilliant
feathers and crest, related to
the cuckoo.
[< French < a West African lan-
guage]

Transkei /'trəens,kei/, n a homeland (region in South Africa set
aside by the government for blacks)
for the Xhosa, located in three
scattered sections of Cape province. Although granted independence by South Africa in 1976,
it is not recognized as a nation
by the United Nations.
  The bill granting statutory
  authority for the independence
  of the 200-mile strip of territory on South Africa's Indian
  Ocean coast provides that any
  person who is "culturally or
  otherwise associated" with the
  Xhosa tribe will cease to be
  a South African citizen on Oct.
  26, the date set for Transkei
  independence. New York Times,
  5/27/76, p 4
  A measure of South Africa's
  reputation in this area has
  just been accorded by Freedom
  House, a respected American
  body which keeps a constant
  watch on levels of political
  rights....In terms of rights,
  our latest ranking is low and
  in terms of civil liberties it
  is worse - in the second-from
  bottom group along with countries such as Cuba, Zaire,
  Transkei and Tanzania. And
  along with Russia. It is not
  enviable company to be in.
  Star (Johannesburg), 1/26/80,
  p 9
[< Latin trans- across + Kei
river in South Africa]

tro-tro /'troutrou/, n a truck or
van in Ghana, especially one
used for carrying passengers.
  Ghanaians run lorries called
  "tro-tros" transporting people
  and goods around the country

with great efficiency. "They
all want feeder roads to meet
up with the main roads, and
this just isn't on," says Mar-
chant. New Scientist, 9/16/76,
p 597
A spokesman for the [State
Transport] corporation said
42 mini-buses currently being
used as "tro-tro" to convey
workers to and from their of-
fices had been drafted to
supplement the fleet. Ghanaian
Times, 4/19/73, p 12
[< Akan, ? reduplication of tro
three-pence (a reference to the
fare); but cf. trotro slippery
(stick) perhaps a reference to
the shifting lever in a truck]

tsama /'tsamə/, n a type of water-
melon from southern Africa.
  They poured the juice of a
  Tsama melon on the hairy side
  of the skin and began to rub
  vigorously with a rock that
  had been worn smooth by usage.
  Maclean's, 2/10/62, p 40
[< Afrikaans < Khoikhoin (Nama)
tsamas; ? ~ Sandawe tanga]

tsavorite /'tsavə,rait/, n a rare,
semi-precious stone similar to
a garnet, first discovered in
the Teita hills near Tsavo Park
in Kenya.
  New kinds of gems also appeared
  during the year. The best of
  these was a vanadium-bearing
  grossular garnet (Tsavorite)
  from near the Tsavo National
  Park in Kenya. Having several
  of the best gem characteristics of emerald, it gained
  instant popularity. Britannica
  Book of the Year, 1976, p 421
[< Tsavo a Kenyan national park
in the southeast + English -ite
mineral suffix]

tsessebe /'tsesə,bi:/, n =
SASSABY.
  "Come where the elephants,
  giraffes, klipspringers and
  tsessebes play...there's no

other playground like it," proclaimed the South African Air-
ways early this year. Maclean's,
3/6/65, p 9
Some of these animals are threatened with extinction in parts
of southern Africa. In Rhodesia,
efforts are being made to save
the last of the tsessebe, the
fleetest of the hartebeest. The
Times, 10/9/65, p 9

tsetse, n the well-known disease-
carrying fly of Africa.
[< a Bantu language ~ seTswana
tsetse ~ Luyia tsiisi flies]

Tshiluba /tʃi'lu:bə/, n = CHILUBA.

tshwala /'tʃwalə/, n a beer made
from maize in South Africa.
For that weekend-long occasion,
105 oxen, 50 antelopes, seven
buffaloes and 20 wildebeests
were slaughtered and eaten,
washed down with thousands of
gallons of tshwala, a native
beer. Time, 12/13/71, p 17
[< Zulu (u)tshwala ~ TJWALA ~
JOALA ~ Luyia amalwa beer]

tsitsinga /tsi'tsingə/, n a West
African dish of marinated beef
skewered and cooked over a grill
and coated with a vegetable mixture with corn flour.
[< a West African language]

tsotsi /'tsoutsi: or 'tsotsi:/,
n a black hoodlum or street thug
in urban South Africa, often
young and flashily dressed.
Every day a quarter of a million
people travel in and out of
Soweto to work in Jo-burg, by
car, taxi, bicycle...They are
terrorized every payday by the
tsotsis, the young thugs who
stab in the back, rob, and
leave the dead jammed upright,
or attack out of the dark on
the street with long sharpened
bicycle spokes, hitting above
the coccyx; instant paralysis.
Maclean's, 9/20/76, p 35

The pickpockets - or tsotsies
as they are known by Africans
- are usually African juveniles
who operate in groups of two
to six. They're as wily as foxes
and as slippery as snakes. Rhodesia Herald, 3/23/73, p 10
[< Nguni (uku)tsotsa (past tense,
-tsotsile) to dress in exaggerated clothing; thought to be ultimately < English zoot suit]

tsumebite /'tsumə,bait/, n an
emerald-green mineral of Namibia.
Formula: $Pb_2Cu(PO_4)(OH_3)$
[< Tsumeb region and town in
northern Namibia + English -ite
mineral suffix]

Tswana /'tswanə or 'tʃwanə/, n a
people of Botswana and South Africa; their Bantu language,
seTswana.

tufuhene /tu:fə'heinei/, n a sub-
chief in Ghana.
[< Akan (o)tufo warrior armed
with a gun + -hene king, chief]

tukl /'tu:kəl/, n = TUKUL (among
the Nuba).
Five Mud Tukls and a Covered
Courtyard Are Home to a Nuba.
Only entrance is the keyhole-
shaped doorway to the tukl at
right, which is a reception
hall. Adjoining, on left, is
a bedroom; next, only partially
shown, a beer storage room;
then a granary; and finally a
cookhouse. National Geographic,
2/51, p 271
[? < Nubian, ? < Arabic]

tukul /'tu:kul/, n a circular
stone dwelling with a thatched
roof (in Ethiopia).
Coptic priests - several hundred of them, to be sure, and
their families - live in tukuls.
R. Kane, Africa A to Z, 1961,
p 126
Where churches had once stood
by the hundreds, there remained
only ashes and blackened stones.

"Most were rebuilt," I was told by Ato Kebbede Mikael, Ethiopian Minister of Antiquities and trustee of the Ethiopian Archaeological Institute. "But strangely, they are in a new style that usually uses a circular ground plan, probably based on the tukul, the omnipresent Ethiopian rural house." National Geographic, 12/70, p 869
[? < Amharic, ? < Arabic]

tulu /tu:lu:/, n a unit of measurement equal to approximately three gallons, used in Nigeria.
[< Hausa tulu bottle, pitcher, ewer]

Tumbian /'tᵊmbi:ᵊn/, adj of or relating to a Stone Age culture of eastern and central Africa.
Any account of the affinities of a new discovery is usually studded with references, oblique or direct, to Choukoutien in north China, the Trinil beds of Java, the Australopithecines of the South African veldt or, worse, the names of the specialized industries of Europe and Africa such as the...Kafuan from Uganda, Natufian from Wadi en-Natuf in Israel, Obanian from Argyllshire or the Tumbian from the Lower Congo basin. New Scientist, 3/25/65, p 798
[< Tumba lake in Zaire where artifacts of this culture were discovered]

tumboa /tᵊm'bouᵊ/, n a plant (Welwitschia) of the Namib desert in southwestern Africa.
[< a language of southwestern Africa]

Tutsi or Tusi /'tutsi: or tu:si:/, n a people of Burundi and Rwanda, also known as WATU(T)SI; their Bantu language.

tuwo /'tu:wou/, n stiff porridge made from guinea corn among the hausa; FUFU.
First my mother sent me to another neighborhood to gather the customers' empty bowls. I also collected the money from our regular customers. My mother put the tuwo in the bowls and told me the amount of money to collect for each. Then I delivered them to the customers. Natural History, 6/81, p 47
[< Hausa]

Twa /twa/, n a "pygmy" people of Rwanda and Burundi.

twala /'twalᵊ/, n = TSHWALA.

Twi /twi: or tʃwi:/, n a people of Ghana; their language, considered a dialect of AKAN.

tzetze /'tsetsi:/, n = TSETSE.

U

Ubangi /yu'bæŋgi:/, n a name given to a woman of the Sara people who uses plugs and discs to distend the lips and ears as a mark of beauty.

The Ubangis' principal claim to the public's curiosity rested on the fact that their women wore plates, or saucers, in their lips. More specifically, they affected a small plate in the nether lip and a smaller saucer in the other. New Yorker, 4/18/53, p 50
[< Ubangi river in West Africa]

Ubangiji /yubaŋ'gi:dʒi:/, n the supreme deity of the Hausa.
[< Hausa, literally, father of the home < uban master]

ubuhake /ubu'hakei/, n a feudal-like system in which Tutsi cattle owners dominated Hutus as serfs, abolished in Rwanda at independence.

Efforts in the direction of overcoming the "Ubuhake" system, under which cattle-holding is a form of wealth, rather than a means of consumption, are slowly making headway, thus enabling breed improvement for dairy and meat. Collier's Encyclopedia Yearbook, 1957, p 598
[? < Kinyarwanda ubu- abstract noun pfx + -hake ~ Swahili haki a just share]

ubuntu /u'buntu:/, n basic humanity; the finer, nobler qualities of mankind or of human nature, especially such qualities found in or exemplified by black (South) Africans.

It seems to me Peter Dreyer sees the blacks of South Africa as Moses to humanity, leading mankind by the African ethos of ubuntu - "the practice of being humane" - out of the 20th-century community of self-destruction....This is an intellectual and spiritual concept of the highest order, and one that puts to shame those who have regarded the African ethos as the sum of superstitious fears from which the black man is released by substitution of imported, imposed spiritual and philosophical concepts. But can one speak of "the African" with this total identification of moral absolutes, assuming that every black lives by his traditional values of ubuntu, any more than one can speak of "the Christian", or "the Jew", assuming these whites live by their traditional values: fully realized, unchanging, as laid down by their prophets and thinkers? New Republic, 8/16/80, p 38
[< Nguni ubu- abstract noun pfx + -ntu ~ Swahili u-tu human nature,

m–tu person~ BANTU, MUNT]

ugali /u'gali:/, n porridge made
from maize (in eastern and central
Africa).
> With his wood ladle he stirs
maize meal into boiling water
to make the thick white paste
called ugali that is subsistence in East Africa; ugali,
eaten with the fingers, is
rolled into a kind of concave
ball used to mop up whatever
is at hand in the way of meat,
vegetables, and gravy. New
Yorker, 9/30/72, p 70
> Several little markets have
since sprang up at various
points, let alone roadside
hawkers who are doing a thriving
business selling anything from
uji to Ugali. The labour force
from both the company and the
outgrowers look forward to
such lunches by the roadside.
Sunday Nation (Nairobi), 2/24/80,
p II

[< Swahili u- (abstract) noun
pfx + -gali (root for) this food]

Uganda /yu"g nd /, n a country
of East Africa bordering on
Rwanda, Zaire, Sudan, Kenya and
Tanzania.
[< Swahili u- (abstract) noun
pfx + ganda; adaptation of BU-
GANDA]

ugubu /u'gu:bu:/, n a one-stringed
musical instrument of the Zulu
with animal skin stretched over
a gourd resonator.
> A visitor from the city makes
himself at home, strumming an
ugubu while his host's wives
prepare the evening meal. The
kraal of a well-to-do Zulu
usually includes a Great House.
National Geographic, 12/71,
p 745

[< Zulu, ? < u- singular noun
pfx + -gubu ~ INGUBU animal skin
(used for clothing)]

Uhuru /u'hu:ru:/, n 1 freedom, in-

dependence from colonial rule.
Kenya will not likely be led
again by so dominating a man
as Kenyatta. He was at least
a generation older than most
African leaders, and he was
working for uhuru (independence)
before some of them were born
...He also gave Kenya a stability and prosperity that most
African states would envy.
Time, 9/4/78, p 25
> In the new states of black Af-
rica the generation of Uhuru
- of independence - has been
replaced by new men - "black
Europeans" - who drive Mercedes-
Benzes and send their children
to European schools and boast
of the number of white teachers.
New Republic, 6/9/79, p 38
2 a holiday celebrated on August
11 by members or followers of
the Afro-American US organization
to commemorate the uprising in
Watts (California). See the quotation under KUZALIWA.
3 an artificial earth satellite
launched off the coast of Kenya
in 1970 to detect and analyze
X-ray emissions.
> The X-ray astronomy satellite
that NASA had approved was...
named Uhuru, the Swahili word
for freedom. "Before Uhuru,
it was really a game," says
Giacconi. "I...had my very own
personal channel of communication, or telephone line, to
nature. Uhuru was really a
lucky child. It was so beautiful, the data coming in." Dis-
cover, 12/80, p 69

[< Swahili u- (abstract) noun
pfx + huru free, emancipated
< Arabic ḥurr free-born, <
ḥurrīya freedom]

ujamaa /u:dʒa'ma(ɔ)/, n 1 a form
of Tanzanian socialism based on
traditional concepts of the extended family, the social community, and self-help projects.
> He began by outlining Julius
Nyerere's ujamaa ("familyhood"

in Swahili) philosophy, the concept of rural socialism based on...self-help and the dignity of the individual, and, as a result, on the gradual transfer of power from the federal government to the local community. New Yorker, 12/6/76, p 129

<u>2</u> a cooperative farm established under this principle.

An "ujamaa" is roughly a community of peasant farmers who have gathered together, pooling their labour and equipment, investing the fruit of their common work in community projects. There are 4,400 such communities in Tanzania and 11 per cent of the mainland population lives in them. Manchester Guardian, 1/6/73, p 17

[< Swahili, literally, familyhood < <u>u</u>- (abstract) noun pfx + <u>jamaa</u> family; ultimately < Arabic <u>jama'a</u>] See NYAYO.

uji /'u:dʒi:/, <u>n</u> a thin gruel or soup of rice served especially for breakfast (in East Africa).

Several little markets have since sprang up at various points, let alone roadside hawkers who are doing a thriving business selling anything from <u>uji</u> to Ugali. The labour force from both the company and the outgrowers look forward to such lunches by the roadside. Sunday Nation (Nairobi), 2/24/80, p II

[< Swahili]

ulendo /u'lendou/, <u>n</u> a trip, journey, or SAFARI (in central and western Africa).

The men of the district administration, living for long periods at small and remote stations and going frequently on "ulendo", or trek, to villages miles from the roads, live close to the people and their everyday problems. Manchester Guardian, 10/22/59, p 5

The writing [The Diary of a District Officer by Kenneth Bradley] is breathless, headlong stuff, much of it jotting on <u>ulendo</u>. Manchester Guardian, 5/12/66, p 10

[< a Bantu language < <u>ul(u)</u>- noun pfx + <u>endo</u> ~ Swahili (w)endo a going < -<u>enda</u> (root of) go]

Umbanda /um'bandə/, <u>n</u> a South American cult with elements of VOODOO, Roman Catholicism, and Indian beliefs.

Sir, You have gone too far in trying to describe spiritism as a pagan cult in Brazil. You have confused African religious rites, such as Quimbanda and Umbanda, which were brought by the slaves, with the Christian religion or spiritism. Time, 1/31/72, p 7

[< Spanish < a West African language, ? < alteration of MBUNDU]

Umbandista /,umban'di:stə/, <u>n</u> a member or follower of UMBANDA.

Dona Isabel ran a foster home, and at Praia Grande girls in white crinolines threw their rings into the sea, like the Doges of Venice. Half a million Umbandistas were on the beach that day, and we saw them. It was like a scene by Fellini. The Times, 11/24/77, p 9

[< Spanish < UMBANDA + -<u>ista</u> -ist]

Umbundu /əm'bundu:/, <u>n</u> a Bantu language of Angola, spoken by the MBUNDU.

umfaan /um'fan/, <u>n</u> a young or small black African boy (in South Africa).

Jim...could tell of an umfaan sent out to herd the cattle within sight of the British camp and draw the troops out raiding while the impis crept round...behind them. Sir P. Fitzpatrick, Jock of the Bushveld, 1907, p 194

[< Afrikaans < Zulu umfana young
boy < um- singular noun pfx +
-fana ~ Swahili (mw)ana child]

Umhlanga /um'hlangə/, n a festival
in which reed dances are performed
in honor of the NDLOVUKAZI of
Swaziland.
    Umhlanga...will now be held on
    Monday September 3. August 27
    will therefore not be a public
    holiday, but Monday September
    3 will be. Girls taking part
    in the ceremony will...collect
    the reeds on August 29 and re-
    turn to Lobamba on September 1.
    Times of Swaziland, 8/17/73, p 1
[< siSwati; ~ Zulu umhlanga reed;
also, God]

umgqashiyo /umga'ʃi:you/, n a
type of jazz music popular in
South Africa.
    Further south the new music
    known by such various names as
    Zulu jive, South African jazz,
    and the local name umgqashiyo
    has made great international
    impact. The Times, 1/18/77, p II
[? < Xhosa]

umiviesa /,umivi'esə/, n = BAZIMO.
[< a Bantu language]

umkhovu /um'kouvu:/, n a familiar
to the ABATHAKATHI of the Zulu.
    The most dreadful is the um-
    khovu - an exhumed corpse with
    animal eyes and a tongue snipped
    off at the tip. As it goes
    about its master's business,
    slipping quietly into kraals
    at night, the zombie's passage
    can be detected - a sound like
    the soft swishing of a skirt.
    National Geographic, 12/71,
    p 760
[< Zulu]

Umkonto We Sizwe /um'kontou wei
'sizwei/, n a radical multi-
racial arm of the African National
Congress of South Africa.
    Dr. Yutar asked who were the
    leaders of the militant group

Umkonto we Sizwe and Sisulu
said he would mention only
those involved in the trial or
who had left the country.
London Guardian, 4/23/64, p 16
Umkonto We Sizwe, the military
wing of the banned African
National Congress, a liberation
movement, is crossing the Lim-
popo River into South Africa,
caching weapons, and fighting
when detected. New York Times
(Sec. 4), 3/18/79, p E21
[< Nguni, literally, spear of
the nation < umkonto spear + we
connective, "of" + sizwe country]

umnumzane /umnəm'zanei/, n the
chief, headman, or head of a
household (in southern Africa).
    When an umnumzane, head of the
    homestead, has a beast slaugh-
    tered, certain parts and or-
    gans are given to members with-
    in the family and among neigh-
    bours and friends. Times of
    Swaziland, 7/20/73, p 5
[< Nguni]

Umoja /u'moudʒə/, n 1 unity; a
principle of NGUZO SABA celebrated on the first day of KWANZA.
    Discussions usually focus on
    community problems. "On the
    first day, when the principle
    is umoja, or unity, the adults
    are likely to talk about watch-
    ing each other's homes to stop
    rip-offs." Wall Street Journal,
    12/24/75, p 6
2 a type of corn-row hairstyle
popular among Africans and Afro-
Americans. See the quotation under
ASHIA.
[< Swahili, literally, oneness
< u- (abstract) noun pfx + moja
one]

umuganda /umu'gandə/, n weekly
communal labor (in Rwanda).
    Umuganda has become a national
    practice, with high officials
    participating. There is some
    resistance by poorer peasants,
    who prefer to direct all their

efforts to eking out a living. Farm sizes continue to diminish because of demographic pressures, and landless peasants are increasing in number. Collier's Encyclopedia Yearbook, 1977, p 483
[< Kinyarwanda umu- singular noun pfx + ganda (root for) this labor]

umwami /um'wami:/, n = MWAMI.

umzimbiti or umzimbete /umzim-'bi:ti:, -'beti:/, n the ironwood tree; its hard wood.
The Cape ebony, white stinkwood ...essenhout and umzimbiti, trees that yield beautiful timber for furniture-making, grow in profusion in every kloof. Cape Argus (Mag. Sec.), 3/18/50, p 7
[< Nguni umsimbithi]

ungalawa /uŋgə'lawə/, n = NGALAWA.

Unkulunkulu /əŋ,kuluŋ'ku:lu/, n the supreme deity of the Zulu.
[< Zulu un- singular noun pfx + -kulunkulu reduplication of -kulu great ~ Swahili -kuu great]

unntu /'untu:/, n a person (among the Fipa in southern Africa).
"The person (unntu) in Fipa theory is a structured entity which analysis shows to be homologous with various supra-personal dimensions of the Fipa cosmos." New Scientist, 7/5/79, p 40
[< Fipa un- singular noun pfx + ntu ~ Swahili (m-)tu person ~ BANTU, MUNT, UBUNTU]

upeygan /u'peig n/, n a common African rhinocerous (Atelodus bicornis); black rhino.
[< Shona]

uputhu /u'pu:tu:/, n a maize

porridge of southern Africa, especially of the Zulu.
One of Mazibe's wives, plump and humble as traditionally a Zulu wife should be, entered on her hands and knees. Permitted to kneel but not to stand, she adroitly balanced a baby strapped to her back in a cloth sling, while serving us roast chicken and uputhu, a kind of hominy that has been a staple Zulu dish for centuries. National Geographic, 12/71, p 746
[< Nguni]

Urundi /u'rundi:/, n former name of BURUNDI.
[? < Swahili u- (abstract) noun pfx + rundi; adaptation of Burundi]

utenzi /u'tenzi:/, n a Swahili poem, especially a religious or heroic poem.
[< Swahili u- (abstract) noun pfx + -tenzi ~ -tenda do, practice]

utshuala or utywala /u't∫walə/, n = TJWALA (among the Xhosa).

uzara /u'zarə/, n the dried root of a woody herb plant (Gomphocarpus Asclepiadaceae) of southern Africa, used as a medicine against dysentery.
[< a southern African language]

uzarigenin /u,zarə'dʒenən/, n a crystalline compound used as an antidiarrheal. Formula: $C_{23}H_{34}O_4$
[< UZARA + -igenin]

uzarin /u'zarin/, n a crystalline substance derived from UZARA, used as an arrow poison in southern Africa. Formula: $C_{35}H_{54}O_{14}$
[< UZARA + -in chemical suffix]

V

Vai /vai/, n a people of Sierra
Leone and Liberia; their Niger-
Congo (Mande) language, used as
a lingua franca in Liberia; a
syllabic script used for this
language, invented by Momolu
Doalu Bukere in the early 1800's.

Venda /'vendə/, n 1 a people of
South Africa; their Bantu language. 2 a homeland (region in
South Africa set aside by the
government for blacks) for the
Venda, Pedi and Shangaan located in two sections of the
northern Transvaal. Although
granted independence by South
Africa in 1979, it is not recognized as a nation by the United
Nations.
　　During the year the government
　　launched the third independent
　　"homeland," Venda, in the north-
　　east, but like Transkei and
　　Bophuthatswana before it, it
　　was refused international recog-
　　nition. Americana Annual, 1980,
　　p 447
　　Three homelands, Transkei,
　　Venda and Bophuthatswana, have
　　accepted independence under
　　terms that only South Africa
　　recognizes as being in accord
　　with international practice.
　　A fourth, Ciskei, is about to
　　do so. "If the Zulus were go-
　　ing the same way as these
　　other people who are going

for this sham independence,"
Chief Buthelezi asks, "then
what would be left actually
in South Africa? Truly, what
would be left?" New York Times,
11/30/80, p 18
[< Venda, literally, land,
world]

vitenge /vi'tengei/, n pl of
KITENGE.
[< Swahili vi- plural noun pfx
+ -tenge (root for) this cloth]

vodun or vodu /vou'du:/, n =
VOODOO.
　　Yet even skeptics admit that
　　there are some who experience
　　the real 'mystery,' that is
　　the vodu. Such persons feel
　　an exaltation, a sense of awe
　　and of unity with the god
　　that, though held in check be-
　　tween ceremonies, wells forth
　　at once if the proper songs or
　　drum rhythms are heard....As
　　they dance, they are no longer
　　themselves, and they remember
　　nothing of what happened when
　　the vodu leaves them. But,
　　when they regain consciousness
　　of the world outside and are
　　themselves once more, they
　　feel as though something heavy
　　had left them. M. Herskovits,
　　Man and Works, 1948, p 376
[< Haitian Creole voodoo <
several West African languages

~ Ewe <u>vodu</u>, Fon <u>vodu</u> spirit, demon, deity]

voodoo /'vu:du:/, <u>n</u> the well-known body of religious rites of African origin, characterized by magic, sorcery and conjuration, and popular especially in the West Indies.

Post Office inspectors put a hex on a Chicago suburban housewife's plan to sell voodoo kits - complete with needles, doll, and "secret incantations"

- by mail. <u>Newsweek</u>, 3/18/57, p 91
[See VODUN]

voudoun /'fu:du:/, <u>n</u> = VOODOO.

<u>Prodigal Prince</u>, then, is... powerful and sensitive in its journey into the life and dreams of a young man who, through visions of a Voudoun goddess and a Christian saint, explores and experiences his African heritage. <u>Saturday Review</u>, 2/10/68, p 45

W

wabaio /wa'baiyou/, n = OUABAIO.
Comparing Mr. Hanley's experi-
ments with those of the writer,
it will be seen that they are
similar to a large degree.
These comparisons are of interest, for although Mr. Hanley
did not say so, Wabaio is a
variety of strophantus. London
Sunday Times, 7/13/58, p 4

wabenzi /wa'benzi:/, n pl owners
of big, powerful automobiles,
especially of Mercedes-Benz cars
(in eastern Africa).
Only beer is served at government receptions, and the swift-
est way to political oblivion
is to be a wa-benzi, or the
owner of a big car like a Mercedes-Benz. Time, 11/1/68, p 57
[< Swahili wa- plural noun pfx
+ benzi (Mercedes) Benz]

walia /'weili:ə/ or walie /'weili:/,
n the Abyssinian ibex (Capra walie).
[< Amharic walia]

wali na nyama /'wali na 'nyamə/,
n an East African dish of rice
and beef.
[< Swahili wali rice + na and +
nyama meat]

wanga /'wangə/, n a charm, spell,
or other sorcery in the VOODOO
cult.
Some 200 Haitians, dressed in
their cotton Sunday best,
watched intently while an old
lady threw object after object
into the flames - bottles to
bubble when a thief is in the
garden, carved wooden bowls
from which to feed the gods,
wanga bags to protect the traveler, love charms, colored
beads, mysterious, headless
dolls. Time, 7/5/54, p 48
[< Haitian Creole OUANGA < a
West African Bantu language ∼
Kimbundu wanga witchcraft, Chiluba buanga medicine, charm,
fetish]

wananchi /wa'nantʃi:/, n pl countrymen (in eastern Africa).
Drawn by 72 soldiers in red
tunics from the Kenya Rifles,
the cortege moved at a stately
pace down Kenyatta Avenue
toward Parliament grounds. Thousands of wananchi lined the
street, trying to glimpse the
passing coffin, which was be-
decked with Kenyatta's military
cap, his sword and his Kikuyu
beaded belt. The mourners were
eerily silent, as though numbed
by grief. Time, 9/11/78, p 40
Mr. Kibaki made it clear that
Kenya was an open society where
the Government was freely elected
by the citizens. "The era of
underground literature was
buried with the attainment of

independence", the Vice-President told "wananchi" outside the Nyeri D.C.'s office. Standard (Nairobi), 11/23/79, p 1
[< Swahili wana children (variant of waana) + nchi country]

warada /'warədə/, n a district (in Ethiopia).
[< Amharic wərrədə, literally, descend]

waragi /wa'ragi:/, n an alcoholic drink of Uganda, much like gin, made from a banana-based liquor.
The currency notes, all of which bear Amin's bejowled and bemedaled portrait, have always been worthless outside the country and now count for nothing inside because people do not want them. Instead, they would rather have scarce butter or a slab of meat or a bottle of waragi. Time, 3/7/77, p 22
Wealthy Lango in their Mercedes and Peugeots...are feeling the effects of Amin's economic war, with restricted supplies of spare parts for cars, and the ferocious Ugandan spirit waragi to drink rather than imported Scotch. Manchester Guardian, 1/27/73, p 20
A spokesman of the East African Distillers, the makers of Uganda Waragi, attributed the shortage of his product to the local enguli distillers who are not delivering enough supplies. He had been asked to comment on the shortage of the liquor – particularly the large bottle. He said there was no problem about bottles or anything else. Voice of Uganda, 3/14/73, p 1
[< Luganda < Swahili wargi an intoxicant, ? < Arabic arak]

wari or **warri** /'wari:/, n = BAO (in West Africa, and in Jamaica).
[< Akan (ɔ) ware]

Waswahili /ˌwaswə'hi:li:/, n pl

the Swahili people.
[< Swahili wa- plural noun pfx + swahili]

wat /wat/, n an Ethiopian sauce or stew of beef or chicken, vegetables, and hot spices.
The guests were served hors d'oeuvres and roast chicken followed by wat, a meat done in hot peppery sauce. With this came injera, an unleavened bread of loose, rather rubbery appearance. The Times, 2/5/65, p 10
Wat is a kind of curried stew made of lamb, beef or chicken and liberally seasoned with red pepper and other spices. The injera is served with the wat – usually for dipping. Time, 6/14/63, p 18
[< Amharic wət']

watu /'watu:/, n pl people; men; a derogatory term for black Africans.
Some units use specially attached police trackers: the King's African Rifles prefer to train their own. As one company commander put it: "Most of the Watu (Africans) are pretty good at this game." The Times, 6/7/55, p 6
[< Swahili wa- plural noun pfx + -tu (root for) person, creature ~ BANTU, MUNT]

Watusi /wa'tu:si:/, n a vigorous, popular discotheque dance of the mid-1960's.
The kids perform the Frug, the Watusi, the Swim, the Mashed Potato, Walkin' the Dog, and other dances that look like tribal rituals because they are. Maclean's, 3/20/65, p 24

--v to dance the Watusi.
No one worked in Fairyland – they scuba-dived and aquaplaned, they fed on lotus and daiquiri, they frugged and watusied, they heli-hopped

between the Virgin Islands and
the Alps. <u>Punch</u>, 7/20/66, p 116
[< the WATUTSI]

Watutsi or Watusi /wa'tu(t)si:/,
<u>n</u> <u>pl</u> the Tutsi people of Rwanda
and Burundi.

wawa /'wawə/, <u>n</u> a tree (<u>Triplo-
chiton scleroxylon</u>) of Ghana; its
wood.
[< Akan ɔ-wáwa]

wazee /wa'zei/, <u>n</u> <u>pl</u> old people,
especially old men (in eastern
Africa); sirs.
The old <u>wazees</u> and <u>mamas</u> and
other fellows in the local
areas who don't understand Kiswahili, English and other languages, except Kisii need to
hear some music which they
understand. It is not their
fault that is the only
language they understand. <u>Daily
Nation (Nairobi)</u>, 1/18/80, p 7
[< Swahili wa- plural noun pfx
+ -zee ~ MZEE < -zaa be born]

wazungu /wa'zuŋgu:/, <u>n</u> <u>pl</u> white
people; Europeans (in eastern
and central Africa). <u>Sg.</u>: MZUNGU.
An old African had told the
Warden that long ago he saw
the strong young <u>Wazungu</u> (Eng-
lishmen") running up this hill
and being killed, as easily
as birds. <u>Atlantic</u>, 2/66, p 75
[< Swahili wa- plural noun pfx
+ -zungu (root for) European]

wereda /'weredə/, <u>n</u> = WARADA.
The PMAC extended its control
by the appointment of several
of its members as regional
administrators. Some 500 political cadres were trained to

replace existing governors at
the lowest (<u>wereda</u>) level of
administration. <u>Britannica
Book of the Year</u>, 1979, p 374

weyna dega /'weinə 'deigə <u>or</u>
'wainə 'deigə/, <u>n</u> the temperate
zone in Ethiopia.
[< Amharic wəynə daga, literally, vineyard highlands; wəyn
grape, ? < English <u>wine</u> + DEGA]

whydah or whidah /'waidə/, <u>n</u>
an African black weaverbird
with white or buff markings,
often kept as cage birds.
[alteration of <u>widow(bird)</u>,
influenced by <u>whydah</u> (Ouidah)
town in southern Benin]

wildedagga /,wildə'dagə/, <u>n</u> =
DAGGA¹.
[< Afrikaans <u>wilde</u> wild +
DAGGA]

woina dega or woyna dega
/'woinə deigə/, <u>n</u> = WEYNA DEGA.
In 1935, Italy, still smarting
from a crushing defeat received nearly 40 years before,
resolved to attempt once more
the military conquest of the
plateau. The points of attraction were (1) a large population, (2) many undeveloped natural resources, and (3) a zone
of cool climate (the woina
dega, between 4,800 and 8,000
feet elevation) suitable for
white colonization. White &
Renner, <u>Human Geography</u>, 1948,
p 392

Wolof /'woulof/, <u>n</u> a people of
Senegal and Gambia; their Niger-
Congo (West Atlantic) language
used as a lingua franca in Gambia.

X

xala /'xalə/, n an evil spell or curse, especially of impotence (in western Africa).

A xala... is laid upon the hero, a Senegalese business-man called El Hadji Kader Bey, on the night of his wedding to his third wife, the young and voluptuous N'Gone. New Yorker, 5/16/77, p 141

The worst, however, is to come. On his wedding night, he discovers that he has the Xala, the curse of impotence. He quickly despairs of new-fang-led pharmaceutical preparations and consults witchdoctors and marabouts. The Times, 11/5/76, p 9

[< a West African language < Arabic]

Xhosa /'kousə or '//ousə/, n a people of South Africa; their Bantu language.

[< Xhosa amaxhosa < ama- plural noun pfx + xhosa (root for) these people]

Xiconhoca /zika'nyoukə/, n a rascally, roguish character in Mozambique whose vices and excesses are to be scorned and despised (said to represent attitudes of the former Portu-guese colonialists).

The survival of Xiconhoca deserves respect. People are even starting to like him. His name is becoming a term of light rebuke for risky behavior (why, you son-of-a-gun!). How can the party propagandists handle his growing notoriety? Manchester Guardian, 11/21/76, p 9

[said to mean roughly "undesir-able fellow" and to be a hybrid < Portuguese Xico ? fellow (~ Spanish chico) + nhoca a Bantu language, literally, snake ~ Swahili nyoka snake]

Y

yam, n the well-known potato-like
tuber.
[< Portuguese inhame or Spanish
name < a West African language,
? Wolof or Mandingo ∽ Fulani
nyami to eat]

yasigine /ˌyasə'giːnei/, n a
woman who is initiated into the
mask society of the Dogon.
Proud face and special headdress bespeak the privileged
status of a yasigine (left),
who is permitted to approach
masked male dancers with food
and drink. Ornamental aluminum
rings pierce her nose and lips.
National Geographic, 3/69,
p 441
[< Dogon, literally, sister to
the mask]

yassa /'yasə/, n a Senegalese dish
of fish, chicken, or other meat
marinated in spices, lemon juice,
vinegar and peanut oil, grilled
or cooked slowly.
[? < Wolof]

yeshimbra assa /yeʃimbrə 'asə/,
n an Ethiopian dish of chick-pea
flour made into dough, shaped into the form of a fish, fried and
served with a red-pepper sauce.
[< Amharic; cf. šimbra chick
peas]

yohimbe /you'himbei/, n an African
tree (Coryanthe yohimbe) whose
bark yields YOHIMBINE.
Australian aborigines fermented
a species of pine nut in urine,
and when they ate them, a veri-
table delirium tremens re-
sulted. Plants of the rue family have been employed to produce temporary psychotic states;
so has yohimbe and ibogaine
gathered by the Ibo tribe of
Central Africa. Harper's,
5/57, p 52
[< a Bantu language ∽ Duala
djombe this tree]

yohimbine /you'himbain/, n a
crystalline compound from the
yohimbe tree having hallucino-
genic effects, also used as an
aphrodisiac. Formula:
$C_{21}H_{26}N_2O_3$
As a native of Cameroon I'm
glad to read that your roving
aphrodisiacs editor, "Gives
Good Ed" Dwyer [High Times,
"I Was A Sex-Crazed Dope Fiend,"
October '78], got off behind
yohimbine, one of my nation's
most prized supernatural resources. High Times, 1/79, p 13
[< YOHIMBE + -ine chemical suffix]

Yoruba /'yorəbə/, n a people of
Nigeria and Benin; their Niger-
Congo (Kwa) language, a national
language of Nigeria.

Z

Z, abbreviation of ZAIRE, ZIMBAB-
WE (when used before a symbol).
  Zaire. Finance. Monetary unit,
  zaire; 1 zaire = US$0.65.
  Budget (1979): revenue Z2,429
  million; expenditures Z2,661
  million. Collier's Encyclopedia
  Yearbook, 1979, p 619
  Zimbabwe....Plans were laid in
  November for a national development scheme costing Z$4,000
  million to restructure the
  economy. Annual Register, 1981,
  p 257

zagaie or zagaye /zə'gaiyə/, n
  = ASSEGAI.

Zaire /zai'i:r/, n a country of
  central Africa bordering on
  Congo, Central African Republic,
  Sudan, Uganda, Rwanda, Burundi,
  Tanzania, Zambia and Angola.
  Formerly called (Belgian) Congo.
  [< Portuguese, said to be al-
  teration of nzadi local name for
  the Congo river]

zaire , n a unit of currency in
  Zaire, equal to 100 MAKUTA.
    They tried to recruit former
    Katangese gendarmees...They
    offered seven zaires (Ł5) to
    every man who enlisted. The
    Times, 11/9/67, p 6
    [< Zaire]

Zambezi shark /zæm'bi:zi:/, n

a bull shark (Charcharhinidae)
of southern Africa.
  The Zambezi shark...is a slow-
  moving fish, but puts on sudden spurts of speed to attack.
  It is very aggressive and will
  attack larger fish as well as
  boats. Grolier Science Supplement, 1976, p 77
  The Zambezi shark of South
  Africa stalks its prey. Time,
  7/23/79, p 52
[< Zambezi river in southern
Africa, said to be < a southern
African language ambei great
waters]

Zambia /zæmbi:ə/, n a country
of southern central Africa, bordering on Tanzania, Malawi, Mozambique, Zimbabwe, Botswana, Angola and Zaire; formerly called
Northern Rhodesia.
[< Zambezi + -ia, as in Namibia]

zambo /'zæmbou/, n = CAFUSO.
[< an alteration of SAMBO]

zamle or zamble /'zam(b)lei/,
n a mask of the Guro representing
a human face, antelope horns,
and jaws of a big game animal.
  The same intention receives
  a somewhat different sculptur-
  al expression in the zamle
  masks of the Guro of the Ivory
  Coast (British Museum, 19-1/2
  in), but here again the

exponential curve of growth
in the antelope horns seems to
run through to condition the
whole form of the sculpture.
W. Fagg & M. Plass, African
Sculpture, 1964, p 153
[< Guro]

zanza /'zanzə/, n a thumb piano.
[Peter] Matthiessen's prose
can also be a mixture of information and fantasy. "The
mbira, or flat-bar zither,
came to East Africa centuries
ago from Indonesia. It is a
hollow box faced with tuned
strips of stiff metal that
produces soft swift wistful
rhythms of time passing..."
What does that mean? He might
have added that this instrument is usually called a thumb
piano, that its most common
African name is zanza, and
that you can buy a kit to make
one in American novelty shops.
Natural History, 12/72, p 92
[< an African language; ultimately < Arabic sanj castanets,
cymbals] See SANSA.

zanzibari /zanzi'bari:/, n a
type of clothing material made
in Zanzibar.
   How many Kikuyu bibis have
   you seen wearing goatskins in
   the last two years, the last
   five years, the last ten years?
   Not a one of them but hasn't
   got a shuka made out of merikani or zanzibari. And shoes
   of a sort. And head kerchiefs.
   And houses with tin tops. R.
   Ruark, Uhuru, 1962, p 189
[< Zanzibari a resident of Zan-
zibar] See MERIKANI.

zar /zar/, n a possession cult of
Ethiopia; a ceremony in this
cult.
   The Zar is a hypnotic, paci-
   fying ceremony for people
   possessed by a spirit....It
   was originally applied to the
   sky god who later degenerated

into an evil spirit. New
Scientist, 11/5/70, p 288
[< Amharic, ? < a Cushitic lan-
guage]

zebra, n the well-known striped
animal.
[< Portuguese < an African
language]

zemetcha /zə'metʃə/, n a national work campaign in Ethiopia
in which students and intellec-
tuals were forced to work in
the countryside for a specified
period.
[< Amharic zemeca campaign]

zeze /'zeizei/, n a stringed
musical instrument of eastern
Africa, somewhat like a guitar
or banjo.
   A member of the Tanzania
   National Dance Troupe playing
   a 13-string zeze in a performance at the Commonwealth
   Institute, London. The Times,
   8/19/78, p 3
[< Swahili]

zilzil /'zilzil/, n an Ethiopian
dish of beef strips braised in
a sauce, served with INJERA.
[< Amharic   zələzzəl   cut
into strips]

zimb /zimb/, n a dipterous fly
(family Tabanidae) of Ethiopia,
resembling the TSETSE in its
destructive effects.
[< Amharic]

Zimbabwe /zim'babwei/, n 1 a
civilization of southeastern
Africa (from 1000 to 1800 A.D.);
the large, stone ruins formerly used as dwellings and compounds of this civilization and
its rulers, found in many parts
of present-day Zimbabwe, but
especially the ruins found in
Fort Victoria.
   The walls of the zimbabwe,
   made of granite blocks and
   no mortar, were 6 to 8 feet

high and 4 to 5 feet thick.
They apparently enclosed
earthen dwellings. Until recently the official version
of the zimbabwe was they were
built by a foreign civilization
(sometimes King Solomon was
mentioned(, the assumption
being that the black were be-
reft of any engineering ability. The word zimbabwe connoted
not only the physical compound,
but also the sovereignty of
the chief. S. Blumenthal,
Bright Continent, 1974, p 488
2 a country of southern Africa
bordering on South Africa,
Botswana, Zambia and Mozambique,
formerly called Rhodesia (and
Zimbabwe-Rhodesia).

Like the phoenix, the legacy
of the ruins of Great Zimbabwe rises to give an African
name to Rhodesia. To blacks
who long to govern, the nation
is already known as Zimbabwe
(meaning "venerated houses").
Here a key city of the Shona
peoples grew and flourished
from the 15th to the 19th
century. National Geographic,
5/75, p 645
The Salisbury accord includes
a number of provisions safe-
guarding white political and
economic privileges for 10
years. Guerrilla leaders cite
those provisions in rejecting
the accord as a sell-out, and
as reasons to continue their
five-year war against a black-
run Zimbabwe, as Rhodesia will
be called after Dec. 31. New
York Times (Sec. 4), 3/26/78,
p 2
[< Shona dzimbahwe, literally,
stone houses or dwellings of a
chief, said to be < earlier
zimbabgi lofty stone houses]
See DZIMBAHWE.

--Zimbabwean, n: Let us work
untiringly for the total mobili-
zation of the four million Zim-
babweans for Chimurenga (war
of liberation). The Times,
12/30/67, p 4

zingana /ziŋ'ganə/, n a grainy,
fine-textured African wood used
in finishing furniture.
Designer Milo Boughman used
the strikingly grained African zingana wood for a line
of luxe pieces. Compton's
Year Book, 1979, p 176
[< an African language]

zombi, n the well-known walking-
dead specter of certain cults.
[< a Niger Congo language < a
Bantu language ~ Kikongo, Kimbundu, Tshiluba nzambi god, ~
Nzambi or Zambi supreme deity;
Kikongo zumbi fetish]

zongo /'zangou/, n urban quarters
set apart for foreign workers
in Benin.
For many the solution lies in
migration to Ashanti, especially to Kumasi, and to the Western and Eastern Regions. Many
towns have their zongos or
immigrant quarters for the
northerners where they live
and look for work as labourers
in public works and industry,
in domestic service, or on
cocoa farms. R. & E. Steel,
Africa, 1974, p 84
[< a West African language,
? < Fon]

Zulu /'zu:lu:/, n a people of
South Africa and Swaziland;
their Bantu language.
[< Zulu, literally, sky,
heaven (a praise name)]

zulu, n an aeronautical term
for Greenwich Mean Time; a
communications term for the
letter z.
[< Zulu]

APPENDIX

INTRODUCTION

This appendix groups related entries
in this dictionary by subject area, so
readers can easily determine semantically
similar terms originating in or found across
Africa. The classificatory headings are not
intended to be rigorous, but are simply
there for the convenience of the reader
who may wish to be directed to other terms
beyond those with which he is familiar. Of
course, there are a large number of mis-
cellaneous entries that simply do not fall
into any of the following headings, but
still this schema will be useful for both
the interested reader and the lexicographer.

ARCHAEOLOGY

afarensis
Gumban
Kamasian
Kanam
kanjera
Kenyapithecus

Magosian
Nachikufan
Namoratunga
Njoroan
Oldowan
Sangoan

Tumbian

BOTANY

abura
afara
agba
akee
amatungula
ayous
bahar zaf

baku
bambarra nut
banana
bango
baobab
bazimo
bolobolo

Appendix

buaze
bubinga
bumbo
calinut
camwood
cola
dattock
dagaa
dika
doka
etua
fonio
fundi
funtumia
ganna
gesho
ghaap
grugru
guarri(boom)
gumbo-limbo
gungo pea
iboga
imfe
imphee
iroko
isano oil
kaffirboom
kamassi
karité
katemfe
kei apple
kevazingo
khaya
kikuyu
kino
koko
kukamakranka
limba
limbo
mafura
majimbi
makoré
malanga
mangwe
marula
mbuni
mesenna
mfuu

milo
miombo
miyembe
mlala
mlanje
mmoza
mninga
mohonono
mongongo
mopani
mpani
msasa
mugongo
mugumu
muhimbi
mvinje
mvule
mzambarau
naboom
naras
nug
num-num
obeche
okoumé
okra
opepe
ouabaio
owala
pangola grass
quashee
quassia
samba
sapele
sassywood
sobosobo
tambookie
tambouti
teff
tocusso
tsama
tumboa
umiviesa
umzimbiti
uzara
wawa
wildedagga
yam
yohimbé

zingana

CHIEFS, RULERS, TITLES

abatembuzi
adontehene

afe negus
akida

192

alafin
Ankyeamehene
ardo
Asofohene
Asantehene
athimaki
athuri
baba
bakungu
balabbat
balopwe
bami
basaza
bataka
bokor
botikela
changamire
cheka
Dagachin
dejasmatch
fituari
Fon(g)
Ganwa
grazmatch
hogon
indlovukati
inkosi
inyenzi
jumbe
kabaka
kantiba
katikiro
kenzasmatch
krontihene
Kyabazinga

kyeame
litunga
mai
mambo^2
mani
Mansa
maulana
Moro Naba
Mtemi
mukama
Mwalimu
Mwami
Mwene
mwinyi
Mzee
Nabagereka
Mdlovukazi
negus
ngola
Ngwazi
Ngwenyama
Ntemi
Nyimi
obi
Omukama
Oni
Osagyefo
ras
Safohene
sarki
shebuja
shum
tufuhene
umnumzane
umwami

CLOTHING, CLOTH

adinkra
adire
agbada
akwete
aladire
alari
americani
aso-oke
awo
batakari
booboo
buba
bubu
buibui
busuti
chamma

chijaga
chikwemba
chirundu
chitenge
danshiki
dashiki
daunha
Dongola kid
duku
emahiya
eta
fula
garra
gele
ingubu
kanga

193

Appendix

kanzu
kapitula
kareba
kaross
kehla
kente
khanga
khanzu
kikoi, -y
kitenge
lappa
lesu
lipute
mahiya
majumboro
malikan

merikani
moochi
muchi
ndoro
ngoi
ngubu
nguo
obitenge
riga
sanyan
shamma
shuka
sokoto
temtem
vitenge
zanzibari

DRINKS

akpeteshie
amasi
bandji
Bangui
bojalwa
busaa
buzaa
chibuku
chiperone
emasi
gavine
joala
kaffir beer
kaikai
konyagi

maas
magou
mahewu
marissa
pombe
puza
shimiyana
sodabi
talla
tej
tembo
tjwala
tshwala
twala
utshwala

waragi

DWELLINGS, HOUSEHOLD FURNITURE, UTENSILS AND TOOLS

badza
banco
banda
barshi
berele
boma
bority
chiromila
dar
debe
debre
dzimbahwe
enkang
fimbo

gumba
jebena
jembe
karai
kia
lapa
mabati
manyatta
mesob
mkeka
nyumba
obi
soukala
sufuria

tata	tukl
tembe	tukul
thingira	tulu

FESTIVALS, HOLIDAYS

afo	Kwanzaa
Ahobaa	Madaraka Day
Akwasidae	Maskal
asikloe	molimo
Bakatue	ngoma
Incwala	Saba Saba
Karamu	sanda
Kuanzisha	Timkat
Kuomboka	Uhuru
Kuzaliwa	Umhlanga
Kwanza	Umoja

FOODS

aano geel	domodah
aboloo	doro wat
adalu	eba
agahuza	eddo
agala dzempkpelle	eddy
agushi	egusi
akadja	ekuru
akara	enjera
akassa	ensete
alecha wat	foofoo
ambasha	fufu
amiwo	funge
ata	gari
atieke	garri
barisse	goober
basi nyebe	ibiharag(w)e
basta	imojo
beer	injera
benachin	irio
benne	Jollof rice
berebere	kashata
bukari	kelewele
buna	kenkey
cala	kungu cake
chere	kwanga
chichinga	maandazi
chiko	mabele
chinchin	mafe
cossa cossa	maharagwe
cramcram	matoke
cush	moamba
dabo kolo	moinmoin
dika bread	mseto

muhogo

nsenene

nshima

ogi

ogusi

papa

pilipili

pinder

piripiri

pombo

posho

putu

sadza

samosa

sik sik wat

simsim

sukuma wiki

tere siga

thiebou dien

tin apa

tsi-tsinga

tuwo

ugali

uji

uputhu

wali na nyama

wat

yassa

yeshimbra assa

zilzil

FORMER KINGDOMS

Amhara

Axsum

Azania

Benin

Buganda

Dahomey

Ghana

Monomotapa

Nok

Nubia

Zimbabwe

GAMES

bao

dolos

ghoen

hagi

lela

mali

nsolo

oware

war(r)i

GEOGRAPHY, TERESTRIAL, CLIMATE, GEOLOGY

amba

balleh

balq

banto faros

bega

bolis

bolilands

bundu

chiperone

chitemene

daga $_2$

dagga

dambo

dambonite

dayr

dega

donga

erg

fadama

firiki

gasha

gu

guban

gumbotil

isokite

harmattan

jilaal

karoo, karroo

kasolite

kenyte

kiva

krempt

kwolla
lusaka
lusuku
magadi
magadiite
mboziite
mbuga
miombo
msitu
murram
niaye
nyanza
nyika

omuramba
otavite
poto-poto
reg
shamba
tabki
tannes
tanzanite
toich
tsavorite
tsumebite
weyna dega
zongo

MEDICINE, DISEASES, DRUGS

akuammine
berberine
bisabol
bisabolene
calumba
Calabar bean
chikungunya
columbin
cusso$_1$
dagga
daktari
dambose
dandy fever
dawa
deiamba
dengue
diamba
eboka
Ebola
eserine
goundou
ibogaine
isangu
jamba

kino
kombe
kosin
koso
kwashiokor
Lassa fever
mesena
mganga
muti
nagana
nakuruitis
nganga
olduvai
olumigumi
onyong-nyong
ouabagenin
ouabain
ouabaio
tabernanthine
uzara
uzarigenin
uzarin
wabaio
yohimbine

MONEY, COMMERCE

ackey
angolar
B
basa
biche
birr
bonsella
butut
C
cedi

chai
dash
D
dalasi
dalasy
duka
dukawallah
E
ekpwele
emalangeni

Appendix

gursha
hongo
K
kalabule
karani
kobo
kumi
kwacha[1,2]
kwanza
likuta
lilangeni
lisente
loti
lwei
M
macuta
magendo
makuta
mali
maloti

maluti
matabiche
N
naira
ndoro
ngwee
P
pesewa
pula
S, Sh, /
sengi
senti
shilingi
sumuni
syli
t
tambala
thebe
Z
zaire

MUSIC, SINGERS, DANCE

ahyewa
amadinda
asunrara
azmari
batuque
balafon
bamboula
banjo
berimbau
bongo[3]
boogie-woogie
calinda
conga
fontomfrom
gidigo
gomgom
goombay
gora
griot
imbongi
irimbako
izibongo
jazz
juke

kalimba
kora
kwela
likembe
limbo
mambo
marimba
mbira
mbongi
nyimbo
patha-patha[1]
samba[1]
sancho
sansa
sanza
sekere
shakaray, -ey
tango
timbila
ugubu
umgqashiyo
Watusi
zanza
zeze

PERSONAL ADDRESS OR REFERENCE

abafazi
abelungu
baba

backra
Bantu
basenji

bashenzi
bibi
Bongo
buckra
bwana
dinge
dudu
efulefu
emakhulungwane
ferengi
frenji
galla
Griqua
hincty
Hottentot
inkosi
izicaza
jazzbo
kaffir
kehla
khotso
Kuke
kwedini
Kyuke
mafuta
makulu

mama
mondele
mtoto
munt
muzungu
mwana
mzungu
ndugu
quashee
ras
sambo
Shangalla
shenzi
Taata
talakawa
tata
toto
toubab
umfaan
unntu
wabenzi
wananchi
watu
wazee
wazungu
zambo

POLITICS, COUNCILS, SLOGANS

amandla
Anya Nya
Arusha declaration
Azania
azikhwela
Bantustan
baraza
bayethe
birane
Bophuthatswana
bunga
bunge
bwalo
CCM
Chama cha Mapinduzi
chimurenga
Ciskei
Dergue
gari
Gazankulu
gombolola
gwacha
harambee
Imbokodvo
indaba

induna
inkatha
inkhululeko
jamhuri
jogoo
kabela
kebele
keftanya
kgotla
kiama
kipande
kujitegemea
kuta
kwacha
Kwandebele
Kwa Zulu
libandla
liqoqo
Lome convention
lukiko
lusendvo
mailo
Maji Maji
majimbo
Mau Mau

Appendix

Nguzo Saba	Sobukwe clause
nyayo	uhuru
pitso	ujamaa
Poqo	Umkonto We Sizwe
Qwaqwa	umuganda
Rukurato	warada
salongo	wereda
saza	zemetcha

RITUAL, RELIGION, FOLKLORE, MAGIC

abathakathi	isanusi
abiku	juju
abiru	jumby
abuna	kalunga
afarsata	kibunzi
Afo-a-Kom	Kimbanguism
amadhlozi	kinara
Anansi-tori	kithitu
azmari	'komfo
babalawo	kra
bafumu	kuanzisha
bahtawi	kujur
bazimu	laibon
bongotol	Legba
bori	liretlo
candomblé	Lisa$_2$
chi	loa^2
chuku	Lucumi
daktari	macumba
dama	malam$_1$
dawa	mambo
debtera	mangu
demera	mawu
dia	mganga
dolos	mkeka
duppy	mojo
eboka	molimo
Engai	mpembe
gbo	Mulungu
Gelede	mumbo-jumbo
goofer	Mungu
grigri	muti
Gu	mwiru
guffer	nancy-story
hadithi	Ngai $_2$
hlonipa	ngola^2
hogon	ngula
hoodoo	Nommo
hungan	obeah
ibeji	obosom
Ifa	ogbanje
inyanga	Ogun
isangoma	orisha

Oshun
ouanga
pembe
Rada
Rasta(farian)
Sango
sangoma
Sardauna
sasabonsam
Shango
sheytani
sunsum
tagati

thahu
tikoloshe
tokoloshe
Ubangiji
Umbanda
umkhovu
vodun, vodu
voodoo
wanga
xala
yasigine
zamle
zar

zombi

SOCIOLOGY

abakwetha
abousan
abusa
abusua
Afagne
asafo
Bwiti
chibaro
chitemene
cibalo
dawa (def. 2)
Dopkwe
egbe
Ekine
Eunoto
Falasha
Gelede
ibeji
Ifa
inkatha

Kawaida
kungena
kyekyema
letsema
Lifa
lobola
Maji-Maji
Mau Mau
Mmo
moran
muran
Niyabingi
Poqo
Poro
Sande
Sekiapu
sharo
simba
ubuhake
ubuntu

WEAPONRY, ARMIES, CRIME

amajoni
askari
assegai
athimaki
bakombozi
banabana
bayaye
boma
bunduki
Difaqane
elongo
emabutfo
fimbo

ilmuran
impi
koboko
kier(r)(i)e
koboko
kondo
magotla
Mfecane
moran
mujiba
muran
panga
ruga ruga

Appendix

rungu   simi
shifta   tsotsi
zagaie

ZOOLOGY

aboma	giraffe
addax	gnu
addra	gogga
angoni	gorilla
angwantibo	guereza
ankole	hadada
aoudad	herola
aoul	hirola
bafaro	impala
Barotse	impoof, -pufu
basenji	impoon
beira	inyala
beisa	ipiti
biddy	jako
bohor	jigger
bonga$_1$	jird
bongo	jocko
bonobo	kaama
bontequagga	kapenta
boran	keitloa
borele	kob
brubru	kokoon
buchu	kongoni
caama	konze
cat	koolokamba
chacma	kori
chama	korin
chambo	korrigum
chigger	kudu
chigoe	kukama
chimpanzee	kuku
chimungu	kungu
chipimbiri	kusimanse
cooter	lechwe
coqui	loa
dauw	macaque
defassa	madoqua
dibatag	mamba
dik-dik	mandrill
dioch	mboloko
djigga	mngwa
dosinia	nakong
drill	Nandi bear
dudu	nandine
emgalla	nanger
fisi	ndagaa
galago	ndagala
gerenuk	ndalawo

N'dama	simba
ngege	simbil
nyala	sitatunga
nyama	songololo
okapi	suni
opah	taha
oribi	tampan
pongo	tolly
poor joe	topi
potto	tora
puku	touraco
quagga	tsessebe
quelea	tsetse
sakabula	tzetze
samango	upeygan
Sanga	walia
Sangu	whydah
sassaby	Zambezi shark
shrimpi	zebra
siafu	zimb

About the Author

GERARD M. DALGISH is an Assistant Professor of English (as a second language) at Baruch College in New York City. He has been Dictionary Editor at C. L. Barnhart, Inc., and a Lecturer in African Languages and Linguistics at the University of Dar es Salaam, Tanzania. His numerous articles on linguistics have appeared in scholarly journals such as *Studies in African Linguistics*, *African Languages*, and *Studies in the Linguistic Sciences*.